ENGRAVED BY T. B. WELCH PHIL.—FROM A DAGUERREOTYPE.

REV. W. G. BROWNLOW.

Very Respectfully, &c.
W. G. Brownlow

THE

Great Iron Wheel Examined;

OR,

ITS FALSE SPOKES EXTRACTED,

AND

AN EXHIBITION OF ELDER GRAVES, ITS BUILDER.

IN A SERIES OF CHAPTERS.

BY

WILLIAM G. BROWNLOW,

EDITOR OF BROWNLOW'S KNOXVILLE WHIG.

"To the law and to the testimony: if they speak not according to this word, it is because THERE IS NO LIGHT IN THEM."—ISAIAH viii. 20.

"For there is nothing covered, that shall not be *revealed;* and *hid*, that shall not be known."—CHRIST.

NASHVILLE, TENN.:
PUBLISHED FOR THE AUTHOR.
1856.

Dedication.

TO

Every honest and impartial reader,
who loves Truth and despises Falsehood,
whether perpetrated by a Priest or a Levite,
for the sake of Fame, or money-making:
To every Protestant Christian, who, to whatever
sect or denomination he may be attached, is unwilling
to see a sister Church pulled down by a collection of tales,
fabrications, and blackguard insinuations, which a decent man
should be ashamed to listen to, and utterly too disgraceful for a
Minister of the Gospel to repeat and publish, this work is confidently

DEDICATED BY ITS AUTHOR:

Who here, most respectfully, as a Local Preacher of the Methodist
Episcopal Church, South, apologizes to the Christian public
for the seeming severity of this work, in some parts, on
the ground that he has performed the painful task
of refuting a series of the most scurrilous
falsehoods, and a collection of the lowest
abuse of the age!

CONTENTS.

CHAPTER IV.

CHAPTER V.

CHAPTER VI.

CHAPTER VII.

CHAPTER VIII.

CHAPTER IX.

CHAPTER X.

CHAPTER XI.

CHAPTER XII.

CHAPTER XIII.

CHAPTER XIV.

CHAPTER XV.

CHAPTER XVI.

CHAPTER XVII.

CHAPTER XVIII.

CHAPTER XIX.

CHAPTER XX.

Preface.

The author of this work does not feel it incumbent upon him to offer an apology for writing this defence of the personal integrity and respectability of Methodist preachers, and of the polity and doctrines of Methodism. He has prepared this work for publication because he believed it *called for*, as a set-off to the "star papers" of unmitigated abuse and calumny, ostentatiously paraded in a book of five hundred and seventy pages, by the notorious *J. R. Graves*, editor of the "Tennessee Baptist," at Nashville, and which are now receiving the praises of the irreligious, vindictive, and more indiscreet partisans of that respectable and numerous denomination of Christians. There are few men in this country who, *in a small way*, have gained so much notoriety, or prostituted a larger stock of *ordinary talents* to baser purposes, than this man Graves! While eagerly seeking for notoriety, and not knowing how to obtain it, on account of the unwillingness of various dignified Christian ministers to come in contact with him—not dreading his talents, but his *irreligious* spirit, his proneness to *prevaricate*, his low and scurrilous *abuse*, and the fact of his general course of conduct not meeting with the approval of the more intelligent and highminded members of his own denomination—his last effort, perhaps the culminating point of *his glory*, has been to throw all the slang of his ill-spent life together in one volume, and adorn its vulgar pages with *pictures*, and by its novelty make some money!

At the close of the *fifth* volume of bound books, as original, upon subjects of controversy, which the author of this work has put forth from time to time, immersed in the cares, anxieties, and arduous duties of the editorial profession, as he is, he had hoped that no event in the exciting religious controversies of the day would impose on him the task of furnishing the world with a *sixth* volume. Besides, wanting the time for much careful reading and patient investigation, he has felt the more reluctant to reply to this series of blackguard assaults on Methodism. Meantime, his attention has been called to the unscrupulous character of Graves's "Iron Wheel," and of the wide circulation given it in the South and South-west, and of the dangerous tendency of its slanders among the really uninformed; and solicitations have come from almost every quarter requesting him to reply. Prompted by these considerations, the work commenced. The design was to meet and refute the most glaring and absurd of these slanders—to exhibit to the world who this man Graves was—to present, without entering largely into the argument, the number of PALPABLE FALSEHOODS this "accuser of the brethren" had perpetrated in one single chapter. It was thought that a few brief chapters, setting forth the most palpable slanders, would accomplish this purpose; but as the writer proceeded, the magnitude of the work increased. He found, from a number of respectable periodicals which came into his hands as the work progressed—both Methodist and Baptist journals—that Graves had laid himself liable to exposures on all hands, and had actually been held up in different States as a general disturber of the religious peace, guilty of numerous misrepresentations. Hence, he has been led, not only to quote a number of authors, but also to multiply quotations from the same authors and editors. This imposed a necessity of going more extensively into an *exposé* of this arrogant and mischievous man than was at first designed. Thus the chapters will be found to be numerous, and some of them are quite long.

The "Iron Wheel" by Graves does not possess even the merit of *originality*, being a re-hash of, and an enlargement upon, a similar work, by FREDERICK AUGUSTUS ROSS, D.D., a more talented man than Graves, but a man of *color*, and a broken-down minister of the New School Presbyterian Church, who, having retreated from the field of his operations in East Tennessee, has taken up quarters in Huntsville, Alabama. This circumstance, in addition to the fact that Graves has quoted largely from Ross, and *filched* from him in other instances without the proper credit—not observing the old adage, that there should be "honor among thieves"—has led the author of this work to occupy several pages in detailing the particulars and also the *points* in the Ross controversy—a controversy in which he acted rather a conspicuous part.

While the writer cannot but hope that the work will be of service to the cause of Truth, or Methodism, or Christianity, he entertains no doubt that, in the press of business, some points have not been fully elaborated, and that it contains imperfections; but he hopes that the importance of the issues will divert attention from whatever defects may appear. The writer does not think an apology is necessary for his entering the arena of religious controversy—not at all! He is not one of those whose superabundant charity would induce him to stand quietly by while a clerical gladiator, wholly unscrupulous, reviles the living and the dead, rather than buckle on the harness in their defence; nor is he one of those who profess an exemption from *sectarianism*, which they fail to exemplify. He believes that had it not been for *controversy*, Romish priests would now be feeding us all with *Latin masses* and with their *wafer gods!*

Not the least weighty, however, among the several reasons which induced the writer to undertake this work, were the *numerous* and *urgent* solicitations from ministers and laymen of the Methodist Episcopal Church, South, known to the writer as men of mature judgments, and of influence and character. He, therefore, concludes this preface with *a few only* of the many calls made upon him in 1855 to furnish such a production. A gentleman writing from Danville, Kentucky, thus concludes his letter:—

The friends of Methodism in this part of Kentucky, or at least a portion of them, are anxious that you should review the "Iron Wheel" by J. R. Graves, a man who has figured in this State in years gone by, but under circumstances by no means creditable to him. His vile and slanderous work is being extensively circulated, and needs just such a reply as we believe you are capable of producing. Either take him up in your widely-circulated paper, or in book form—the latter, I should say. In the first place, demonstrate, and this will not be hard to do, that whatever of talents Mr. Graves may possess, God never intended he should *specially* and *solemnly* devote them to the interests of the Church of Christ, else he would have accompanied them with a moderate *revelation of grace!* You should next demonstrate that he has forgotten the age and country in which he lives by three hundred years, or he would feel comfortable while others think for themselves. Men in this age do not expect to share the fate of *Servetus*, though they should differ from Mr. Graves. I will not say what men ought to expect when they are so fortunate as *not* to differ with him!

A gentleman writing on other business from Somerville, Tenn., thus concludes:—

Brownlow, can't you find time to overhaul the "Iron Wheel" of the notorious Graves? I have heard the wish expressed here and at Memphis that you would take him in hand and discuss his merits, either in pamphlet form or through the columns of your excellent paper. I have long believed him to be a very bad man, and his book displays the very worst features of his character. The intelligent and pious portion of the Baptist Church are truly sick of the man, and put up no defence of him or his writings. To be brief, and at the same time candid, you must take him in hand, though I am aware that you have but little leisure.

A gentleman of intelligence and great weight of character thus introduces a letter from Wilmington, N. C.:—

Mr. Brownlow:—Though I have no personal acquaintance with you, I know you well, and have known you for years, agreeing with you both in religious and political belief. I write you now, hurriedly, in reference to a book being circulated here, known as the "Iron Wheel," and as the production of a certain *Mr. Graves* of your State. It contains an immense amount of false and slanderous matter concerning the ministry, the polity and doctrines of the Methodist Episcopal Church. With the understanding we have as to the unreliable character of the author, we should feel inclined to let it pass; but the "Publishing Society of the Baptist Church" in North Carolina have adopted the work, and are extensively circulating it, thereby making its lies and calumnies their own. For *their sakes*, we desire it answered; and *you* are the man for the work. Enough of such a work as you could produce can be sold in this State alone to defray the expenses of publishing a large edition. What say you? Graves's work is nothing more nor less than an *enlargement* upon the slanders and abuse of *F. A. Ross*, whom you put to silence, and, as we understand here, have actually driven out of your State.

One in whose judgment the author of this work places great reliance thus addresses him from Buckingham Co., Virginia:—

My dear Sir:—You doubtless receive in exchange the "Richmond Christian Advocate," and if so, you have perused the articles written by our old and distinguished friend, Rev. Peter Doub, in reply to *some* of the thousand and one unblushing falsehoods contained in the "Iron Wheel" of *J. R. Graves*, of Nashville. But for the fact of its official adoption by the "Publishing Society of the Baptist Church" in North Carolina, its very gross slanders and vulgar abuse, both of the living and the dead, entitle it to no more notice at the hands of the leading men of our Church than a *comic almanac*, that may have gone out of date, with the death of Davy Crockett! As, however, this really *filthy* book is recognized as a *standard work on Methodism*, by the pious and peace-promoting "Publishing Society of the Baptist Church" in the old North State, it is due to them that they should see how many revolting falsehoods they have endorsed, and what sort of a man they have selected to *edit religious works for them!* You must, then, undertake a defence of Methodism, and an exposure of Graves and his endorsers. It is agreed on all hands that *you* are the man for this "work of faith and labor of love"—a castigation these accusers of the brethren have so richly merited.

Among the several letters received from different States, none has had more influence in determining the author to prepare this work than one from Albany in Georgia, from which an extract only is given:—

Reverend Sir:—Your friends and the friends of Methodism in Georgia very generally desire you to show up Graves and his "Iron Wheel," either through your journal or in a separate publication. J. L. Baker, the pastor of the Baptist church here, is publishing eulogies of this miserable volume of lies through the "Tennessee Baptist," and representing to Graves that his book "has given to Methodism a terrible shock in these parts." I quote from memory. Others are saying that the "Wheel" is unanswerable, and that the Methodist ministers are not able to answer it; and, if they are, that they are afraid to undertake Graves! I tell all such that *you* will yet undertake the work, and that when you do, they will see their man Graves in quite a different light. A book written in your best and severest style—for he deserves no child's play—will sell rapidly and extensively in Georgia. Indeed, an entire edition can be sold in Georgia! Such a work by you, thrown into this market by next spring, would destroy the religious comforts of that class of Baptists who delight in retailing the slanders of such men as Graves. We look anxiously for the work!

The author could multiply similar extracts from letters received from gentlemen in Georgia, Alabama, Mississippi, and even Texas, to an almost indefinite extent; but the foregoing will be deemed amply sufficient. He repeats, that in presenting this work to his fellow-countrymen of the South and South-west, he does it not with a cold indifference, but with his most ardent wishes for their enlightenment and prosperity, and for the continued increase of the piety, learning, and the social, political, moral and religious elevation of the several Protestant denominations of Christians in our country.

The Author.

KNOXVILLE, *March*, 1856.

THE

"GREAT IRON WHEEL" EXAMINED.

CHAPTER I.

Graves seeking notoriety—Desires a controversy with Dr. M'Ferrin—Has the impudence to address Forty Epistles to Bishop Soule—Edits the Tennessee Baptist—The nature and character of the man to be fully disclosed in the sequel.

WHO has not heard the name, and read more or less about the discussions, abuse, and bigoted intolerance of the notorious and self-conceited J. R. GRAVES, editor of the "Tennessee Baptist!" Entering upon the career of his public life some twelve or fifteen years ago, figuring now in Kentucky and then in Tennessee, at a time of religious excitement and of deep interest among partisans—taking an active part in and most generally conducting the abusive and more ungentlemanly parts of the controversies which from time to time have agitated the Churches—possessing talents of only an *ordinary* grade, and these overrated in consequence of his bold, daring, insolent, and really irreligious temperament and demeanor—having a heart, as I honestly believe, unrenewed by grace, and deeply imbued with the hatred, malice, and ambition of a man seeking to rally to his standard a host of sectarian bigots—a nature inclining him to battle and skirmish among sects for the sake of *glory*—this man Graves, I say, has occupied an unenviable position in society, and made a conspicuous figure among a class of men who, like himself, have fomented brawls wherever they have figured; and likewise done much toward increasing the hatred and zeal of ignorant Baptists and bad men toward Methodism, and impeding the progress of the pure gospel of Jesus Christ.

J. R. Graves edits the "Tennessee Baptist" at Nashville, a paper published at Nashville, having quite a large circulation, and being now in the twelfth year of its existence. His paper is a low, dirty, scurrilous sheet, and is so regarded by many of the intelligent Baptists of the country, who refuse to patronize it. And why? Because, as they say, it is conducted by a man who cannot elevate himself above the level of a common blackguard—a man who habitually indulges in language toward other Christian denominations which would hardly be tolerated within the precincts of Billingsgate, or the lowest fish-market in London! No epithet is too low, too degrading, or disgraceful, to be applied to the bishops, ministers, and *usages* of the Methodist Church. The contemporaries of the "Baptist" usually shun coming into contact with it as they would avoid a *night-cart*, or other vehicle of filth; and decent men of the Baptist persuasion have been known to throw the slanderous sheet from their doors with shovel or tongs, disdaining to touch it with their hands. As some fish are said to thrive only in muddy water, so the paper of which I am speaking would not exist one year out of the atmosphere of slang and vituperation. It administers to the very worst appetites of mankind; and whether speaking of the most eminent bishop or minister, the purest of the sainted dead, the venerable FOUNDER of Methodism, or the excellent institutions of said Church, it pursues the same strain of vulgar and disgusting abuse. It is enough for a man, woman, or child to have been baptized by a Methodist minister, or by one received into their Church, to insure the ill-will and contemptuous denunciations of the editor of that vehicle of falsehood and defamation; whilst, on the other hand, he can see no demerit in one who has been *immersed* by a Baptist preacher, and he can take into his fellowship a prostitute, and hug to his bosom a burglar, if they have been baptized by immersion! With him, the Baptist Church is the only kingdom of God on earth, and to find fault with any of its doctrines, ordinances, or abusive preachers, is to sin against the Holy Ghost! With him, no virtue, no honor, no truth, exists anywhere but in the breasts of partisans of his own "faith and order," and no vice or immorality is found but with the members of other Churches. He would surrender his religion (if he ever had any!) and deny his God, if it would bring him in money, or build him up a faction of which he could remain the acknowledged head. Whilst such men continue in the control of a public newspaper, passing as a Church organ, ministers and members of other Churches can have no justice at their hands, and the courtesies of life and the principles of honor will continue to be violated. Believing this, the more intelligent and pious portion of the Baptist membership in Nashville seriously contemplate setting on foot a decent religious paper. From this or some other cause, the intelligent and high-toned portion of the Baptists of East Tennessee have started, at Knoxville, the "Baptist Watchman," which is being edited by the Rev. Mr. Hillsman; while other leading Baptist journals, in different States, as I shall hereafter show, openly denounce this man Graves as the false accuser of his brethren, and hold up his paper as a malignant vehicle through which its editor sends out his illogical conclusions, loosely prepared misstatements, elaborated perversions, and atrocious falsehoods. Several leading Baptist journals have come out and avowed that for Graves they have no sympathy, and no feelings but those of scorn and contempt!

With a view to gain as much notoriety as possible, the noted Graves has challenged first one minister and then another, of different denominations, to meet him in public discussions touching the mode and subjects of Christian Baptism, and the several forms of Church government under which they are associated; and in these squabbles, generally, he has violated the courtesies of debate, zigzagged through a mass of contradictions and inconsistencies: in his waywardness and vanity, he has grown from bad to worse, fomenting neighborhood brawls wherever he has met a competitor, until he has become a sort of *Hindoo leader* of the warlike wing of his Church. In almost every public discussion he ever had, he came off *second best*, though, in *his* account of his several engagements, he was victorious, storming the "Sebastopol" of the enemy, and placing *hors du combat* all the staff officers and superior officers who dared to lead their troops to the attack! He has, in the course of his career, avoided being driven back at the point of the bayonet, on more occasions than one, by deserting his "advanced trenches," and by "scaling the parapet and *penetrating into the interior* of the redoubt." Indeed, his bump of *caution* has led him to dodge sundry "engagements," on the ground that

"He that fights and runs away
Will live to fight another day."

From the time he first came to Nashville, and undertook the editorial management of his "Tennessee Baptist," until now, he has sought, by coaxing, by attacks, and by unblushing falsehoods, to draw Dr. John B. M'Ferrin, the able, gentlemanly, truly Christian editor of the "Advocate," one of the official organs of the Methodist Church, South, into a controversy with him. Dr. M'Ferrin has never gone through the formalities of an introduction to the man—never, I believe, even spoken to him. It is, however, very evident that the courteous editor of the "ADVOCATE" has experienced no inconsiderable solicitude in his endeavors to avoid a personal controversy with such a man. Time after time he passed by the malignant attacks of Graves with the most extraordinary forbearance, considering the skill and acknowledged ability of the Doctor to overturn the illogical conclusions of Graves, his bungling falsehoods, elaborated perversions of truth, and the smallness of his calibre. Not observing the tone of moderation and truth in the conduct of his paper, the editor of the "ADVOCATE" does not, I presume, exchange with him, or read his paper. The policy which has been followed by the conductor of the organ of the General Conference, at Nashville, of treating such assaults with the contempt they deserve, and leaving the shafts of malice to rebound upon the assailant, I feel confident has been the proper course, and, I am now convinced, has met with the approval of the Church, but especially with the Methodist community in and around Nashville, *who know Graves!*

The whole tenor of Graves's course, editorially, has been that of a vagabond politician who expected to live only by excitement—making ruffian-like attacks upon private character, committing all manner of excesses, standing preëminent in selecting themes for lying, and the lowest and most scurrilous abuse of Methodist preachers. He has made repeated attacks upon me, through his paper, with a view to engage me in a controversy upon points of doctrine and Church polity. I was engaged in defence of one of the political parties of the country, and in promoting the internal improvement schemes of our State, and did not choose to occupy my columns in a controversy of this kind with a humiliating spectacle of vice and depravity literally crawling in the dust of contention! This unwillingness of mine to bandy epithets with an inflated *gasometer*, whose brain I believed to be a mass of living, creeping, crawling, writhing, twisting, turning, loathsome vermin, he politely construed into a want of *courage* on my part to encounter the *caitiff* of the "Tennessee Baptist." I confess to a want of moral courage to meet one who eats carrion like the buzzard, and then vomits the mass of corruption upon decent human beings!

There *is* a point, however, at which even such assaults become harmful, and deserve rebuke. The appropriate quarter from which such rebuke should emanate would seem to be a member of the Church this bad man has sought to vilify, and a member of the editorial fraternity. Under this conviction, I have taken him in hand; and by the time I am through with the task, I flatter myself that I will be able to satisfy the candid and impartial of every sect, that the aforesaid editor of the "Tennessee Baptist," and author of the "Great Iron Wheel," has no reverence whatever for truth, and that his warped and biased soul has been steeped in infamous falsehoods and vile calumnies during the greater part of his inglorious career!

Through the columns of the "Tennessee Baptist" this man addressed a series of FORTY Letters to "JOSHUA SOULE, SENIOR BISHOP OF THE METHODIST EPISCOPAL CHURCH, SOUTH;" and, at the earnest solicitations of "thousands who read many of them" in his paper, he places them before the world in book form, constituting a volume of 570 pages. These "star papers," then, any thing but creditable to the character of a clergyman, have been ostentatiously paraded in a book, interspersed with *pictures* ridiculing and misrepresenting every feature of Methodism, which, of course, receive the praises of such sectarians as envy a moral excellence they cannot imitate. This last effort, perhaps the culminating point of *his glory*, has even met with the sanction of the "Baptist Publishing Society of North Carolina."

The venerable "Senior Bishop," though residing in the vicinity of Nashville, it is within my certain knowledge, up to this good hour never has perused one of these FORTY epistles, or any portion of one of them. What a rebuke! And I put the question, in all candor, to men of reflection, Ought Bishop Soule to have done otherwise than treat with the most unmitigated contempt any thing and every thing coming from the pen of *j. r. graves?* Bishop Soule entei into a controversy with a man daily in the practice of discarding the ordinary restraints of society! Bishop Soule, the scholar and Christian divine, of dignified ministerial bearing, and of unblemished personal and ministerial character, the venerable and venerated Superintendent of a great and popular Church, who has ministered at her altars for more than half a century, *condescend* to controvert great questions with a *clerical blackguard*, whose grovelling passions assume full sway on all occasions, and whose innumerable moral delinquencies are enveloped in clouds of moral prostitution—lost to every truly Christian restraint, degraded in his taste, immoral in some of his practices, villainous in his nature, corrupt in his principles, sold to the enemy of God and man, and displaying, in all his hideous deformity, how pitiful, how sordid, how little, and how wretched is this apology for a Christian minister!

Think of a *tom-tit* challenging to mortal combat a *hawk!*—of a *monkey* encountering an *elephant!*—or of a miserable *owl* threatening to demolish the *soaring eagle*, the "proud Bird of Liberty," who, soaring above the mountains and leaving the clouds beneath her shadow, and basking still higher in the full blaze of the sun, and, while thus employed, scarcely remembers the dust she shook from her feet! Think of an *astronomer*, when engaged looking at the moon and stars, almost forgetting this little globe: his great mind nearly absorbed, and his imagination carrying him beyond those bright regions to the great Author of the universe, whose glory fills the heavens, and whose eyes see all things, from the tallest seraph to the least reptile or insect in his vast dominions—think of such a one condescending to controvert astronomical truths with an uneducated *mill-boy!* Think of these contrasts, gentle reader, and then with me turn your eyes to one still more striking—that of BISHOP SOULE controverting points of religious faith and practice with *J. R. Graves!*

After this introductory chapter, I shall proceed to notice the contents of the "Iron Wheel;" and in the conclusion of the work, I will deal upon my adversary blows undoubtedly warranted by his assaults, and clearly within the range justified by strict defence. The Carthaginian general was of opinion that it was a legitimate defence of Carthage to carry the war into the territories and to the gates of Rome; and had he been duly sustained, Rome would have been razed instead of Carthage, and from the pens of Carthaginian historians, *Romana fides* might have been handed down for the execration of posterity, in the place of *Punica fides.* I say to this war-horse, in the language of Hamlet:

> Be thou a spirit of health, or goblin damned,
> Bring with thee airs from heaven, or blasts from hell,
> Be thy intents wicked, or charitable,
> Thou com'st in such a questionable shape,
> That I will speak to thee.

Take *J. R. Graves* in his length and breadth, in his height and depth, in his convexity and concavity, in his manners and in his propensities, and he is a very little man; but in that littleness there is combined all that is offensive and disagreeable among Christian gentlemen. For several years past, in portions of several States, with an unearthly din, this man has been barking, neighing, bleating, braying, mewing, puffing, swaggering, strutting; and in every situation, an offensive *smell*, to gentlemen of refined tastes and Christian habits, has gone out from him! And believing the homely old adage, that "he who lies down with dogs must rise up with fleas," he has been permitted to pass unwhipped by justice.

CHAPTER II.

Elder Graves misrepresents Mr. Wesley's views—These slanders endorsed by the North Carolina Publishing Society—Mr. Wesley's difficulties in Savannah—Indicted by a jury for repelling a lady from the holy communion—Twelve of the jurors defend him—His return to England—Some beautiful incidents in the life of Elder Graves!

On page 102 of the "Wheel," under the caption of "Methodism in Georgia in 1736," Elder Graves, as he is called by the "North Carolina Publishing Society of the Baptist Church," attacks, in a coarse, vulgar, and ungentlemanly manner, the private and ministerial character of John Wesley; and after making him out a very bad man, says that he can bear testimony that his *people* in America are like him—thus reflecting upon the personal integrity and Christian character of all who identify themselves with the Church which, under God, was founded by this great and good man! As this clerical calumniator makes war upon the now sainted founder of Methodism, charging him to have been a corrupt man, and arguing therefrom a want of virtue and integrity on the part of his numerous followers in Europe and America, I have deemed it proper to consider this issue in the early part of this work—not considering his numerous FALSEHOODS in the consecutive order in which they appear. If I shall succeed in satisfying the candid and impartial reader that John Wesley was a great and good man, whose labors were owned and blessed of God in a preëminent degree, and that he was not that vile hypocrite and adulterous sinner he is represented to have been by this man Graves, why then his charges against the members of the Methodist Church generally, fall harmless at their feet!

The sentences from Mr. Wesley's Journal, as quoted by Elder Graves, are not exactly nonsensical; but wicked injustice is done to a deceased author, by interpolations and by omissions. This fact alone presents, though imperfectly, the disingenuousness of the quotations, and the character of the man. He knew that not one in ten of his readers would ever see Mr. Wesley's Journal, and that not one-third of *his* readers would likely ever see any reply that might come from the pen of a Methodist preacher. His villainy, of which I complain, and for which he deserves to be driven from decent society, consists in separating the sentences he frequently quotes, from that portion of the chain of thought and argument with which they were connected; in other words, in garbling them—an operation which, according to lexicographers, is "*to pick out what may suit a purpose.*" This operation renders nearly all his quotations *false*, and many of them *every way false*—false by *suppression*, false by *denial*, and false by *misrepresentation*. Though not a lawyer, I nevertheless possess enough of legal knowledge to warrant the assertion, that it is a principle in municipal law that the *suppression* of truth is equivalent to the *expression* of falsehood; or, as the law-books express it, "the former is more artful knavery." In Paley's System of Moral and Political Philosophy, the same sentiment is corroborated in strong and unmistakable language; and in the Bible, upon which Elder Graves *professes* to build his hopes of eternal life, we find the same idea perfected.

Now, I have seen with regret a card in the "Biblical Recorder," a partisan paper published at Raleigh, N. C., in which a Committee, on behalf of the "Baptist Publication

Society of North Carolina," acting, as they say, under the appointment of that Society, and doing what the Society directed—I say I have seen in this card, or "challenge," a full endorsement of the flimsy, slanderous, and disingenuous production on which I am commenting. Nay, this Committee commends to public favor the "Iron Wheel," and challenges Methodist ministers to defend themselves and their Church against its assaults! This endorsement, I will demonstrate before I close this volume, is any thing but creditable to the Christian patriotism and gentlemanly bearing of these *pious* lovers of truth, charged with this "work of faith, and labor of love," by the "Baptist Publication Society of North Carolina."

In this connection, and lest the idea escape my mind, I will submit two questions only to the members of this Committee. Are there not, in the world, false doctrines and wicked practices enough to employ the time and talents of their reforming brethren of the "Publishing Society," without wasting their strength on the "polity and doctrines of Methodism," even admitting that they may not be all they could desire? And can it be a commendable work of Christian piety, for such cause, or in retaliation for supposed wrongs, to endeavor to spread and foment disaffection among those who at present may be peaceful as neighbors, and satisfied with their Church relations? If human passion be consulted, which I think in all likelihood governed the "Publishing Society," I know the answer. If, on the contrary, we consult conscience and the Divine word, with an eye to eternity, the answer will be different.

Now, all this abuse of Mr. Wesley's private and ministerial character, this misrepresentation of Methodist polity, and this array of pictures, caricaturing Methodist itinerancy, in which its beauties are concealed, and its blemishes are exaggerated, —this, I say, may all be very amusing to my gracious brethren of the Baptist Church. They may laugh in their sleeves at the depravity that can suggest such ideas; the meaning smile may light up their countenances, and they may even rejoice with the same assurance with which the untutored savage exults, while he sings his favorite triumph of death around the bonfire he has enkindled for his dying captive; but is there illustrated in it the spirit of Christ Jesus, the charity "that hopeth all things," or that "*thinketh* no evil?" Is there displayed in all this the manly, ingenuous feeling of brotherly love and Christian probity?

But our champion of the "Wheel" I am endeavoring to take the *spokes* out of, commences the chapter under consideration with this heading, in part:—"*Trouble with a lady—Mr. Wesley a rejected lover—His revenge—Is apprehended, tried, and condemned—Flees from justice, and leaves Savannah by night—Seeks the sea-coast, and sails for England.*"

Further on in the chapter, he adds, "We can testify that LIKE FOUNDER, LIKE PEOPLE;" and continues, "It was so with their father John, whether in England or Georgia!" This blackguard allusion is made in reference to the difficulty with the lady, namely, that she "swore to and signed an affidavit, *intimating much more than it asserted*"—italicising just as I have done!

The only remaining quotations I need give from this chapter, are these two:

> Mr. Wesley is tried by a grand jury of forty-four, upon an indictment of ten specifications, and the jury was charged to beware of *spiritual tyranny*, and to oppose the *new illegal authority which was usurped over their consciences.* Mr. Wesley was naturally tyrannical. The jury found a true bill against John, the founder of Methodism, for his conduct towards Mrs. Williamson, and nine other charges. Poor man, he was surrounded by difficulties—unconverted, *unmarried*, a woman prosecuting him for his conduct towards her, far from home, and his own people thoroughly disgusted with his conduct, and outraged by his arrogance and imperial *dictation!!*

> What does the great Wesley think of *running away from America*, and away from a court trial, for the ill treatment of a woman, and unwarrantable spiritual dictation, and a public nuisance?!!

In the profusion of vilification heaped upon the venerable founder of Methodism by Elder Graves, I might be expected to quote more largely; but as the extracts I have given set forth the *points* to which I will be expected to reply, candid and sensible men will not expect me to quote more largely from the vituperation, and most wanton personal attacks, of this last and filthiest of assailants. True, from first to last, he embodies most of the slang against Mr. Wesley, of Southey, Smollet, Nightingale, Lord John Russel, and even *F. A. Ross;* and in many instances without giving these, his "illustrious predecessors," the proper *credit*.

I must ask the indulgence of the reader, for extending this chapter to a length I would gladly have avoided. It treats of the most important event in the life of Mr. Wesley—his residence of near two years in Georgia, his difficulties while there, and certain legal proceedings instituted against him—every particular of which is misrepresented by this man Graves, and none of which, when properly understood, reflects the least dishonor upon Mr. Wesley.

I premise further, that I gather all my facts from the Life of the REV. JOHN WESLEY, by REV. JOHN WHITEHEAD, M. D., the author of the discourse delivered at Mr. Wesley's funeral, by appointment of a Committee, his brother in the ministry, and a physician who stood by his bedside when he breathed his last. I have before me the London edition, printed by STEPHEN CONCHMAN, MDCCXCIII. When the Methodist Conference assembled in London, in August, 1792, after the death of Mr. Wesley, the Committee met and resolved in favor of Dr. Whitehead executing this work, and which was not at variance with the following extract from Mr. Wesley's last will and testament:

"I GIVE all my manuscripts to THOMAS COKE, DOCTOR WHITEHEAD, and HENRY MOORE, to be burnt or published, as they see good." (See Arminian Magazine for January,

1792, page 29.) I am the more particular in stating that I resort to Dr. Whitehead's Life of Wesley, because some of the friends of Mr. Wesley, and of Methodism, both in Europe and America, have objected to the work, on the ground that it gives both the *good* and the *bad*, in reference to his life and labors—if I may be allowed the use of such terms in reference to SUCH A MAN.

The settlement of a colony between the rivers Savannah and Alatamaha, was meditated in England in 1732, for the accommodation of poor people in Great Britain and Ireland, and for the further security of Carolina. Humane and wealthy men suggested a plan of transporting a number of poor families to this part of America, free of expense. For this purpose they applied to the king, George II., and obtained from him letters patent, bearing date June 9th, 1732, for legally carrying into execution their project. They called the new province *Georgia*, in honor of the king, who favored the scheme. A corporation of 21 persons was constituted by the name of "The Trustees for establishing the Colony of Georgia." In November, 1732, 116 settlers embarked for Georgia, conveyed thither free of expense, and furnished with every thing requisite for building, and cultivating the soil. JAMES OGLETHORPE, one of the Trustees, and an active promoter of the enterprise, embarked as the head of these settlers, and they arrived at Charles*town*, as Charleston was then called, early in the next year. It was on the 6th of February, 1736, Mr. Wesley first set foot on American ground, on a small uninhabited island over against *Tybee*, and thence took a boat for Savannah. He entered on his ministry at Savannah, Sunday, March 7th, 1736. In December, 1738, he took leave of America for England, having preached the gospel at Savannah ONE YEAR AND NINE MONTHS. He arrived there, it will be seen, 120 years ago, as a missionary, and a minister of the Established Church of England. He came over on board the *Simmons*, commanded by Mr. Oglethorpe—all which is set forth in his Journal.

Feeling a deep interest in every event connected with the history of Mr. Wesley, and being a great admirer of the man, when in Savannah, several years ago, I visited the wharf, in the business portion of that city, where he first landed, and viewed the spot. I have also been in the large livery stable, on the corner of President and Whitaker streets, where Mr. Wesley's chapel stood—where he regularly preached and administered the sacraments; and the very spot on which he gave offence to an aristocratic family, by repelling a MRS. WILLIAMSON from the holy communion, the particulars and *facts* of which will hereafter appear. The old Fort *Frederica*, five miles below, one of Mr. Wesley's regular preaching-places, is still standing—the identical house—and is a venerable specimen of British architecture. Close by, among the cypress swamps, is *Thunderbolt*, another of his preaching-places, to both of which he was accustomed to *walk*, for bodily exercise. In that vicinity stands a portion of the "Whitefield Orphan Home," which, but a few years ago, was used as a *kitchen*, and was the property of a Methodist preacher. When I was last in Savannah, Rev. Mr. Godfrey, a worthy Methodist minister, presented me with a walking-stick, made of a portion of the *English cherry bedstead* on which Mr. Whitefield slept, and which he brought over from England!

The descendants of Mr. Wesley's persecutors are still living in Savannah—the Williamsons and Caustons—clever, intelligent, and respectable people, connected in part with the Presbyterian and Methodist Churches. He publicly refused to administer the sacrament to Mrs. Williamson, a niece of Mr. Causton, an influential and respectable gentleman, out of which grew the fierce persecution so basely misrepresented by *Elder Graves*. For repelling this lady from the holy communion, in his little chapel, a presentment was made to the Grand Jury, containing ten specifications or *counts*, charging him with "breaking the laws of the realm, contrary to the peace of the sovereign lord, the King, his crown and dignity." These specifications were—

1. By speaking and writing to Mrs. Williamson, (relative to her improprieties,) against her husband's consent.
2. By repelling her from the holy communion.
3. By not declaring his adherence to the Church of England.
4. By dividing the morning service on Sunday.
5. By refusing to baptize Mr. Parker's child, otherwise than by dipping, except the parents would certify it was weak, and not able to bear it.
6. By repelling Wm. Gouch from the holy communion.
7. By refusing to read the burial service over the body of Nathaniel Polhill.
8. By calling himself *Ordinary* of Savannah!
9. By refusing to receive Wm. Agliondy, not a communicant, as a godfather.
10. By refusing Jacob Mathews for the same reason, etc., etc.

Among the enemies of Mr. Wesley at Savannah, there were some desperate persons, evidently as ill-minded as *Graves* is; and their hatred, like that of Graves, rose to a degree hardly credible. Every species of defamation likely to prejudice the people against him was propagated with diligence. The worst constructions which malignity itself could invent were put upon his actions, and reported as facts: it even seems that the giving away his own private income in acts of charity, was construed into the embezzlement of the Society's money!

And now, I will let Dr. Whitehead be heard in further defence of Mr. Wesley, and in reply to the calumnies of Elder Graves. I quote from page 306 to page 314, inclusive; and ask all who may have read the quotations from Graves, to "read, mark, learn, and inwardly digest," the eight pages I copy.

Mr. Causton, the chief magistrate of Savannah, seems to have been of a warm and rather violent temper: impatient of contradiction, overbearing, and fickle in his attachments. He had hitherto not only shown a decent civility towards Mr. Wesley, but even a friendly regard for him. This regard seemed increased during a fever he had in the end of June, in which Mr. Wesley attended him every day. On the third of July, Mr. Wesley reproved Mrs. Williamson for some things which he thought wrong in her conduct. The reproof was resented by the lady, who said *she did not expect such usage from him.* This was the beginning of strife, which, as the wise man tells us, "is as when one letteth out water." The next day Mrs. Causton called, and apologizing for the behavior of her niece, desired Mr. Wesley to inform Mrs. Williamson in writing what he had to object against her conduct. He accordingly wrote to her on the 5th, and here the matter rested for a few weeks. In the meantime, however, Mrs. Williamson miscarried, and Mrs. Causton reported that the miscarriage was occasioned by Mr. Wesley's reproof, and the letter he had sent; but Mrs. Williamson frankly acknowledged that, her husband having been sick, it was occasioned by the hurry and anxiety his sickness had produced. During this time Mr. Causton showed the same friendly attention to Mr. Wesley as if nothing had happened. On this occasion Mr. Wesley writes in his private journal: "July 23.—The strange esteem which Mr. Causton seemed to show for us, by which means we had nothing without but ease and plenty, occasioned my expressing myself thus in a letter to a friend—'How to attain the being crucified with Christ, I find not; being in a condition which I neither desired nor expected in America: in ease, and honor, and abundance. A strange school for him who has but one business, *Γυμνάξειν σεαυτὸν πρὸς εὐσέβειαν.*' "*

In the beginning of August, he joined with the Germans in one of their love-feasts. This, I believe, was the first time he ever saw a love-feast. He speaks thus of it: "It was begun and ended with thanksgiving and prayer, and celebrated in so decent and solemn a manner, as a Christian of the apostolic age would have allowed to be worthy of Christ." He afterwards adopted love-feasts into the economy of Methodism.

August 7.—Mr. Wesley repelled Mrs. Williamson from the holy communion, for the reasons specified in his letter of the 5th of July, as well as for not giving him notice of her design to communicate, after having discontinued it for some time. On the 9th, a warrant having been issued and served upon him, he was carried before the Recorder and magistrates. Mr. Williamson's charge was: 1. That Mr. Wesley had defamed his wife: 2. That he had causelessly repelled her from the holy communion. The first charge Mr. Wesley denied; and the second, being purely ecclesiastical, he would not acknowledge the magistrate's power to interrogate him concerning it. He was told that he must, however, appear at the next court holden for Savannah.

---

* To exercise himself unto godliness

In the mean time Mr. Causton, having become Mr. Wesley's bitter enemy, required him to assign his reasons in writing for repelling his niece. This he accordingly did, in the following letter to Mrs. Williamson: "At Mr. Causton's request, I write once more. The rules whereby I proceed are these: so many as intend to partake of the holy communion, shall signify their names to the curate at least some time the day before. This you did not do.

"And if any of these—have done any wrong to his neighbor by word or deed, so that the congregation be thereby offended, the curate shall advertise him, that in any wise he presume not to come to the Lord's table, until he hath openly declared himself to have truly repented.

"If you offer yourself at the Lord's table on Sunday, I will advertise you, as I have done more than once, wherein you have done wrong; and when you have openly declared yourself to have truly repented, I will administer to you the mysteries of God."

On the 12th of August, and the following days, Mr. Causton read to as many as he conveniently could, all the letters Mr. Wesley had written to himself, or Miss Sophy, from the beginning of their acquaintance; not, indeed, throughout, but *selecting certain passages*, which might, being *detached from the rest*, and aided by *a comment which he supplied*, make an impression to Mr. Wesley's disadvantage. Such methods as these of oppressing an individual, are detestable; and yet they have too often been practiced, even by persons professing religion; but they always afford sure evidence of a bad cause.

While Mr. Causton was thus employed, the rest of the family were assiduous in their endeavors to convince all to whom they spake, that Mr. Wesley had repelled Mrs. Williamson from the communion out of revenge, because she had refused to marry him. "I sat still at home," says Mr. Wesley, "and I thank God, easy, having committed my cause to him; and remembering his word, 'Blessed is the man that endureth temptation; for when he is tried, he shall receive the crown of life, which the Lord hath promised to them that love him.' I was at first afraid that those who were weak in the faith would be turned out of the way, at least so far as to neglect the public worship, by attending which they were likely to suffer in their temporal concerns. But I feared where no fear was: God took care of this likewise; insomuch that on Sunday the 14th, *more were present at the morning prayers than had been for some months before.* Many of them observed those words in the first lesson, 'Set Naboth on high among the people; and set two men, sons of Belial, before him, to bear witness against him.' No less remarkable were those in the evening lesson: 'I hate him, for he doth not prophesy good concerning me, but evil.' O, may I ever be able to say with Micaiah, 'What the Lord saith unto me, that will I speak; and that, though I too should be put into prison, and fed there, with bread of affliction, and with water of affliction.'"

August 16. At the request of several of the communicants, he drew up a short relation of the case, and read it after the evening prayers, in the open congregation. And this evening, as Mr. Wesley supposed

Mrs. Williamson was prevailed upon to swear to and sign a paper containing many assertions and insinuations injurious to his character. During the whole of this week, Mr. Causton was employed in preparing those who were to form the grand-jury at the next court-day. He was talking with some or other of them day and night: *his table was free to all:* old misunderstandings were forgot, and nothing was too much to be done for them, or promised to them. Monday, the twenty-second, the court was formed, and forty-four jurors were sworn in, instead of fifteen, to be a grand-jury to find the bills. This was done by Mr. Causton, who hereby showed his skill in the management of a controversy like this. He knew well that numbers would add weight to every thing they transacted, and induce them to take bolder steps than a few would venture upon. To this grand-jury he gave a long and earnest charge, "to beware of spiritual tyranny, and to oppose the new illegal authority which was usurped over their consciences." Mrs. Williamson's affidavit was read; and he then delivered to them a paper, entitled a List of Grievances, *presented by the* grand-jury for Savannah, this day of August, 1737. In the afternoon Mrs. Williamson was examined, who acknowledged that she had no objections to make against Mr. Wesley's conduct BEFORE HER MARRIAGE. The next day Mr. and Mrs. Causton were also examined, when she confessed that IT WAS BY HER REQUEST Mr. Wesley had written to Mrs. Williamson on the 5th of July; and Mr. Causton declared, that if Mr. Wesley HAD ASKED HIS CONSENT TO HAVE MARRIED HIS NIECE, HE SHOULD NOT HAVE REFUSED IT!! The grand-jury continued to examine these ecclesiastical grievances, which occasioned warm debates, till Thursday; when Mr. Causton being informed they were entered on matters beyond his instructions, went to them, and behaved in such a manner, that he turned forty-two out of the forty-four into a fixed resolution to inquire into his whole behavior. They immediately entered on that business, and continued examining witnesses all day on Friday. On Saturday, Mr. Causton finding all his efforts to stop them ineffectual, he adjourned the court till Thursday, the first of September, and spared no pains, in the mean time, to bring them to another mind. September 1. He so far prevailed, that the majority of the grand-jury returned the List of Grievances to the court, in some particulars altered, under the form of two presentments, containing ten bills, only two of which related to the affair of Mrs. Williamson; and only one of these was cognizable by that court, the rest being merely ecclesiastical. September 2, Mr. Wesley addressed the court to this effect: "As to nine of the ten indictments against me, I know this court can take no cognizance of them; they being matters of an ecclesiastical nature, and this not an ecclesiastical court. But the tenth, concerning my speaking and writing to Mrs. Williamson, is of a secular nature; and this therefore I desire may be tried here, where the facts complained of were committed." Little answer was made, and that purely evasive.

In the afternoon he moved the court again for an immediate trial at Savannah; adding, "That those who are offended may clearly see whether I have done any wrong to any one; or whether I have not rather deserved the thanks of Mrs. Williamson, Mr. Causton, and of the whole family." Mr. Causton's answer was full of civility and respect. He observed: "Perhaps things would not have been carried so far, had you not said, you believed if Mr. Causton appeared the people would tear him in pieces: not so much out of love to you, as out of hatred to him for his abominable practices." If Mr. Wesley really spake these words, he was certainly very imprudent, considering the circumstances in which he was placed. But we too often find, in disputes, that the constructions of others on what has been said are reported as the very words we have spoken; which I suspect to have been the case here. Mr. Causton, however, has sufficiently discovered the motives that influenced his conduct in this business.

TWELVE of the grand-jurors now drew up a protest against the proceedings of the majority, to be immediately sent to the trustees in England. In this paper they gave such clear and satisfactory reasons, under every bill, for their dissent from the majority, as effectually did away all just ground of complaint against Mr. Wesley, on the subjects of the prosecution. As Mr. and Mrs. Williamson intended to go for England in the first ship that should sail, some of Mr. Wesley's friends thought *he ought to go likewise;* chiefly to remove the bad impressions which misrepresentation and ill-natured report might make on the trustees, and others interested in the welfare of the colony. But September 10 he observes: "I laid aside the thoughts of going to England; thinking it more suitable to my calling still to commit my cause to God, and not to be in haste to justify myself: only to be always ready to give to any that should ask me, a reason of the hope that is in me."

Immoderate zeal is always to be suspected; especially when it appears in pursuing such measures as tend to injure or ruin an individual. A bad cause, which originated from hatred or malice, will almost always be carried on with more intemperate zeal and bolder measures, than a consciousness of acting right will ever produce. The pursuit of any end in view, when governed by the passions, is always more violent than when directed by reason and truth. On this principle we may account for the proceedings of the magistrates of Savannah. They sent the affidavit they had procured, and the two presentments of the grand-jury, to be inserted in the newspapers in different parts of America. The only purpose this could answer, was to injure Mr. Wesley in the opinion of a large body of people, who could not easily come at a true knowledge of the case. That these advertisements might make a deeper impression on the minds of the multitude, the pomp of legal form was preserved; the following words being added at the end of each bill—"CONTRARY TO THE PEACE OF OUR SOVEREIGN LORD THE KING, HIS CROWN AND DIGNITY." Persons of discernment saw through the artifice; and in the end of September, Mr. Wesley received a letter from a gentleman of considerable abilities and learning in Charlestown, in which are the following observations: "I am much concerned at some reports and papers concerning you from Georgia. The papers contain some affidavits made against you by one Mrs. Williamson; and *a parcel of stuff called presentments of you by the grand-jury*, for matters chiefly of your mere office as a clergyman. Has our sovereign lord the king given the temporal courts in Georgia ecclesiastical jurisdiction? If he has not, then sure I am, that whatever your failings in your office may be, a grand-jury's presentment of them, being repugnant to the fundamental laws and constitution of England, is a plain '*breach of his peace*,' and an open insult on 'his crown and dignity;' for which they themselves ought to be presented,-if they have not incurred a *premunire*.* The presentments, a sad pack of nonsense, I have seen; but not the affidavits. They were both designed to have been published in our Gazette, but our friends here have hitherto prevented it. I shall be glad to have some light from yourself into these matters, and wherewith to oppose the reports industriously spread here to your disadvantage; meantime, I remain your most obedient humble servant,

"S. Garden."

Mr. Wesley received some consolatory letters from those of his friends to whom he had represented his situation. A letter of this kind from Dr. Cutler, a clergyman of Boston, contains some thoughts so just, and not very commonly to be met with, that I think it worthy of a place here. It is dated the twenty-second of October. "I am sorry, sir," says he, "for the clouds hanging over your mind, respecting your undertaking and situation; but hope God will give a happy increase to that good seed you have planted and watered, according to his will. The best of men, in all ages, have failed in the success of their labor; and there will ever be found too many enemies to the cross of Christ; for earth will not be heaven. This reminds us of that happy place, where we shall not see and be grieved for transgressors; and where, for our well-meant labors, our judgment is with the Lord, and our reward with our God. And you well know, sir, that under the saddest appearances, we may have some share in the consolations which God gave Elijah; and may trust in him that there is some wickedness we repress or prevent; some goodness by our means, weak and unworthy as we are, beginning and increasing in the hearts of men, at present; perhaps like a grain of mustard-seed, that in God's time may put forth, and spread and flourish; and that, if the world seems not the better for us, it might be worse without us. Our low opinion of ourselves is a preparative to these successes; and so the modest and great Apostle found it.

"No doubt, sir, you have temptations where you are, nor is there any retreat from them: they hint to us the care we must take, and the promises we must apply to; and blessed is the man that endureth temptation.

"I rejoice in the good character you give, which I believe you well bestow, of Mr. Whitefield, who is coming to you; but I question not but his labors will be better joined with than supersede yours; and even his and all our sufficiency and efficiency is of God.

* To incur a premunire, is to be liable to imprisonment and loss of goods.

"It is the least we can do to pray for one another; and if God will hear me, a great sinner, it will strengthen your interest in him. I recommend myself to a share in your prayers, for his pardon, acceptance and assistance; and beg that my family—may not be forgotten by you."

Mr. Wesley, in the midst of this storm kept up by the arts of his avowed enemies, without a shilling in his pocket, and three thousand miles from home, possessed his soul in peace, and pursued his labors with the same unremitting diligence, as if he had enjoyed the greatest tranquillity and ease. October 30. He gives us an account of his labors on the Lord's-day. "The English service lasted from five till half an hour past six. The Italian (with a few Vaudois) began at nine. The second service for the English, including the sermon and the holy communion, continued from half an hour past ten till about half an hour past twelve. The French service began at one. At two I catechised the children. About three began the English service. After this was ended, I joined with as many as my large room would hold, in reading, prayer, and singing. And about six the service of the Germans began; at which I was glad to be present, not as a teacher, but as a learner."

November 1. He received a temporary relief from his pressing wants. "Col. Stephens," says he, "arrived, by whom I received a benefaction of ten pounds sterling;* after having been for several months without one shilling in the house, but not without peace, health, and contentment."

November 3. He attended the court holden on that day; and again at the court held on the twenty-third; urging an immediate hearing of his case, that he might have an opportunity of answering the allegations alleged against him. But this the magistrates refused, and at the same time countenanced every report to his disadvantage: whether it was a mere invention, or founded on a malicious construction of any thing he did or said. Mr. Wesley perceiving that he had not the most distant prospect of obtaining justice, that he was in a place where those in power were combined together to oppress him, and could any day procure evidence (as experience had shown) of words he had never spoken, and of actions he had never done; being disappointed, too, in the primary object of his mission, preaching to the Indians, he consulted his friends what he ought to do; who were of opinion with him, that, by these circumstances, Providence did now call him to leave Savannah. The next day he called on Mr. Causton, and told him he designed to set out for England immediately. November 24, he put up the following advertisement in the great square, and quietly prepared for his journey:

"Whereas John Wesley designs shortly to set out for England, This is to desire those who have borrowed any books of him, to return them as soon as they conveniently can, to

JOHN WESLEY."

November 30. He went once more to Mr. Causton, to desire money

* I suppose the ten pounds mentioned in Dr. Burton's letter the 15th of June.

to defray his expenses to England, intending to set out on Friday, the second of December. It appears to me that this was an event which the magistrates most ardently wished to take place, and to which all their proceedings had been solely directed. It is no objection to this opinion, that they published an order to prohibit him from leaving the province. It is manifest that they had no intention of bringing the matter to a fair hearing before them, and of giving it a legal decision. They knew well that the evidence was so strong in Mr. Wesley's favor, that they could not even invent a plausible pretence for giving the cause against him. But to give it in his favor would have been cause of rejoicing to him and his friends, and would have covered his enemies with shame; and they had no way of preventing this but by delaying the trial as long as possible. On the other hand, they easily foresaw that if, by cutting off all prospect of terminating the affair, and multiplying false and injurious reports concerning him every day, they could weary out his patience, and induce him to quit the province of his own accord, the triumph would be left to his enemies; and he leaving the province pending a prosecution against him, and in opposition to a prohibition of the magistrates, would bring a censure upon him, and make his conduct and character suspected among all those who did not know the circumstances of the case. Finding him now determined to go for England, they had a fine opportunity of giving their plan its full effect. Mr. Wesley intended to set out about noon, the tide then serving; but about ten o'clock the magistrates sent for him, and told him he should not go out of the province till he had entered into recognizance to appear at the court, and answer the allegations laid against him. Mr. Wesley replied, that he had APPEARED AT SIX COURTS SUCCESSIVELY, and had openly desired a trial, but was refused it. They said that he must, however, give security to appear again. He asked, what security? After a long consultation together, they agreed upon *a kind of bond*, that he should appear at Savannah, when required, under a penalty of *fifty pounds*. But the Recorder added, You must likewise give bail to answer Mr. Williamson's action of one thousand pounds' damages. "I then began," says Mr. Wesley, "to see into their design of spinning out time and doing nothing; and so told him plainly, *Sir, I will sign neither one bond nor the other: you know your business, and I know mine.*"

The magistrates finding him quite resolved to go for England, saw their plan was secure, and that they might carry on the farce, to keep up appearances in their own favor, without danger of disappointment. In the afternoon, therefore, they published an order requiring all officers to prevent his going out of the province, and forbidding any person to assist him so to do. The day was now far spent: after evening prayers, therefore, the tide again serving, Mr. Wesley left Savannah, IN COMPANY WITH THREE OTHER PERSONS, NO ONE ATTEMPTING TO HINDER HIM. Indeed, I have no doubt but the magistrates were heartily glad to get rid of a man whose whole manner of life was a constant reproof of their *licentiousness*, and whose words were as *arrows sticking fast in them.*

If we candidly review all the circumstances of this affair, we shall perhaps be led to conclude that Mr. Wesley might have acted with more caution, and more regard to his own ease and character, than he did when he first saw the storm gathering, and likely to burst with violence upon him. But his constant rule was, to ascertain, to the satisfaction of his own mind, that particular line of conduct which duty required him to pursue, as a Christian and a minister of the gospel, and then steadily to walk in it, regardless of consequences. And there is every evidence which the case will admit, that he acted in this conscientious manner towards Mrs. Williamson. It does not appear that any one ever charged him with repelling her from the holy communion *out of revenge because she would not marry him*, EXCEPT HER RELATIONS, who now thought it necessary to injure his reputation as much as possible, to cover themselves from reproach. But this charge not only wants positive proof: it is even destitute of probability. It was about five months after her marriage when this circumstance happened; during the former part of which time *he had frequently administered the sacrament to her*, without showing any symptoms of revenge; and about three months after her marriage, he saw such things in her conduct as, in his private Journal, which was never printed, *induced him to bless God for his deliverance in not marrying her.* Now let me ask any candid man, if it is probable that Mr. Wesley could be actuated by a spirit of revenge for a disappointment at the end of five months, which had no influence on his conduct at the end of three months; and even after he had been convinced that the disappointment itself was a mercy, for which he secretly thanked God? I think no man will say it is probable: I apprehend it is impossible this should be the case. In his pastoral character, Mr. Wesley acted by one rule towards all the communicants. If any one had discontinued his attendance at the Lord's table, he required him to signify his name some time the day before he intended to communicate again; and if any one had done wrong to his neighbor, so that the congregation was thereby offended, he required him openly to declare that he had repented. *This rule the order of the Church of England required him to observe*, and he acted by it invariably in all cases, whether the persons were rich or poor, friends or enemies. Mrs. Williamson did not conform to this established order, which must have been well known to all the communicants in so small a place. Mr. Wesley was therefore reduced to this alternative, either to break an order he held sacred, in her favor, and thereby incur the censure of a blamable partiality for her, after being married to another; or to repel her from the holy communion, and incur the censure of having done it out of revenge, because she would not marry him. Censure was inevitable, whichever way he had acted; and having well considered the matter, he determined to follow the rule he had always observed, and leave the consequences to God.

I have elsewhere omitted to state, that the substance of Graves's abuse of Mr. Wesley, on account of this affair at

Savannah, is taken from *Lemprière's Universal Geography*. Lemprière was at heart an infidel, an enemy to Mr. Wesley; and he speaks as contemptuously of Whitefield as of Wesley: resolving his ardent piety and flaming zeal in the cause of God, into *enthusiasm* and a spirit of proselytism!

Even *Mr. Southey*, in his Life of Wesley, on this subject has done himself honor and Mr. Wesley justice. Graves quotes Southey in other matters, but in this Savannah affair he passes him by, because Southey vindicates Mr. Wesley's character against this vilest of all other slanders!

It is very certain, says Mr. Southey, that the magistrates designed nothing more than to make him withdraw; but in order to keep up appearances, and to stigmatize his departure as if it were a flight from justice, they published an order that afternoon, requiring all the officers and sentinels to prevent him from leaving the colony, and forbidding any person to assist him to do so. *This order was not meant to be obeyed.* Indeed, Mr. Wesley had still zealous friends in the colony. Even among the jurors, (fifty were summoned,) though every means was taken to select men who were likely to prove his accusers, and no means of prepossessing them against him were spared, twelve persons were found (a sufficient jury) who, in a paper addressed to the trustees, *protested* against the indictment as a scheme for gratifying personal malice by blackening Mr. Wesley's character.

Now, there are a few points I wish the candid reader to bear in mind:

1. This *slanderer* alleges that Mr. Wesley "*flees from justice and leaves Savannah by night.*" The proof is that he left late in the afternoon, having waited for the rising of the tide, in company with "three other persons," but not without having previously put up a bold and manly advertisement on the GREAT SQUARE, to the effect that he would leave for England, and asking the return of all the books persons had borrowed of him! He left openly and above-board, according to a previous notice, but not until he had "appeared at SIX COURTS SUCCESSIVELY, and had openly desired a trial;" and besides, not ntil he had called on Mr. Causton in

person, and "told him that he designed to set out for England immediately." He went to Mr. Causton, last of all, and applied for money to defray his expenses to England, TELLING HIM THE DAY ON WHICH HE WOULD SET OUT!

2. Elder Graves says that "his own people were thoroughly disgusted with his conduct." In Roberts's Narrative of the Life of GEORGE WHITEFIELD, who arrived at Savannah the following May, and entered upon his ministry, at page 56, we learn that Mr. Whitefield "found many serious persons, the fruits of Mr. Wesley's ministry, glad to receive him, and regretting the return of the former to England"—that "he had now an opportunity of inquiring, *upon the spot*, into the circumstances of the late disputes, and bears witness to the ill-usage Mr. Wesley had received." And to this good day, to my own certain knowledge, the citizens of Savannah have great veneration for the name and memory of JOHN WESLEY; and the influence of his example and teachings are yet to be seen in the liberality of the people, both in supporting the gospel and contributing to other benevolent objects. The Methodists have several fine houses of worship there, and as many large and respectable societies, who thank God most sincerely that ever a Wesley labored in that city!

3. Elder Graves says, "The jury found a true bill against John, the founder of Methodism," etc. The proof is, that the jury were coaxed, lectured, feasted, and their meetings were adjourned over from day to day, until, *worried* by the importunities of Mr. Causton, a wealthy, talented, vindictive man, they returned a bill against him, but with great reluctance! Mr. Wesley defended himself, or "APPEARED AT SIX COURTS SUCCESSIVELY," but could get no hearing, because neither Mr. Causton nor the magistrates ever intended he should have a trial! A minority of the jurors defended him successfully, and their defence was transmitted to the trustees in England, which document appears in his Journal. Did I

not feel that his defence is complete, I would copy that document!

4. Elder Graves says that Mrs. Williamson "swore to and signed an affidavit, *intending much more than it asserted!*" The connection in which this language is used, and the manner in which it is *italicised,* leave no doubt that a most *villainous insinuation* is intended! The proof is, that the *chastity* of Mr. Wesley never was called in question: Mrs. Williamson testified upon oath that she had no objection to the conduct of Mr. Wesley toward her *before her marriage:* Mrs. Causton made oath that it was at her request Mr. Wesley wrote the letter to her niece that gave them offence; and Mr. Causton testified on oath that if Mr. Wesley had asked his consent to marry his niece, he would have given it! The virtue of Mrs. Williamson, formerly *Miss Sophy Causton,* never was doubted; and if Mr. Wesley had ever made an ungentlemanly or dishonorable proposition to her, would she have continued, both before and after her marriage, and through a period of more than eighteen months, to have received, at regular and stated periods, and according to the usages of the Church of England, the holy communion at his hands? Certainly not!

5. Mr. Wesley, though "prosecuted" by a woman and her friends, for enforcing the rigid rules of the Church of England, of which he was a minister, never *kept house in Nashville*—employed an unmarried woman to live with his wife, who turned out to be "possessed"—not only of a devil, but also of a *most loathsome disease*—all which came before his Church—was rehearsed from beginning to ending, until "his own people became thoroughly disgusted with his conduct!" I repeat that Mr. Wesley never was in a scrape of this kind; but *J. R. Graves* cannot say, and tell the truth, that such an affair never came off in his family and Church!

6. Mr. Wesley, though presented to the Grand Jury, by

an ill-natured and irreligious family, for refusing to administer the holy communion to a woman who refused to comply with the rules and regulations of the Church, never was indicted for *a gross libel* upon a respectable gentleman (through the columns of the filthy "Tennessee Baptist") at Lexington, Tennessee—convicted and punished to the tune of SEVEN THOUSAND FIVE HUNDRED DOLLARS AND COSTS; never appealed to the Supreme Court of Tennessee at Jackson—there had the decision of the Court below affirmed, and *mortgaged all his effects away*, to avoid the payment of this fine and costs. But all this has happened with *J. R. Graves*, during the last twelve or eighteen months, as the records at Lexington, Jackson, and Nashville will show!

7. Mr. Wesley was indicted more than one hundred years ago, in the Province of Georgia, for refusing to administer the holy communion to a lady, in violation of the rules and usages of his Church; but he never was *publicly cudgelled on the streets of Nashville*, by an ex-member of Congress, for wanton abuse and insults of female character, through the columns of that great receptacle of filth, the "Tennessee Baptist." But this merited castigation was inflicted upon the reckless and notorious *J. R. Graves!* And no sympathy was felt for him in that community, nor could any redress be had at law. He had unfrocked himself as a clergyman—he had dragged female character before the public, and done that which derogated from the dignity of his high calling—and the brother-in-law of the lady taught him the gracious lesson of moderation, by *publicly mauling him with a stick!* This is the man, however, who has been endorsed by the "North Carolina Publishing Society of the Baptist Church"—an endorsement their consciences may trouble them for in the future, unless they find consolation in the truthful words of the poet:

Lives of great men all remind us
We can make our lives sublime;
And, departing, leave behind us
Footprints on the sands of Time!

Intending in the next chapter a further consideration of the character and labors of Mr. Wesley, I shall not extend my remarks in this. The reader must have discovered ere this the blind impetuosity and cherished hostility of "Elder Graves," as his North Carolina associates style him, to the doctrines, polity, and interests of Methodism. Even *truth*, when he utters it, is couched in such language, and written under the influence of such a spirit, as scarcely to entitle it to credit. How lost to all that is virtuous, to all that is dignified or interesting in the character of man, that state of feeling must be which can feast with pleasure upon the supposed foibles or even wickedness of human nature, I need not pause to tell; and I should tremble to relate the destiny of him who cherishes it! How truly it may be said of the indulgence of such feelings, when seen in one passing for a grave "Elder" in the ministry, who arrogates to himself distinguished powers of mind and the advantages of an education, that learning loses its dignity, religion its sanctity, and talents their merited respect!

CHAPTER III.

Mr. Wesley's early training—Character of his mother—His ordinations—His intercourse with the Moravians—Preaches in the open fields with great power and effect—The organization of the first Conference—Introduction of Methodism into America—Preachers sent over to America—First Conference held in Philadelphia—Appeal to the "North Carolina Publishing Society of the Baptist Church"—Fruits of Methodism—Statistics—Comparative strength of Methodists and Baptists in Georgia—Closing scenes of Mr. Wesley's life—His triumphant death—Inscription on his tomb—Description of his person.

"METHODISM," says Mr. Watson, in his Observations on Southey's Life of Wesley, "has been usually assailed by a violence so blind and illiberal, that those writers who have attempted to confute its principles, or to exhibit it alternately as an object of ridicule and alarm, have, in most cases, sufficiently answered themselves, and controversy has been rendered unnecessary. A few and only a few defences of Mr. Wesley and his opinions have, therefore, been published. The time of those best qualified for such a task has been better employed in works of active piety and benevolence. They have held on their way '*through good report and evil report*,' thinking it enough that, by the writings of their founder and other subsequent publications, the candid might acquaint themselves with their views of Christianity; and that a people spread through the land presented points of observation sufficiently numerous to enable unprejudiced persons to form an accurate estimate of their character and influence."

Now, what I have to say touching these judicious observations of that very eloquent and excellent divine is, that they are as forcibly applicable in America as ever they were in England. A high sense of the merits of Mr. Watson is entertained in this country, as well as his own, both of his talents and his virtues, and of the distinguished services which, as well by his pulpit eloquence as by his various works from the press, he has rendered, not to "Methodism" only, but to Christianity and to the world. And to all those who think proper to assail "Methodism" or "Wesley," through such mediums as *F. A. Ross* and *J. R. Graves,* I beg leave respectfully to recommend a perusal of Mr. Watson's review of the Life of Wesley by Southey. It will be found an ample antidote; and will convince any *Christian gentleman,* I think, that Southey's work, as well as the more vulgar productions of *Ross* and *Graves,* made up in part by quotations from the former, are as direct a stab at all evangelical and vital godliness as at "Methodism" or "Wesley."

The representations of "facts" given by Elder Graves, which go to make up his proofs of charges, are not correct, nor are they consistent with the authors he professes to rely upon; and among these there are those of the very worst character, because of the most decided hostility both to Mr. Wesley and to Methodism. Of these authorities, it is sufficient barely to mention the names of *Southey, Toplady,* and *Ross!*

In this chapter, I desire to continue my defence of Mr. Wesley, and to supply some important omissions, which were allowed, rather than increase the length of the former chapter to an extent that might tend to weary the patience of the reader.

The Rev. JOHN WESLEY was the second son of Samuel and Susannah Wesley, and was born at Epworth, in Lincolnshire, England, June 17, 1703, (*Old Style.*) He received his first lessons of instructions from his mother, one of the first women of the last century, and a woman admirably qualified for the proper education and training of her children. Truly did Bonaparte say, "The future destiny of the child is the work of the mother." His father was a learned and pious minister of the Established Church of England; and his mother was not less strenuously attached than his father to the doctrines, usages, and formularies of that Church. The Wesley family were all resolute and determined. In these principles JOHN WESLEY was educated, and the impressions made upon his mind, under the skilful management and pious teachings of one of the noblest mothers of that century, and the guidance and examples of such a father, were not only never erased, but became the guiding principles of his subsequent life.

To give the reader an idea of the MORAL COURAGE of Samuel Wesley, I give the following incident, strictly true:

The Rev. Samuel Wesley, father of the celebrated John Wesley, being strongly importuned by the friends of James II. to support the measures of the court in favor of Popery, with promises of preferment, absolutely refused even to read the King's declaration; and though surrounded with courtiers, soldiers, and informers, he preached a bold and pointed discourse against it from these words: "If it be so, our God whom we serve is able to deliver us out of thine hand, O King. But if not, be it known unto thee, O King, that we will not serve thy gods, nor worship the golden image which thou hast set up."

At the age of sixteen years, John Wesley entered college at Oxford, and by his rapid progress soon gave evidence of his superior powers of intellect, and sternness of virtue, which so distinguished him in after life. In 1725 he was ordained a deacon, and in 1726 he was elected Fellow of Lincoln College. He took his degree in 1727, and in 1728 was ordained a presbyter in the Church of England.

Passing over the events of his life which occurred during the remainder of the brief period he spent at Oxford, and which were characterized by his devotion to the Church, love of literature, wise and prudent counsels, and his constant charity to the poor, I come down to his missionary voyage to America; and which has been, in connection with his brief sojourn in Savannah, the subject of such abuse, slander, and wicked insinuations, as never were heaped upon any man since that period. As set forth in the preceding pages, I repeat, that Mr. Wesley was baffled in his pious designs of preaching the gospel to the North American Indians, misrepresented and persecuted by those who ought to have been his friends and defenders; and seeing but a dull prospect of succeeding in his main design, he took leave of the Georgians under the circumstances herein before detailed, and arrived in London in February, 1738, having spent two years in America.

On his passage to America, Mr. Wesley made the acquaintance of some pious Moravians on board the same ship. He had frequent opportunities of conversing with them—gave into their sound and scriptural views of the doctrine of justification through faith in Jesus Christ, and the necessity and privilege of the DIRECT WITNESS, and the fruits of the Holy Spirit. On his return to England, he renewed his acquaintance with some of the Moravian ministers, and held frequent and profitable conversations with them. To these interviews, and the prayerful reading of Luther's Preface to the Epistle to the Romans, he attributes his being made a partaker of greater spiritual blessings than he had ever before enjoyed. With a view to strengthen himself in the faith of the Moravian Church, by whose conversations and prayers he had been much edified, and even signally blessed, he performed a journey to their principal settlement in Germany, attended their meetings, and had free and full conversations with their most eminent men on the subject of experimental and practical godliness, by which his mind was much enlightened, and his heart entirely established in the great doctrine of justification by faith, and of the DIRECT WITNESS and FRUIT of the

Holy Spirit. After thus holding communion with these pious and orthodox Christians for some time, he returned to London in the fall of 1738; and from that day to the day of his death, which was in the spring of 1791, a period of FIFTY-THREE YEARS, no other plan of operations ever entered his head, than simply to get and communicate all the good in his power. He ever, after that, preached with power and effect the great and soul-saving doctrine of justification by faith in Christ, and the witness and fruit of the Holy Spirit. So pointed were his appeals, and earnest his exhortations to repentance, that he soon learned what was meant in the Scriptures by the "offence of the cross," for he was refused the use of this, and of that, and then of another church, to preach in! Then it was that, like the eloquent and pious Whitefield, he went into the open fields, Kensington Commons, and other places, and preached the glorious doctrines of faith in Christ, which set all England in a blaze! Success crowned his efforts wherever he labored. Those who were awakened under his preaching—and their names were Legion—came to him for advice; and as the number of these rapidly increased, he found it necessary to form them into a society; and in 1743 he drew up those rules of his societies, which have continued to be the GENERAL RULES of the Methodist societies, both in England and America, to this day, with scarcely an exception.

This was the first regular organization of societies by Mr. Wesley, and the formation of *classes* followed soon after this. Among those who were converted under his ministry, and joined his societies, were some talented and educated young men, and others with but limited education, but "full of faith and of the Holy Ghost," whom, notwithstanding his devotion to the *established order of things*, he started out to preach. Hence originated his employment of lay-preachers, an irregularity for which, though he suffered much persecution, thousands had cause to be thankful in Europe. As the work increased under the labors of John and Charles Wesley, and the preachers in their employ, it became necessary, in order to avoid confusion, to reduce their operations to *system*, and to have a more digested plan. This led to the calling of all the preachers together for *a Conference*, the first of which was held in London in June, 1744, or *one hundred and twelve years* ago; although Elder Graves says—" Methodism cannot be called a Church of Christ, because too young—it being only *sixty-eight* years old!"

After the organization of a Conference, the work went on more rapidly than ever, and soon spread over different parts of England and Wales. In his evangelical labors, Mr. Wesley was assisted by several pious and learned clergymen of the Established Church, not the least efficient of whom were his brother Charles and Mr. Fletcher. The work spread over Ireland and Scotland; but it is by no means necessary in this sketch to enter into further details as to the rise and progress of Methodism in Great Britain.

In 1766, Providence opened the way for the introduction of Methodism into America; and the first Methodist society was established in the city of New York in that year. The first preacher of the Methodists who labored in New York was Philip Embury, a local preacher who emigrated from Ireland. But Elder Graves asserts, time and again, that Methodism is *"only sixty-eight years old,"* and is therefore too young to be called a Church of Christ! The proof is that its first appearance in New York was *eighty-eight* years ago, showing a mistake on the part of Elder Graves of *twenty* years, dating its origin only back to its introduction into the United States! This blunder was not a *slip of the pen*, for the writer dwells upon it, occupies several pages upon this *assumed* fact, and drives to various conclusions. He has taken this position either through ignorance or a love of lying —the reader may decide which.

At the Conference at Leeds, in 1768, Mr. Wesley sent over to the aid of the cause in America two additional preachers, Richard Boardman and Joseph Pillmore; and about that time, Robert Strawbridge, a local preacher from Ireland, came over and settled in Frederick county, in Maryland. In 1771, Francis Asbury and Richard Wright were sent over to the work in America. At page 109, vol. iii., of Mr. Asbury's Journal, in 1773, he speaks of the numbers in their societies where he had labored—not having any report from Mr. Strawbridge in Maryland, and others—after this wise: "About three hundred in New York, two hundred and fifty in Philadelphia, and a few in New Jersey."

Mr. Asbury was constituted "general assistant" by Mr. Wesley, in 1772, and began to hold quarterly meetings, and hear reports from his brethren in the ministry. This designation is better understood when it is remembered that Mr. Wesley being, under God, the founder of the societies, was considered the head of the whole body, both in Europe and America; and all having charge of circuits under him were styled his "*assistants*," and those under these assistants were styled "*helpers*." In appointing Mr. Asbury a *general assistant*, he constituted him the head of all the preachers and societies in America, with power to station the preachers; but under the general direction of Mr. Wesley himself, to whom he made his regular reports.

The first regular Conference ever held in America convened in Philadelphia, July 4th, 1773, *eighty-three* years ago, notwithstanding Elder Graves asserts that Methodism is "only 68 years old," and the "North Carolina Publishing Society" endorses his assertion! The numbers in society, as reported in the general minutes, were ELEVEN HUNDRED AND SIXTY-SIX, and the preachers in the work were TEN, laboring in New York, Pennsylvania, New Jersey, Maryland, and Virginia.

These conferences were held every year, sometimes in one

State and sometimes in another—the membership and ministry increasing rapidly, until the arrival of a very important period in the history of Methodism in this country, the organization of the METHODIST EPISCOPAL CHURCH, which was in 1784. Dr. Coke, Richard Whatcoat, and Mr. Vasey, arrived in America in this year, and proceeded to New Jersey, where they met with Mr. Asbury and others, and announced to them their intention to organize the Methodists of this country into an independent Episcopal Church; and it was at once agreed to call a General Conference at Baltimore the ensuing Christmas. In conformity with this arrangement, December 25th, 1784, SIXTY out of the EIGHTY-THREE travelling preachers then in the connection assembled in the city of Baltimore, where Dr. Coke presided, assisted by Mr. Asbury; and the first act of this General Conference was to elect Dr. Coke and Mr. Asbury, by a unanimous vote, General Superintendents. Though Mr. Asbury had been appointed to that office by Mr. Wesley, he was too much devoted to the mutual rights of ministers and of *republican* principles, to act any longer in that capacity independently of the suffrages of his brethren over whom he must preside. He did so willingly when there was a *necessity* for it, but no longer than was indicated by the providence of God. The validity of Mr. Asbury's ordination by THOMAS COKE, Doctor of Civil Law, Presbyter of the Church of England, and Superintendent of the Methodist Episcopal Church in America, as well as the Methodist form of Church government, all of which are ridiculed and misrepresented by Elder Graves, will form the subject-matter of a future chapter in this work.

I again resume the consideration of the character and labors of Mr. Wesley, than whom no man, since the days of the apostles, ever was clothed with such a panoply as that with which he was armed. *Bigoted Calvinistic Baptists*, however, will no more pardon Mr. Wesley for the wounds he inflicted on their favorite theory, than the Roman Catholics will forgive Calvin and Luther for striking such a death-blow at the sale of indulgences and other mummeries sanctioned by that corrupt Church. But despite the malicious slanders of such men as Elder Graves, the name of John Wesley will ever be associated in the minds of the good and great, who best know his worth, with all the excellences which adorn and beautify the human character, when sanctified by grace, as well as those qualifications which originate from profound learning, an acute and penetrating mind, and a heart deeply imbued with the grace of God, and also a life unweariedly devoted to the best of all causes. That he was encompassed with those infirmities which are inseparable from humanity, his friends and admirers never denied; and this detracts nothing from his character, any more than the offensive *epithets* applied to him, and *vulgar charges* preferred against him, by the miserable calumniator of the "Tennessee Baptist;" which can never lessen him in the estimation of those who impartially estimate worth.

I do not ask Elder Graves to contemplate the glorious achievements of Methodism, under the direction of John Wesley, but I call upon the "North Carolina Publishing Society of the Baptist Church" to look calmly at its rise and progress! I ask the members of that Society to go with me, as one of the admirers of Mr. Wesley, to the humble dwellings of the miners of Cornwall, to the homely tents of the colliers of Kingswood and Newcastle, and to the equally humble workshops of the manufacturers of Yorkshire, in England, who are still rejoicing in God their Saviour that a Wesley was ever born into this sin-stricken world, and ask them if they believe he lived and died an unconverted man? Go with me, gentlemen of the "Publishing Society," among the backwoodsmen of North America, and examine them in their lonely tents; go among the honest settlers on our western frontiers, and amid the interminable forests of our far-off western wilds, where multiplied thousands reside who were brought into the fold of Christ through the instrumentality of Wesleyan ministers, and ask them if they think the founder of their Church, under God, was a hypocrite? Go with me to the rich pastures and luxuriant harvest-fields of your own native Carolina; enter the neat cottages and stately mansions of the glorious Old North State, and ask the intelligent and educated females who are rejoicing in God, to this very day, in hope of future and eternal life, through the instrumentality of the sermons and prayers of Wesleyan ministers, if they believe the venerable founder of their Church was *a wicked adulterer?* Go with me to the distant islands of different seas, to the burning sands of Africa, to Ceylon, and other pagan countries, and ask the benighted converts from heathenism, through the instrumentality of Wesleyan ministers, if they believe the venerable founder of the Church of which they are now happy members was a man of God, or an ambitious candidate for fame? Enter the dwellings of the rich and fashionable planters of our own "sunny South;" ride through and around their extensive sugar and cotton plantations, among the sable sons and daughters of Africa, and witness the blessed fruits of the orthodox teachings, pious life, Christian integrity, and triumphant death of the great and good Wesley! Meet me, gentlemen, half way between Knoxville and Raleigh, our respective places of abode, and together let us enter the log-cabins of the virtuous, pious, happy peasantry of the "hill-country" of Western Carolina, and ask them whether they believe the facts set forth in Mr. Wesley's Journal, or the misrepresentations of Elder Graves! Ask any one of them upon a dying-bed, whether they desire one of Wesley's sermons read to them, or a chapter from the "Iron Wheel" you have so graciously condescended to endorse!

Whether we send the religion and Church government which God has handed down to us through a Wesley, an Asbury, a Coke, and others, among the neat cottages and stately mansions of New England, or among the wilds of Missouri, Arkansas, or Texas, the wilderness and solitary places are made glad for them, and the desert is made to rejoice and blossom as the rose! Methodism weathered the storm of persecution brought upon it by Southey, Smollet, Toplady, Nightingale, and even Lord John Russell, of the British Parliament; and most assuredly it is not to be demolished west of our Alleghany range of mountains by *j. r. graves*, a vindictive little Baptist preacher, of exceedingly doubtful piety, as well as of questionable veracity, and without that force of character requisite to build up or pull down any sect! Let Baptist malice, with its grim concomitants, envy and hatred, tremble as it plots the ruin of Methodism, and seeks to build up its own perfidious and exclusive system; and, above all, let this bread-and-butter patriot of the nineteenth century, *J. R. Graves*, remember that his day for fasting and humiliation is close at hand!

The Reformation dawned with Luther in Germany, but the sun of its glory rose with Methodism in England: the first streaks of *Protestant* light were seen on the horizon of the sixteenth century, but the meridian sun of the Reformation shone in all its brightness on the Wesleys and Whitefield! But the United States, or more properly North America, has been the land of its triumph and its glory; and in America God has shown the world what Methodism can suffer unharmed, and what Methodism can accomplish. Yes, here, in the glorious nineteenth century, after slander and persecution have done their vilest work, and have tried in vain to crush Methodism beneath the "Iron Wheels" of the chariot of perdition, she is still "going forth conquering and to conquer," as the right arm of the Lord, when his enemies bow before him, and the kingdoms of this world become the kingdoms of God and of his Christ:

"O! 't is a flower that cannot fade,
That no *rude blast can chill:*
It blossoms in the sheltered shade,
And on the bleakest hill;
And every changing form of time
Moves on, and sees it in its prime!"

That what I have said may not appear as "vain boasting," I will give the FACTS and FIGURES, as these will deceive no one. The self-styled prophet, *J. R. Graves*, has put on record the prediction that Methodism *must ere long die out.* He has discovered, in a dream by night, signs of a decreasing membership, ominous of death. I am able to show, and to *prove*, that the increase of Methodism, for half a century past, has been steady and onward! This can be easily shown; and the able editor of ZION'S HERALD does the work effectually in his issue of the 24th of October, 1855. He says:

The following table covers over half a century. We are governed in our selection of the starting-points of our decades by the dates of the national census. Our numbers for each decade are for the year immediately following that on which each census was taken:

Increase of the Methodist Episcopal Church, by decades, from 1791 *to* 1854.

In 1791, Memb. M. E. Church,	63,269,	*An increase in* 10 *years of*
" 1801, " "	72,874,	9,605, or 15⅛ per cent.
" 1811, " "	184,567,	111,693, or 153½ "
" 1821, " "	281,146,	96,579, or 52⅓ "
" 1831, " "	513,114,	331,968, or 82½ "
" 1841, " "	859,811,	346,697, or 67½ "
" 1851, (North & South,)	1,251,198,	391,388, or 45½ "
" 1854, (North & South,)	1,386,661,	135,463 *for the last* 3 *years.*

The next table shows how the *per centage* of our increase compares with that of the entire population of the country:

The population	increased from	1790 to 1800	35.02 per cent.
Methodism	"	1791 to 1801	15.20 "
The population	"	1800 to 1810	36.45 "
Methodism	"	1801 to 1811	153.50 "
The population	"	1810 to 1820	33.13 "
Methodism	"	1811 to 1821	52.33 "
The population	"	1820 to 1830	33.49 "
Methodism	"	1821 to 1831	82.50 "
The population	"	1830 to 1840	32.67 "
Methodism	"	1831 to 1841	67.50 "
The population	"	1840 to 1850	25.87 "
Methodism	"	1841 to 1851	45.50 "

Thus it appears that the per centage of our increase has been decidedly greater than that of the aggregate population of the country.

A comparison of our *numbers* with the whole population will show a rapidly increasing ratio. Thus, beginning with 1791, seven years after the organization of our Church, we have the following results:

In 1791	one Methodist	to about every	62½	of the	whole population.
" 1801	"	"	72½	"	"
" 1811	"	"	39¼	"	"
" 1821	"	"	30	"	"
" 1831	"	"	25	"	"
" 1841	"	"	19½	"	"
" 1851	"	"	18½	"	"

These ratios, which do not include the members of various seceding Methodist bodies, but only the Methodist Episcopal Church, and the Methodist Episcopal Church, South, show, that in the sixty years previous to 1852, our ratio to the entire population has increased from *one* in *sixty-two and a half*, to *one* in *eighteen and a half;* or, including the various branches of Methodism not embraced in the above table, but numbering over one hundred and thirteen thousand communicants, our ratio has advanced from one in sixty-two and a half to one in seventeen; which exhibits a very gratifying increase on the population of the country.

But Elder Graves tells the world, *boastingly*, on page 109 of his "Iron Wheel," that Mr. Wesley's own people in Georgia were "thoroughly disgusted with his conduct, and outraged by his arrogance and imperial dictation." He informs the public, in a note to be found on page 108, that a certain *Judge Warren*, of Albany, Georgia, informed *him* that the bill of indictment found against Mr. Wesley, at the instance of *Mr. Causton*, "is still preserved in the Court House at Savannah, where it can be seen!" Wonderful preservation this! And for the information of Judge Warren, we can say that the bill of indictment upon which J. R. Graves was *convicted* and fined $7,500 and costs, is still preserved in the Court House at Lexington, Henderson county, Tennessee, "where it can be seen" likewise! A further record of the fact can be found in the office of the Supreme Court at Jackson, Tennessee, where the decision of the court at Lexington was *affirmed;* and to evade the payment of this fine and these costs, J. R. Graves *mortgaged* his property to some Baptist friends at

Nashville, where the record is still preserved, and "can be seen." What a country ours is for preserving bills of indictment and records of *fraudulent* mortgages!

But Elder Graves tells us that "Methodism is only sixty-eight years old," and is therefore too young to be a Church of Christ; while the Baptist Church is an old and venerable Church, as old as the hills, and therefore *is* the Church of Christ! Let us compare the strength of the two denominations in Georgia, where the founder of one is in such bad odor!

I have procured the published Minutes of the late Baptist Convention of Georgia, and also the Minutes of the Georgia Conference of the Methodist Episcopal Church, South, for the same year, (1855,) and I presume them both to be correct, as they are the *official* reports of these grave bodies of men. According to these statistics, the *Missionary* Baptists, who hold their connection with the Convention—and with this wing of the numerous Baptist family Elder Graves is associated—these number in Georgia 35,130 whites, and 19,510 colored, after *deducting* 2000 whites and colored of an association within the bounds of the State of Florida, who are likewise connected with said Convention. These Minutes next set forth that there are 11,968 "Primitive Baptists," whites and colored—commonly called *Hard Shells* or *Iron Jackets*—a race of men who "play upon a harp of a thousand strings, spirits of just men made perfect!" Next in order these minutes report 3,964 Baptists, white and colored, who hold no connection with either of the former, but set up "on their own hook." These numbers include all in the State of Georgia who hold to *the exclusive mode of baptism by immersion!*

Now, let us turn to the Minutes of the Georgia Conference, and see what the strength of the Methodists is. They set down the numbers as follows:—50,213 whites; 21,857 colored; 552 local preachers—making in all, whites and colored, within the bounds of the Conference, 72,622. Add to this 6000, the number in sixteen counties in Georgia, included in the Florida Conference, and not reported in these Minutes, we have the number of 78,622. There are 11,000 Protestant Methodists in Georgia, who may be numbered with the Episcopal Methodists, as the 11,968 Hard Shells are with the Missionary Baptists. Adding, then, this 11,000 to the former, we have the number of 89,622 Methodists in Georgia. But include the 552 local preachers and 200 travelling preachers, who are as legitimately members of the Church as the Baptist clergy are, and we have 90,374 Methodists in Georgia!

Now, gentle reader, the comparative numerical strength of these contending denominations in the State of Georgia is as 90,374 to 70,572; or, deduct the 70,572 Baptists from the 90,374 Methodists, and the *young* Church exhibits a majority of 19,802 over the *old* Church, and emphatically *the* Church, to the exclusion of all others! I will add that the people of Georgia place a different estimate upon the doctrines and polity of Methodism from that given in the vile production of this man Graves. It will not be contended that the "lower classes" constitute the Methodist forces in Georgia. I know, of my own knowledge and from actual personal observation, that there is as much of wealth, talents, respectability, and influence in the Methodist Church in Georgia as any Church can boast of, and, if the reader please, *a little more*, because their numbers are greater than those of any other Church.

Many more particulars of Mr. Wesley's life, both of a public and private nature, might have been detailed; but it will be remembered that I am not writing out his life, but *defending* certain of his acts; and, I hope, in such a manner as to enable the intelligent reader, by this time, to form a correct opinion of his character. Let us remember that some particular circumstances, or a few occasional acts in a man's life, do not form his character, but the *general tenor of his conduct;* because this shows some fixed principle that uniformly operates upon him, which, with a correspondent *practice,* forms his character. (I am aware that Elder Graves will object to this rule, because, in his case, it would expel him from any tolerably civilized Church in America!) And when a long, virtuous, and useful life is crowned with AN END suitable to it, as was the case with John Wesley, death puts a stamp upon his virtues, which shows us they were not *spurious coin,* but genuine. If the candid reader will judge of Mr. Wesley by this rule, he will agree with me that, whatever failings as a man he may have had, he possessed a degree of excellence, and acted it out, to which few men have attained in this life.

But, to complete the picture which I have intended to draw, it is necessary, now, only to contemplate him as he delivered up his commission into the hands of his great Master. Passing over a variety of thrilling incidents, I give the copy of a letter he addressed to the Lord Bishop of London, some of whose clergy had forbid Mr. Wesley's preachers occupying their pulpits:—

MY LORD,—I am a dying man, having already one foot in the grave. Humanly speaking, I cannot long creep upon the earth, being now nearer ninety than eighty years of age. But I cannot die in peace before I have discharged this office of Christian love to your Lordship. I write without ceremony, as neither hoping nor fearing any thing from your Lordship, or from any man living. And I ask, in the name and in the presence of Him to whom both you and I are shortly to give an account, why do you trouble those that are quiet in the land?—those that fear God and work righteousness? Does your Lordship know what the Methodists are? that many thousands of them are zealous members of the Church of England? and strongly attached, not only to his Majesty, but to his present ministry? Why should your Lordship, setting religion out of the question, throw away such a body of respectable friends? Is it for their religious sentiments? Alas, my Lord, is this a time to persecute any man for conscience' sake? I beseech you, my Lord, do as you would be done to. You are a man of sense, you are a man of learning; nay, I verily believe (what is of infinitely more value) you are a man of piety. Then think, and let think. I pray God to bless you with the choicest of his blessings.—I am, my Lord, etc., JOHN WESLEY.

After this, Dr. WHITEHEAD, on page 540 of his Life of Wesley, makes these remarks:—

Mr. Wesley began now to feel the infirmities of age increase fast upon him, though he continued his usual labors without complaint. But in January, 1790, he observes, "I am now an old man, decayed from head to foot. My eyes are dim: my right hand shakes much: my mouth is hot and dry every morning: I have a lingering fever almost every day; and my motion is weak and slow. However, blessed be God, I do not slack my labor. I can preach and write still." And on June 28, his birthday, he further observes, "This day I enter into my eighty-eighth year. For above eighty-six years, I found none of the infirmities of old age: my eyes did not wax dim, neither was my natural strength abated. But last August, I found almost a sudden change: my eyes were so dim that no glasses would help me; my strength likewise quite forsook me, and probably will not return in this world. But I feel no pain from head to foot, only it seems nature is exhausted, and, humanly speaking, will sink more and more, till

"'The weary springs of life stand still at last.'"

After this he began to sink—was confined to his own room and his bed; and I will let Dr. WHITEHEAD finish the melancholy narrative, which terminates, however, in the triumphant Christian death of JOHN WESLEY:—

He asked what the words were from which he had preached a little before at Hampstead. Being told they were these: "For ye know the grace of our Lord Jesus Christ, that though he was rich, yet for your sakes he became poor, that ye through his poverty might be rich," he replied, "That is the foundation, the only foundation, and there is no other."—This day I desired he might be asked if he would have any other physician called in to attend him; but this he absolutely refused. It is remarkable that he suffered so little pain, never complaining of any during his illness, but once of a pain in his breast. This was a restless night.—Tuesday morning, he sang two verses of a hymn: then lying still, as if to recover strength, he called for pen and ink; but when it was brought he could not write. A person said, "Let me write for you, sir: tell me what you would say." He replied, "Nothing, but that God is with us." In the forenoon he said, "I will get up." While they were preparing his clothes, he broke out, in a manner that astonished all who were about him, in singing,

I'll praise my Maker while I've breath,
And when my voice is lost in death
  Praise shall employ my nobler powers:
My days of praise shall ne'er be past
While life, and thought, and being last,
  Or immortality endures!

Having got him into his chair, they observed him change for death But he, regardless of his dying body, said with a weak voice, "Lord, thou givest strength to those who can speak, and to those who cannot. Speak, Lord, to all our hearts, and let them know that thou loosest tongues." He then sang,

To Father, Son, and Holy Ghost,
  Who sweetly all agree—

Here his voice failed. After gasping for breath, he said, "Now we have done all." He was then laid on the bed, from whence he rose no more. After resting a little, he called to those who were with him "to pray and praise." Soon after he said, "Let me be buried in nothing but what is woollen, and let my corpse be carried in my coffin into the chapel." And again called upon them to "pray and praise;" and taking each by the hand, and affectionately saluting them, bade them farewell. Attempting afterwards to say something which they could not understand, he paused a little, and then, with all the remaining strength he had, said, "The best of all is, God is with us." And again, lifting his hand, he repeated the same words in a holy triumph, "The best of all is, God is with us." Something being given him to moisten his lips, he said, "It will not do: we must take the consequence. Never mind the poor carcase." Being told that his brother's widow was come, he said, "He giveth his servants rest;" thanked her as she pressed his hand, and affectionately endeavored to kiss her. His lips being again wet, he repeated his usual grace after a meal: "We thank thee, O Lord, for these and all thy mercies: bless the Church and King, grant us truth and peace, through Jesus Christ our Lord." After some pause, he said, "The clouds drop fatness. The Lord is with us: the God of Jacob is our refuge." He again called them to prayer, and appeared fervently to join in their petitions.

Most of the following night he often attempted to repeat the psalm before mentioned, but could only get out, "I'll praise! I'll praise!" On Wednesday morning his end drew near. Mr. Bradford, his old and faithful friend, who, with the affection of a son, had attended him for many years, now prayed with him; and the last word he was heard to articulate was, "Farewell!" A few minutes before ten, on the second day of March, while a number of friends were kneeling around his bed, died Mr. John Wesley, without a groan. He was in the eighty-eighth year of his age, had been sixty-five years in the ministry; and the preceding pages will be a lasting memorial of his uncommon zeal, diligence, and usefulness in his Master's work for more than half a century. His death was an admirable close of sc laborious and useful a life.

March the 9th was the day appointed for his interment. The preachers then in London, to my utter astonishment, insisted that I should deliver the funeral discourse; and the executors afterwards approved of the appointment. The intention was to carry the corpse into the chapel, and place it in a raised situation before the pulpit during the service. But the crowds which came to see the body while it lay in the coffin, both in the private house, and especially in the chapel the day before the funeral, were so great that his friends were apprehensive of a tumult if they should proceed on the plan first intended. It was therefore resolved, the evening before, to bury him between five and six in the morning. Though the time of notice to his friends was short, and the design itself was spoken of with great caution, yet a considerable number of persons attended at that early hour. The late Rev. Mr. Richardson, who now lies with him in the same vault, read the funeral service, in a manner that made it peculiarly affecting. The discourse, which was afterwards printed, was delivered in the chapel, at the hour appointed in the forenoon, to an astonishing multitude of people, among whom were many ministers of the gospel, both of the Establishment and the Dissenters. The audience was still and solemn as night; and all seemed to carry away with them enlarged views of Mr. Wesley's character, and serious impressions of the importance of religion and the utility of Methodism.

The death of Mr. Wesley attracted the public notice beyond any former example, perhaps, of a clergyman, however dignified. It being generally known that he died as he had lived, and evinced in death the uprightness and integrity of his life, the impression on the public mind in favor of his character and of Methodism was almost universal; so that some persons said Mr. Wesley will do more good by his death than he did in his whole life. This, however, is certain, that a door of usefulness was now opened to the Methodist preachers unknown at any former period.

The following inscription, though in my judgment not worthy of Mr. Wesley, has since his interment been put on his tomb:—

To the Memory of
THE VENERABLE JOHN WESLEY, A. M.,
Late Fellow of LINCOLN College, OXFORD.

This GREAT LIGHT arose
(By the singular Providence of God)
To enlighten THESE NATIONS,
And to *revive, enforce,* and *defend*
The Pure, Apostolical DOCTRINES and PRACTICES of
THE PRIMITIVE CHURCH:
Which he continued to do, by his WRITINGS and his
LABORS,
For more than HALF A CENTURY:
And, to his inexpressible Joy,
Not only beheld their INFLUENCE extending,
And their EFFICACY witnessed,

In the hearts and Lives of MANY THOUSANDS,
As well in the WESTERN WORLD, as in these
KINGDOMS:
But also, far above all human Power or Expectation,
Lived to see PROVISION made, by the singular Grace
of GOD,
For their CONTINUANCE and ESTABLISHMENT,
TO THE JOY of FUTURE GENERATIONS!
READER, if thou art constrained to bless the INSTRUMENT,
GIVE GOD THE GLORY!

*After having languished a few days, He at length finished
his* COURSE *and his* LIFE *together: gloriously
triumphing over* DEATH, *March* 2, *An.
Dom.* 1791, *in the eighty-eighth Year
of his Age.*

The following is the inscription on the marble tablet erected to his memory in the chapel where he labored so long and so successfully, City Road, London:—

Sacred to the Memory
OF THE Rev. JOHN WESLEY, M. A.,
SOMETIME FELLOW OF LINCOLN COLLEGE, OXFORD:
A Man in Learning and sincere Piety
Scarcely inferior to any:
In Zeal, Ministerial Labors, and extensive Usefulness,
Superior, perhaps, to all Men,
Since the days of ST. PAUL.

Regardless of Fatigue, personal Danger, and Disgrace,
He went out into the highways and hedges,
Calling Sinners to Repentance,
And Publishing the GOSPEL of Peace.

He was the Founder of the Methodist Societies,
And the chief Promoter and Patron
Of the Plan of Itinerant Preaching,
Which he extended through GREAT BRITAIN and IRELAND,
The WEST INDIES, and AMERICA,
With unexampled Success.

He was born the 17th of June, 1703;
And died the 2d of March, 1791,
In sure and certain hope of Eternal Life,
Through the Atonement and Mediation of a Crucified Saviour

He was sixty-five Years in the Ministry,
And fifty-two an Itinerant Preacher:

He lived to see, in these KINGDOMS only,
About three hundred Itinerant,
And one thousand Local Preachers,
Raised up from the midst of his own People;
And eighty thousand Persons in the Societies under his care.

His Name will be ever had in grateful Remembrance
By all who rejoice in the universal Spread
Of the Gospel of Christ.

Soli Deo Gloria.
[Glory to God alone.]

INSCRIPTION ON HIS COFFIN:—

JOHANNES WESLEY, A. M.,
OLIM SOC. COLL. LIN. OXON.

Ob. 2 do. die Martii, 1791.
An. Æt. 88.*

It would be superfluous, in closing this account of a man at once so extraordinary and so great, to attempt any further delineation of his character, since this has been done so ably by Messrs. Whitehead, Moore, and Watson, that nothing can easily be added with good effect. I have enlarged to the extent herein found, because this work will fall into many hands, and be read by many persons, who otherwise might never see the facts, and still be annoyed by quotations from the vile, not to say infamous and slanderous production of *J. R. Graves!* The injustice done to Mr. Wesley's memory by the work I am replying to, is calculated to prepossess many a youthful mind with strong and early prejudices against one of the most devoted and the most honored ambassadors of Christ that have ever graced any age or nation since the days of the holy apostles. The influence of such prejudices can only be met by a cheap work of this kind, extensively circulated, as I have reason to believe this will be. Moreover,

* "John Wesley, Master of Arts, formerly Fellow of Lincoln College, Oxford, died on the second day of March, 1791, in the eighty-eighth year of his age."

in order to counteract the influence of such prejudices, even against the Christian denomination of which that eminent man was, under God, the founder, it has been of the utmost importance that I should show *who J. R. Graves is*, and to what degree of credit his *assertions* are entitled. This is at once my apology and justification for the seeming *severity* and manifest *personalities* I use.

The following description of Mr. Wesley's person, which is taken from his life by Dr. Whitehead, will be full of interest to most readers of the preceding pages; and certainly will be more agreeable to those who are members of the great religious family of which he was, under God, the *father*:—

The figure of Mr. Wesley was remarkable. His stature was low: his habit of body, in every period of life, the reverse of corpulent, and expressive of strict temperance and continual exercise; and notwithstanding his small size, his step was firm, and his appearance, till within a few years of his death, vigorous and muscular. His face, for an old man, was one of the finest we have seen. A clear, smooth forehead, an aquiline nose, an eye the brightest and most piercing that can be conceived, and a freshness of complexion scarcely ever to be found at his years, and impressive of the most perfect health, conspired to render him a venerable and interesting figure. Few have seen him without being struck with his appearance; and many, who had been greatly prejudiced against him, have been known to change their opinion the moment they were introduced into his presence. In his countenance and demeanor, there was a cheerfulness mingled with gravity; a sprightliness, which was the natural result of an unusual flow of spirits, and yet was accompanied with every mark of the most serene tranquillity. His aspect, particularly in profile, had a strong character of astuteness and penetration.

In dress, he was a pattern of neatness and simplicity. A narrow plaited stock, a coat with a small upright collar, no buckles at his knees, no silk or velvet in any part of his apparel, and a head as white as snow, gave an idea of something primitive and apostolic: while an air of neatness and cleanliness was diffused over his whole person.

But one conclusive evidence of the greatness and goodness of the deceased Wesley is, that, though dead and gone to his reward in heaven, he is still the object of the most malignant, wicked, and ungentlemanly abuse from sectarian bigots of all Churches, and especially the *pig-pen orators* and *whisky-shop saints* of the Baptist denomination! Go on, ye insignificant revilers! spit your venom at his fair fame, spew your slime upon the escutcheon of his character, empty your polluted stomachs of all the pent-up spleen that is in you, for you cannot harm the illustrious dead. An enlightened public know his history, his principles, his ability, and his unexampled usefulness; and the tongues and pens of slander cannot detract from either!

CHAPTER IV.

Opposition to Methodism—Methodism "an accident, and of human invention"—Methodism not the work of design, but of Providence—Mr. Wesley the author of Episcopacy—Ordination of Dr. Coke—Deacons, elders, and bishops, considered as orders in the ministry—Testimony of Clarke, Watson, Emory, Stillingfleet, and Dr. Miller, in reference to Episcopacy—The Baptist the only Church of Christ on earth!

THE gross misstatements of Lord John Russell, both in the British Parliament and through the press, and of other designing politicians and wicked men, show that Methodism has been a prominent object of attack by the enemies of Christianity, as well in Europe as in America. Sectarian bigotry, too, and ambitious and corrupt clergymen, have never ceased their warfare against Methodism, as may be seen by a reference to the coarse and bitter attacks of such men as *J. R. Graves.* In America, as also in Europe, her doctrines were first assailed, and then her polity. But on both continents, and in each case, she has maintained her ground; and the struggle has both added to her strength and increased her glory.

That objections and anathemas should be gravely thrown out against the ecclesiastical economy of Methodism, by Episcopalians and Presbyterians, and other sects having themselves *forms of Church government,* might reasonably enough be expected; but for Baptists, whose government is "without form and void," as was our earth before the Creator restored it to order, to be lecturing against the government of the Methodist Church, is certainly ridiculous!

The loud and often-reiterated clamor of heresy in doctrines, had scarcely died upon the ear of Methodism, until she was able to discover, from pretty clear and unequivocal indications, that it had only yielded to a different mode of attack; and that, while opposition was thus changing its character, it was abating nothing, either of its rancor or its activity. As Methodists, we can boast, with the Reformers of the sixteenth century, that the popular voice is with us in *doctrines;* and a knowledge of this fact on the part of other denominations has forced them to take our DOCTRINES kindly by the hand, and bid them God-speed! No sooner did this suspension of hostilities against our *doctrines* take place, than an open attack upon our *Church government* was brought about.

I am within bounds, I think, when I affirm, as I now do, that 300 out of the 570 pages of Elder Graves's book, are abuse and misrepresentation of the *government* of the Methodist Episcopal Church; and as much of this is a repetition of the same slang, some original, some from other authors, both with and without credit, I need only take up the main points, and in answering these, I answer the whole work.

On page 66, Elder Graves charges—"Methodism is an accident—Mr. Wesley was opposed to Episcopacy—did not believe in three orders—the system of Methodism is purely of human invention."

And on page 73, in continuing the subject, he says: "We understand by Episcopacy, THREE SEPARATE AND DISTINCT ORDERS IN THE MINISTRY, and that of Bishops as the THIRD ORDER, POSSESSING A DIVINE RIGHT TO OVERRULE ALL."

1. The evidence is before the world, that the distinguished founder of Methodism was fully qualified for and regularly called to his work—a work which has proved to be eminently

the work of God; and whether by "accident" or design, matters not.

2. The measures and means adopted by Mr. Wesley for carrying on this work were sanctioned of God, for the spiritual good of mankind, to an extent that no other man's labors have been since the days of the apostles. But Mr. Wesley was led into this work without any previously digested plan of his own, and was conducted forward, not by "accident," but by the indications of *Divine providence* and *grace*.

3. Mr. Wesley was so far from setting out in his career, as charged by this man Graves, with a view of putting himself at the head of a *sect*, that his sole object was to do good—to revive primitive Christianity in the Established Church, of which he was a minister, in conformity to the letter and spirit of its own articles of faith and formularies of devotion, which had been shamefully departed from and neglected for years. And for this work he was fiercely opposed, and bitterly persecuted, by the corrupt, dissipated, and carnal clergy of his own Established Church, as well as by the Dissenters and papists, who were still more corrupt, and with whose *loose code of morals* Mr. Wesley's teachings were at war, as they still are with the manner of life led by J. R. Graves! Here a crisis arose in Mr. Wesley's affairs, which forced him either to act contrary to the teachings of God's word and Spirit, and relinquish his good-begun work, or to become the leader of a new and a DISTINCT SECT. He chose the latter, as I think, wisely; for which bad men and designing hypocrites will long continue to abuse him, and for which good men and true will as long admire him in this life, and multiplied thousands will bless God for it in eternity! Well may I exclaim, in the delightfully poetic language of Charles Wesley—

When he first the work begun,
  Small and feeble was his day:
Now the word doth swiftly run,
  Now it wins its wid'ning way.

4. Nor is Methodism, though "an accident," indebted for any part of this success to any unworthy compromise with either the follies, the errors, or the vices of the age. In a steady, firm, and uncompromising opposition to them all, and in zealous and persevering efforts for the recovery of those who have been unhappily lured into their destructive paths, she yields to no other Church in Europe or America. She has interposed her instructions, her exhortations, her prayers and her tears, between the impious offenders of God's laws, and the dreadful catastrophe with which they were threatened; and without regard to rank, character, wealth, or circumstances, she has pursued the vicious into all their retreats. Into the most degraded abodes of human wretchedness she has found her way, and has been made the honored instrument of diffusing, with distinguished and unequalled success, the blessings of the gospel of peace; to which blessings, in all probability, they would have remained entire strangers, but for the existence of "an accident!"

5. From among the miners and colliers of Europe, and the poor of America, and the poor everywhere, for whose souls none seemed to care, she has succeeded in rescuing thousands from the dominion of destructive habits, and from the very confines of a dreadful ruin; and if to be the instrument of converting multitudes from the error of their ways, and of turning them from Satan to God, be desirable and praiseworthy, in this honor a Church, the creature of "an accident," has participated more largely than any other in the land. Indeed, some of her brightest ornaments are those who, through her instrumentality, have been rescued from ignorance, obscurity, and vice. And there are, at this day, thousands in the communion of the *Baptist* Church who are indebted, under God, to the influence of Methodism, not only for their awakening and conversion, but for the essential improvement of their *morals;* though the "*accident*" of *immer-*

sion, as introduced into the United States by old *Zeke Holliman*, in Rhode Island, induced them to go in search of "a more excellent way"—the route by *water!* This ends my "chapter of accidents," at least for the present.

I shall now proceed to speak of the *providential origin* of all the peculiar institutions of Methodism, and indeed of her whole ecclesiastical superstructure. Boldly as the opposite has been asserted, and often as that assertion has been reiterated, I hesitate not to say that the Church does not exist, in the institutions and government of which there is to be found *less of human contrivance and worldly policy*, than in the Methodist Episcopal Church. It is so far from being true that we are indebted to any previous calculation and management of Mr. Wesley, such as Mr. Graves styles "human invention," for our excellent and scriptural institutions, that he never for one moment contemplated the organization of a separate Church, or even the formation of *societies*, as shown in the opening of this chapter. Mr. Wesley set out influenced by the single and engrossing purpose of doing good. And so ardent was his zeal, that neither a parish nor a realm could set limits to it: the WORLD was his field of labor. And while he was steadily pursuing his toilsome way, *a providence*, evidently to himself as extraordinary as unlooked for, gave birth, in regular succession, to that variety of most excellent institutions by which Methodism has been always so greatly distinguished: to the organization of societies, lay preachers, a regular itinerancy, class-meetings, band-meetings, love-feasts, watch-nights, etc.; until he, no less than others, was astonished to behold a system unfolding itself, which, for correctness of symmetry and beauty of proportion, was unequalled by any thing that had preceded it. Nor was it, as already stated, the result of previous theoretical speculations, or of conversational deliberations. Each arrangement grew up out of the *necessities* of the case, and was adopted from a practical demonstration of its utility; and the *providence* by which many of them were introduced, had even the prejudices of Mr. Wesley *himself* to overcome in their establishment. Even our "Episcopacy" had the weighty argument of *necessity* to recommend it, and was adopted as the best alternative—the wisest expedient—that in an urgent and important case could be thought of. Nor did Mr. Wesley claim any other merit in relation to any of the institutions of Methodism, than that of rightly interpreting the indications, and embracing and following up the openings, of the *special providence* by which the whole business was evidently superintended.

Not a great many years after the separate organization in America took place, a third branch of the same family was organized in Canada. The local circumstances of the three branches of the Wesleyan family rendered it necessary for each to control its own concerns, for the furtherance of the general work; but this never implied any difference in matters of faith and doctrine—only in government and internal regulations. When the American Episcopal organization took place, in 1784, Mr. Wesley endorsed it, and said of the societies: "They are now at full liberty simply to follow the Scriptures and the primitive Church; and we judge it best that they should stand fast in the liberty wherewith God has so strangely set them free."*

The intelligent reader will perceive that it is not at all necessary for me to examine the *whole* of the regulations which Mr. Wesley framed and recommended to the Methodist societies in America, but to notice the prominent feature assailed by this man Graves, to wit, the *episcopal office*. It is, in effect, stoutly denied by Graves that Mr. Wesley ever established that office in the Methodist Church in America; and he asserts, in so many words, that our episcopal form of

* London edition of Moore's Life of Wesley, vol. ii. p. 327.

government is a *surreptitious* addition to the rules and regulations of Mr. Wesley. The facts connected with what is called Methodist *Episcopacy* I will set forth in the words of English Wesleyan writers themselves, whose testimony no sane man will call in question. The Rev. Mr. Drew, editor of the Imperial Magazine, states the whole case thus:

Mr. Wesley was now far advanced in years, and having made provision for the government of the societies in England after his decease, he thought this a providential call for something of a similar nature to be done for America. Having therefore weighed with much deliberation the various circumstances in which his transatlantic followers were placed, he was perfectly satisfied that the form of government which he had provided for England was by no means adapted for America. And, finally, it was obvious to him that no form of government could be acceptable unless it included a satisfactory authority, vested in the preachers, to administer baptism and the Lord's supper. And nothing of this kind could possibly be permanent unless some *general superintendent* should be appointed: in the first instance from hence to transmit that authority to posterity, by what name soever he might be distinguished.

To accomplish these purposes, after revolving all the possible forms of Church government in his mind, he could find none so well adapted to the exigencies of their condition as that which is *episcopal*. On this, therefore, he finally fixed his eye; and proceeded to take measures for executing his resolution. This resolution was, however, not the result of a momentary impulse. More than a year had elapsed since he had begun to revolve it in his mind; during which time he had communicated his thoughts to several persons. But how formidable soever the objections were which any one could raise, he found none equal in magnitude to the evil that his plan was designed to remedy; and he could learn from none a better form than that which he was about to adopt.

The zeal, the activity, and the piety which Dr. Coke had for several years manifested, both in England and Ireland, in conjunction with his being a regularly ordained minister of the Church of England, all combined to point him out to Mr. Wesley as the most suitable person in the connection to engage in this arduous work, and to assume that character with which he was about to invest him. Accordingly, in the month of February, 1784, he called Dr. Coke into his private chamber, and, after some preparatory observations, introduced the important subject to him in nearly the following manner:

"That as the revolution in America had separated the United States from the mother country for ever, and the Episcopal Establishment was utterly abolished, the societies had been represented to him as in a most deplorable condition. That an appeal had also been made to him through Mr. Asbury, in which he was requested to provide for them some mode of Church government suited to their exigencies; and that, having long and seriously revolved the subject in his thoughts, he intended to adopt the plan which he was now about to unfold. That as he had invariably endeavored, in every step he had taken, to keep as closely to the Bible as possible, so on the present occasion he hoped he was not about to deviate from it. That, keeping his eye upon the conduct of the primitive Churches in the ages of unadulterated Christianity, he had much admired the mode of *ordaining bishops* which the Church of Alexandria had practiced. That, to preserve its purity, that Church would never suffer the interference of a foreign bishop in any of their ordinations; but that the presbyters of that venerable apostolic Church, on the death of a bishop, exercised the right of ordaining another from their own body, by the laying on of their own hands; and that this practice continued among them for two hundred years, till the days of Dionysius. And, finally, that being himself a presbyter, he wished Dr. Coke to accept *ordination* from his hands, and to proceed in that character to the continent of America, to superintend the societies in the United States."

Dr. Coke was at first startled at a measure so unprecedented in modern days; and he expressed some doubts as to the validity of Mr. Wesley's authority to constitute so important an appointment. But the arguments of Lord King, which had proselyted Mr. Wesley, were recommended to his attention; and time was allowed him to deliberate on the result. Two months, however, had scarcely elapsed, before he wrote to Mr. Wesley, informing him that his objections were silenced, and that he was ready to coöperate with him in any way that was calculated to promote the glory of God and the good of souls.

At the ensuing Conference, which was held in Leeds, 1784, Mr. Wesley stated his intention to the preachers present; and from that period he considered the appointment as actually made, although the ratification did not take place until a few days afterward. At this Conference Mr. Whatcoat and Mr. Vasey offered their services to accompany Dr. Coke in the character of missionaries; and being accepted, they became his companions in his first voyage to America.

When the Conference in Leeds in 1784 ended, Mr. Wesley repaired to Bristol, and Dr. Coke to London, to make arrangements for his departure. He had not, however, been long in London before he received a letter from Mr. Wesley, requesting him to repair immediately to Bristol, to receive fuller powers; and to bring with him the Rev. Mr. Creighton, a regularly ordained minister, who had long officiated in Mr. Wesley's chapels in London, and assisted him in various branches of his ministerial duties. "The Doctor and Mr. Creighton accordingly met him in Bristol, when, with their assistance, he ordained Mr. Richard Whatcoat and Mr. Thomas Vasey presbyters for America; and, being peculiarly attached to every rite of the Church of England, did afterward *ordain* Dr. Coke a superintendent, giving him *letters of ordination* under his hand and seal." Of these letters of ordination the following is a faithful copy, carefully transcribed from the original in Mr. Wesley's own handwriting, preserved among the papers of the late Dr. Coke:

"To all to whom these presents shall come, John Wesley, late Fellow of Lincoln College in Oxford, Presbyter of the Church of England, sendeth greeting.

"Whereas, many of the people in the southern provinces of North America, who desire to continue under my care, and still adhere to the doctrine and discipline of the Church of England, are greatly distressed for want of ministers to administer the sacraments of baptism and the Lord's supper, according to the usage of the same Church; and whereas, there does not appear to be any other way of supplying them with ministers—

"Know all men that I, *John Wesley*, think myself to be providentially called at this time to set apart some persons for the work of the ministry in America. And therefore, under the protection of Almighty God, and with a single eye to his glory, I have this day set apart as a Superintendent, by the imposition of my hands and prayer, (being assisted by other ordained ministers,) Thomas Coke, Doctor of Civil Law, a Presbyter of the Church of England, and a man whom I judge to be well qualified for that great work. And I do hereby recommend him to all whom it may concern, as a fit person to preside over the flock of Christ. In testimony whereof, I have hereunto set my hand and seal, this second day of September, in the year of our Lord one thousand seven hundred and eighty-four.

"JOHN WESLEY."

Thus far Mr. Drew has gone. On the foregoing I beg leave to offer the following remarks, and ask the candid reader to consider them:

1. It clearly appears that the *ordination* which Mr. Wesley requested Dr. Coke to accept at his hands, and which he did accept, was the *ordination of a bishop*, and was the same with that which was performed by the presbyters of the Church of Alexandria for more than two hundred years.

2. This same ordination Mr. Wesley calls the *"ordaining of bishops;"* and although he chose to distinguish those whom he set apart by the imposition of hands, being assisted by other presbyters, by the title of *superintendents* for the government of the societies in America, he considered them officers of the Church precisely similar to those whom he calls *bishops* in the Church of Alexandria!

3. Dr. Coke was already a regularly ordained presbyter or elder, which is substantially the same, of the Church of England: it would, therefore, have been nothing but solemn mockery for Mr. Wesley to have ordained the Doctor a presbyter *a second time*, had he not intended to set apart Dr. Coke to an office of a higher grade, or, to say the least of it, one altogether distinct from an ordinary presbyter or elder. Besides, Dr. Coke believing his ordination as a presbyter of the Church of England to be scriptural and valid, he would not have submitted to a second ordination at the hands of any man, no, not even the Lord Bishop of London.

4. It is as clear as a noonday's sun that the office with which Mr. Wesley invested Dr. Coke was quite different from that to which he appointed Messrs. Whatcoat and Vasey; and these he calls at different times "presbyters," or "elders." Dr. Coke's office, then, was the *episcopal* office, and he himself was a *bishop* ever after this last ordination, though Mr. Wesley styled him a *General Superintendent* of the societies in America.

5. Mr. Wesley, as I have more than once asserted, was peculiarly attached to every rite of the Church of England, and wished to conform the government of the societies in America, as nearly as possible, to the rites of that Church, without entangling them with the national establishment, and hence he called Dr. Coke *superintendent*. With a view to this he ordained him. And if Dr. Coke's office were not designed to answer to the *episcopal* office in the Church of England, Mr. Wesley was not able to employ words expressive of his meaning!

6. Mr. Wesley felt perfectly satisfied, from the practice of the Church of Alexandria, and that of the apostolic Churches, that the right of ordination was possessed by the presbyters, or elders; that they had a right jointly to invest any one of their own number with the *episcopal* office; that the person

so ordained was not advanced to a degree of *spiritual* authority which he did not possess before, but was only set apart to a *more extensive ecclesiastical jurisdiction*, for the general good of the Church, by the solemn ordinance of the imposition of hands and prayer.

7. All these circumstances taken together will, I feel confident, satisfy the candid and intelligent reader—and I address myself to no other class of persons—that the *episcopal* office in the Methodist Church is of *Mr. Wesley's own appointment*, and that all statements to the contrary are founded in gross error or a love of lying!

8. Mr. Wesley abridged the form of Common Prayer for the use of the "Methodists in North America," had the work printed in 1784, by his own press in London, and sent it over by Dr. Coke. In this work he also gives the forms for ordaining ministers, which Dr. Coke, Mr. Asbury, and others used. The *first* ministerial office named is entitled, "The form and manner of making of Deacons." The *second* office is, "The form and manner of ordaining of Elders." The *third* is, "The form and manner of ordaining a SUPERINTENDENT."

9. To these facts and arguments I will now add the testimony of the English Wesleyan Magazine for 1825, page 183:

Mr. Wesley, in point of *fact*, did *ordain bishops* for the American societies, though he intended them to be called superintendents. Whether the *name* (bishop) had or had not the sanction of Mr. Wesley, is now of the *least possible consequence*, as the *Episcopacy* itself *was of his own creating*. Mr. Wesley's intimate friend and biographer says: "Mr. Wesley gave to the *episcopoi* (*bishops*) whom he *ordained* the modest but highly expressive title of *superintendents*, and desired that no other might be used. That God has greatly blessed this boon (*Episcopacy*) to the American societies, is evident by their great and continued increase. The numbers in the various societies, when Dr. Coke went over, were about *fifteen thousand*. *Six* years after they had increased to nearly *seventy thousand;* and in the year 1820 they were *two hundred and eighty thousand!*" They are now nearly *four hundred thousand*.

"About this period," (1784,) says the Rev. Jonathan Crowther, in his *New and Complete Portraiture of Methodism,* "Mr. Wesley, assisted by other ministers, set apart Dr. Coke, and by him Mr. Asbury, to be *bishops* or superintendents of what was *henceforth* termed the Methodist *Episcopal* Church in America: as also Thomas Vasey and Richard Whatcoat to act as *elders* among them;" and in the *second* English edition of this work, p. 413, Mr. Crowther observes: "Dr. Coke was *ordained bishop,* and brothers Whatcoat and Vasey *presbyters.*"

10. If the setting apart of *superintendents,* as such, were not intended by Mr. Wesley to establish the ordination of such an order of ministers among us, neither was the setting apart of *deacons* and *elders* intended to establish *those* orders. Similar forms and solemnities were recommended for the former as for the latter. Any sensible man who will examine this Prayer Book will say, either that Mr. Wesley intended to establish the ordination of an order of *superintendents,* to act as *bishops in fact,* though with the title of "superintendents," or that he did not intend to establish the ordination of any orders of ministers at all; and that Bishops Coke and Asbury, and their successors in the Episcopacy, utterly mistook the whole matter!

11. The late lamented Bishop Emory records the following, of his own knowledge:

> At the British Conference held in Liverpool, in 1820, we heard the profoundly learned Dr. Adam Clarke, and Rev. Richard Watson, that most amiable and eloquent divine, express themselves publicly before the Conference, in relation to our *Episcopacy,* as a *true, actual, scriptural Episcopacy,* of the most *genuine* and *apostolic* kind.

Finally, other authorities might be added to the same effect, and I have them at command; but it is presumed that the above are quite sufficient to satisfy all candid minds that Mr. Wesley did ordain Dr. Coke *bishop.* And if *Elder Graves* had had any regard for truth, or his own moral character, he would never have published that Mr. Wesley did not establish *Episcopacy* among the Methodists in America.

As to the terms *bishop* and *superintendent,* the one is derived from the Greek, the other from the Latin tongue;

but they signify precisely the same thing in the original, as well as in the English. I need not extend this chapter to adduce authorities on this point. If the reader should wish to pursue it further, he is referred to any common English lexicon, especially Johnson's Quarto Dictionary, where he will find the meaning of these words illustrated by several examples; to Bishop Emory's "Defence of our Fathers," page 66; to Parkhurst's Greek Lexicon, on the word *episcopos;* to Dr. Adam Clarke's Commentary on 1 Tim. chap. iii. v. 2; and to the *Critica Biblica,* vol. iii. page 209, London edition. Bishop Emory says: "When the title *bishop* was introduced into the minutes, in 1788, it was sanctioned by the *Conference,* as meaning precisely the same thing with *superintendent.*" See Emory's Defence, page 49.

Mr. Wesley disapproved of the term *bishop,* not because he was opposed to the *office*—for he considered it, to use his own words, "well agreeing with the writings and practice of the apostles," and, as I have shown in the preceding pages, appointed it for the furtherance of the work of God in America—not because such a title was inapplicable or unscriptural, for it is both appropriate and scriptural, and it is used by Presbyterians at the present day. In Dr. Samuel Miller's Letters, etc., page 9, this paragraph will be found:—"In the form of government of the Presbyterian Church, the pastors of the churches are expressly styled *bishops,* and this title is recommended to be retained, as both scriptural and appropriate." See also the Presbyterian "Digest-Book of Discipline," on the regulations to be observed in the "translation of a *bishop* from one church to another."

It is not true, as stated by Mr. Graves, that the Methodists teach that "bishops are a *third order,* possessing a *divine right* to overrule all." Methodists acknowledge *two orders only* of ministers, *deacons* and *elders,* and a superior minister denominated a *bishop,* possessing a delegated jurisdiction, chiefly of an *executive* character. When the Methodists ordain a *bishop*, they only intend to confer upon him *fuller powers*, for the government of the Church, than they do upon those whom they denominate *deacons* and *elders*. And if the word *order* is applied to bishops as above defined, they are willing to have it understood that they acknowledge *three orders* of ministers—deacons, elders, and bishops. For in the use of the term *order*, the Methodists mean nothing more, in this connection, than that bishops are invested by consent of the eldership with a power to preside over the flock of Christ, and to discharge other duties not so convenient for the elders or presbyters to discharge. They believe, moreover, that the primitive Church, in the age immediately succeeding the apostles, recognized an *order* of ministers denominated *evangelists;* that these were really *itinerating superintendents*, having a general oversight of the whole Church; and that these differed but little, if any, from the bishops of the Methodist Episcopal Church in the United States!

The *Irenicum* of Dr. Stillingfleet, subsequently *Bishop Stillingfleet*, will be admitted to rank and distinction in America equal in celebrity, as an ecclesiastical work, to the "Iron Wheel" of a second-rate Baptist preacher, both of limited acquirements and doubtful veracity. The object of Stillingfleet in this work, as he avows, was to discuss and examine the *divine right* of the different forms of Church government—contrasting them with the positive laws of God, the practice of the apostles and the primitive Church, citing all the best authorities then extant. For ability, excellence of temper, and sound scriptural views, his work certainly has no equal in Protestant Christendom.

I assert (says Dr. Stillingfleet) any particular form of government agreed on by the governors of the Church, consonant to the general rules of Scripture, to be by divine right; that is, God, by his own laws, hath given men a power and liberty to determine the particular form of Church government among them. And hence it may appear that though one form of government be agreeable to the word, it doth not follow that another is not, or because one is lawful, another is unlawful; but one form may be more agreeable to some parts, places, people, and times, than others are. In which case, that form of government is to be settled which is most agreeable to the present state of a place, and is most advantageously conducible to the promoting the ends of Church government in that place or nation.—*Irenicum*, pp. 9, 10. 2d edit. Lond., 1662.

Matters of fact, and mere apostolical practice, may, I freely grant, receive much light from the records of succeeding ages; but they can never give a man's understanding sufficient ground to infer any divine law arising from those facts attested to by the practice or records of succeeding ages.—*Ibid*, p. 151.

In relation to arguments drawn from the testimony of antiquity, before their authority can be admitted in this controversy, Dr. Stillingfleet affirms: These things must be manifested,—*that such things were unquestionably the practice of those ages and persons; that their practice was the same as the apostles; that what they did was not from any prudential motives, but by virtue of a law which did bind them to that practice.* Which things are easily passed over by the most eager disputers of the controversy about Church government; but how necessary they are to be proved, before any form of government be asserted—so necessary, that without it there can be no true Church—any weak understanding may discern.—*Ibid*, p. 152.

The *reason* of apostolical practice binds still, though not the *individual action:* that as they regulated churches for the best conveniency of governing them, so should the pastors of churches now.—*Ibid*, p. 181.

Any one particular form of government in the Church is neither expressed in any direct terms by Christ, nor can be deduced by just consequence; therefore, no such form of government is instituted by Christ.—*Ibid*, p. 182.

The *extending* of any ministerial power is not the appointing of any *new office;* because every minister of the gospel hath a relation in *actu primo* [primarily] to the whole Church of God—the restraint and enlargement of which power is subject to positive determinations of prudence and conveniency; and therefore if the Church see it fit for some men to have this power enlarged, for better government in some, and restrained in others, that *enlargement* is the appointing *no new office*, but the making use of a power already enjoyed for the benefit of the Church of God. This being a foundation tending so fully to clear the lawfulness of that government in the Church, which implies a superiority and subordination of the officers of the Church to one another, and the Church, using her prudence in ordering the bounds of her officers, I shall do these two things: *First*, Show that the power of every minister of the gospel doth primarily and habitually respect the Church in common; *secondly*, That the Church may, in a peculiar manner, single out some of its officers for the due administration of ecclesiastical power.—*Ibid*, p. 195.

The officers of the Church may, in a peculiar manner, attribute a larger and more extensive power to some particular persons, for the more convenient exercise of their common power—grant to some the *executive part* of that power, which is originally and fundamentally common to them all. For our better understanding of this, we must consider a twofold power belonging to church officers—*a power of order* and *a power of jurisdiction.—Ibid,* p. 197.

Under this distinction, he shows that though every presbyter, primarily and inherently, as to *order*, possesses a capacity for the highest ministerial acts, yet some further authority is necessary in a church *constituted* [or organized] besides the power of order; and when this power, either by consent of the pastors of the church, or by the appointment of a Christian magistrate, or both, is devolved to some particular persons, though *quoad aptitudinem* [as to the capacity or fitness] the power remain in every presbyter, yet *quoad executionem* [as to the actual discharge or execution of it] it belongs to those who are so appointed. And therefore Camero determines that ordination doth not belong to the power of order, but to the power of jurisdiction, and therefore is subject to positive restraints, by prudential determinations. By this we may understand how lawful the exercise of an *episcopal* power may be in the Church of God, supposing an *equality* in all church officers as to the power of *order;* and how incongruously they speak who, supposing an equality in the presbyters of churches at first, do cry out that the Church takes upon her the office of Christ, if she *delegates* any to a more *peculiar* exercise of the *power of jurisdiction.—Ibid,* pp. 197–8.

When the apostles were taken out of the way, who kept the main power in their own hands of ruling the several presbyteries, or delegated some to do it, (who had a main hand in planting churches with the apostles, and thence are called in Scripture sometimes fellow-laborers in the Lord, and sometimes evangelists, and by Theodoret *apostles*, but of a *second order*)—after, I say, these were deceased, and the main power left in the presbyteries, the several presbyters enjoying an equal power among themselves, the wiser and graver sort considered the abuses following the promiscuous use of this power of ordination; and withal, having in their minds the excellent frame of the government of the Church under the apostles and their deputies, and for preventing of future schisms and divisions among themselves, they *unanimously* agreed to *choose one out of their number* who was best qualified for the management of so great a trust, and to *devolve the exercise of the power of ordination and jurisdiction* to him; *yet so as that he act nothing of importance without the consent and concurrence of the presbyters,* who were still to be as the *common council* to the bishop. This I take to be the *true* and *just* account of the *original of episcopacy* in the primitive Church, according to Jerome: which model of government, thus contrived and framed, sets forth to us a most lively character of that *great wisdom* and *moderation* which *then* ruled the heads and hearts of the primitive Christians, and which, *when men have studied and searched all other ways,* (the abuses incident to this government through the corruptions of men and times being retrenched,) *will be found the most agreeable to the primitive form, both as asserting the due interest of the presbyteries, and allowing the due honor of episcopacy;* and, by the *great harmony of both,* carrying on the affairs of the Church with the greatest unity, concord, and peace. *Which form of government, I cannot see how any possible reason can be produced by either party why they may not with cheerfulness embrace it.—Ibid,* pp. 281–2.

Thus we have once more cleared Jerome and the truth together. I only wish that all that are of his judgment for the practice of the primitive Church were of his temper for the practice of their own; and while they own not episcopacy as necessary by a divine right, yet (being duly moderated, and joined with presbyteries) they may embrace it, as not only a lawful, but very useful constitution in the Church of God. By which we may see what an excellent temper may be found out most fully consonant to the primitive Church for the management of *ordinations* and *church power;* namely, BY THE PRESIDENCY OF THE BISHOP AND THE CONCURRENCE OF THE PRESBYTERY.—*Ibid,* p. 283.

DR. SAMUEL MILLER, a divine of acknowledged talents and learning, and a writer on whose researches all parties may rely, informs us that among those who espouse the *episcopal* side upon the question of Church government, there are *two* classes who make themselves prominent. Here is what he says of these classes :—

The first consists of those who believe that neither Christ nor his apostles laid down any particular form of ecclesiastical government to which the Church is bound to adhere in all ages—that every Church is free, consistently with the Divine will, to frame her constitution agreeably to her own views, to the state of society, and to the exigencies of particular times. These prefer the episcopal government, and some of them believe that it was the primitive form; but they consider it as resting on the ground of *human expediency* alone, and not of *Divine appointment.* This is well known to have been the opinion of Archbishops Cranmer, Grindal, and Whitgift; of Bishop Leighton, of Bishop Jewel, of Dr. Whitaker, of Bishop Reynolds, of Archbishop Tillotson, of Bishop Burnet, of Bishop Croft, of Dr. Stillingfleet, and of a *long list* of the *most learned and pious divines* of the Church of England, from the Reformation down to the present day.

Another class of Episcopalians go farther. They suppose that the government of the Church by *bishops,* as a superior order to *presbyters,* was sanctioned by apostolic example, and that it is the duty of all churches to imitate this example. But while they consider Episcopacy as necessary to the *perfection* of the Church, they grant that it is by no means necessary to her *existence;* and accordingly, *without hesitation*, acknowledge as true Churches of Christ many in which the Episcopal doctrine is rejected, and Presbyterian principles made the basis of ecclesiastical government. The advocates of this opinion, also, have been numerous and respectable, both among the clerical and lay members of the Episcopal churches in England and the United States. In this list appear the venerable names of Bishop Hall, Bishop Downham, Bishop Bancroft, Bishop Andrews, Archbishop Usher, Bishop Forbes, the learned Chillingworth, Archbishop Wake, Bishop Hoadly, and many more.

A third class—not of *Episcopalians*, but of sectarian bigots, commonly called *Baptists*—go beyond either of the former. While they grant that God has left men at liberty to modify every other kind of government according to circumstances, they contend that one form of government for the Church is unalterably fixed by Divine appointment; that this form is the *loose congregational form adopted by the Baptists;* that it is absolutely *essential* to the *existence* of a Church; that, of course, wherever it is wanting, as among Methodists, Presbyterians, Episcopalians, Lutherans, and others, there is no Church, no regular ministry, (baptism by immersion included!) no valid ordinances; and that all who are united with religious societies *not* conforming to their views of *baptism, close communion*, and a sort of *Indian council-ground form of government*, are "aliens from the commonwealth of Israel, and strangers to the covenant of promise"—strangers to Christ, "out of the appointed way to heaven," and have no hope but in the "uncovenanted mercies of God!"

Now, it is confidently believed that the two former classes, taken together, embrace at least *nineteen parts* out of *twenty* of all the Episcopalians in Great Britain and the United States; while, so far as my observation goes—and I have had some experience in the world—*two-thirds* of all the Baptists in the United States hold the extravagant opinion I have assigned to them! And that I may not seem to be making *bold assertions* on this point, I submit one single paragraph from the book of Elder Howell, a standard work with the Baptist Publishing Societies throughout the South. He says, on page 275 of this rather *notorious* book:—

> We are not *Protestants*, nor Dissenters, Lutherans, Calvinists, Arminians, nor *Reformers*, but what we *have been in all ages*, THE CHURCH OF OUR LORD JESUS CHRIST!!

With this, and similar declarations by Mr. Graves, with which his book abounds, before me, to contend for the validity of Methodist *ordinations* is to contend for our existence as a Church of Christ, and not for ours only, but also for that of all other Churches, except the Baptist Church. A principle, then, which involves such important conclusions, should be supported by the most indubitable evidence—by evidence far more indubitable than the Baptists are able to bring forward. And whether the sentiments of the Baptists on this subject, as expressed by Graves and Howell, be thus supported or not, will be the subject-matter of the next chapter.

CHAPTER V.

Coke and Asbury not qualified to found a Church of Christ—Holliman and Williams were!—Baptists in a regular line of succession from John the Baptist—The Church in Mesopotamia—Benedict's History of the Baptists—Holliman baptizing Williams—Peculiarities of Roger Williams—Baptist members all Christians—Rare specimens of Baptist conversions!

THE great "Bombastes Furioso" Graves, of the "Tennessee Baptist," and author of *Forty Letters* to "J. Soule, Senior Bishop of the M. E. Church, South," informs the public, on page 138 of his book, that "it is clear as noonday that Methodist Episcopacy is *spurious;* and the palming of it off upon the world is a *fraudulent* operation, performed by an ambitious, aspiring, and power-loving clergy."

On page 142 he concludes Letter No. 12 with this remarkable revelation: "I close this letter with the conviction that such men as Coke and Asbury were not qualified to found a Church of Christ, *and I cannot recognize Methodism as such!*"

The reader will bear in mind that these extracts are from the pen of a minister belonging to a denomination that admits *three distinct orders of church officers:* messengers or ministers, elders, and deacons! And before I close this chapter, I will endeavor to show that Coke and Asbury were as well qualified to found a Church of Christ as old *Zeke Holliman* and *Mr. Williams* were, of the State of Rhode Island, the founders of the Baptist Church in America! I will therefore proceed to examine the *divine right* of the Baptist ministry, and the validity of their claim to a *regular succession from John the Baptist.* It is said by many of the Baptist ministers that their Church and its customs have regularly descended from John the Baptist, Christ, and his apostles; and as these bold assertions and extravagant pretensions have had great influence over the minds of those who have read but little history, and have been chiefly confined to the ministry of Baptists, I deem it in point here to give a brief sketch of the facts as they are.

As to the claim, then, of being the regular descendants of John the Baptist, it is not only without proof to sustain it, but it is directly contrary to the records of history. The Baptists, though Mr. Graves boasts of their *ancient* origin, can be traced back but a few centuries, and certainly no nigher to "John in Jordan" than the *fifteenth* century. The Baptists constituted, in England, one of "the three denominations of Protestant Dissenters." No traces of a Baptist church can be found in Scotland, excepting a small one formed out of a part of Cromwell's army, previous to 1765. Still this sect claims to have descended regularly from the *Old Baptist* whose "raiment" was of "camel's hair," whose "meat was locusts and wild honey," and who preached repentance in the wilderness of Judea! They are not alone, however, in setting up these arrogant claims. The Church in *Mesopotamia,* an extensive province of Asia, situated between the rivers Euphrates and Tigris, in Scripture called Aram, tenaciously claims to have descended from John the Baptist; and yet this Church baptizes *children* at thirty days old, and her *mode* of baptism is *sprinkling.* Who is in the right—our American Baptists, or the Church in Mesopotamia? I should say the latter, as they are a more *ancient* sect, lived more nearly to the age in which John the Baptist figured, and were therefore better posted in reference to the customs of that day. The Greek name of Mesopotamia signifies "between the rivers:" a territory extending as far as the bend formed by the Euphrates near Cunaxa. Mesopotamia is supposed to have been the seat of the earthly paradise; and all geographers agree that here the descendants of Noah settled immediately after the flood. No country or climate on earth was ever more favorable to baptism by *immersion* than this; but this Church of Mesopotamia, though claiming to have descended from John the Baptist in a regular line of succession, practiced *sprinkling!*

But this man Graves asserts—and Baptists generally take the same high and untenable ground—that none are *legal* administrators of the ordinance of baptism, or expounders of the word of God, but those who have been *immersed;* and, to make their baptism *valid*, they must have been immersed by an *immersionist*, who has himself been *plunged!* Now I wish to try them by this their own rule. In the first settling of this country, the Baptists were without any administrator at all. For the truth of this declaration, I refer all interested to their own historian, REV. DAVID BENEDICT. On page 473, vol. i., of Benedict's History of the Baptist Church, an account of the origin of the Baptist Church in the United States is given in the words and figures following, to wit:

> We shall now give a brief account of some of the Baptist churches which have arisen in this State, (Rhode Island,) and beginning with the FIRST CHURCH IN PROVIDENCE. This Church, which is the OLDEST OF THE BAPTIST DENOMINATION IN AMERICA, according to Gov. WINTHROP, was planted in the year 1639.

On page 475, and in the same volume, Mr. Benedict gives an account of the formation of the "First Church"—of the difficulty they found in trying to organize—their want of an administrator. It was in the city of Providence, Rhode Island. I have been on the very spot, and have a distinct recollection of the locality. On this point Benedict says:

To obtain a suitable *administrator* was a matter of consequence: at length, the candidates for communion *nominated* or *appointed* Mr. Ezekiel Holliman, a man of gifts and piety, to baptize [immerse] Mr. Williams, and who, *in return*, [acting upon the principle that one good turn deserves another!] baptized Mr. Holliman *and the other ten!!!*

Now I am aware that some of the Baptists deny that this history contains any such statements. If such will bring me the first volume of the *first* edition of this work, published by Lincoln & Edmunds, Boston, 1813, I will point out these two extracts. I copy from the book itself, and not from a newspaper. David Benedict was the pastor of the Baptist church in Pawtucket, Rhode Island, where he certainly had all the means of knowing the facts in the cases he reports. He completed his history but a short time before its publication in Boston. And I know very well that the Baptist Church in this country has all along recognized it as a correct history of their sect.

Candid reader, is it not as plain as the nose on a man's face, from their own history, that the Baptists should be the last denomination in America to *unchurch* others, or to annihilate the clerical character of other ministers for the want of *validity of ordination?* Mr. Graves is an ordained elder in the Baptist Church, in a *regular line of succession*—not from John the Baptist—but from *old Zeke Holliman* and his "true yoke-fellow," *Mr. Williams!* And, pray, were they better qualified to found a Church of Christ than "such men as Coke and Asbury?" Who authorized Mr. Holliman to immerse Mr. Williams in the name of the Father, Son, and Holy Ghost? And whence did Mr. Williams derive authority to immerse *"the other ten?"* True, "the other ten" were immersed by a man who had himself been immersed, but he was immersed by *old Zeke*, who had never been immersed until this same man Williams immersed him, so as to make a *starting-point* for this "first church" in America, and in the *regular line of succession!* This affair constituted

Williams and Holliman the regular successors of the old preacher of repentance, "whose meat was locusts and wild honey," though he flourished sixteen hundred years before them!

The State of Rhode Island was first settled in 1636, only three years before the founding of this "first church" by Holliman, Williams, and "the other ten." Roger Williams and his followers fled from the persecutions of Massachusetts, and settled at Providence; and Williams gave the place this name, as being expressive of their escape and deliverance. From Providence, since 1636, two hundred and twenty years ago, the Baptists, according to their own showing, have been extending their operations, until they have spread over the South and West, and have taken that stand they now occupy. They have descended, then, in a regular line in the United States, not from John the Baptist, or the apostles, or Christ, but from *one Ezekiel Holliman*—a clever old man, I have no doubt, and, if the reader please, even a pious man, but an old gentleman who had no sort of authority to baptize in the name of the Holy Trinity. If, then, the facts and arguments given upon this point are true and legitimate, am I not warranted in saying that the American Baptists, who descended from Holliman and Williams, *are all out of order?* Or, to use the language of Graves, "such men were not qualified to found a Church of Christ."

This *proscriptive* spirit of Baptists generally, and of Mr. Graves in particular, seems to have come down to them from Roger Williams. While he was pastor of a Baptist church, he declared his intention to separate from his congregation, if they would not separate from the "antichristian churches in the bay," meaning all who opposed his views of baptism! He rebelled against the civil authorities, and because his congregation would not sustain him in this violation of the command of God, he separated from his congregation. His wife still adhered to the congregation; for which he refused to let her join him in any acts of worship! A warrant was issued for Williams, for his rebellious course, and Capt. Underhill was dispatched with fourteen men to execute it; but Williams fled from the province, and found refuge with *Massasoit*, the head chief of the Wampanoag Indians. From this chief he obtained a small grant of land on the east side of Narraganset river, where water was abundant for purposes of baptism! He used to say that he "could not endure the Lord's bishops," and that he liked the "Lord's brethren" just as little—meaning the members of other Churches, Puritans, Quakers, etc. This hatred for *bishops* seems to be characteristic of the sect of which Williams was the founder in America. For proof of the foregoing statements, I refer to pages 227 and 230, vol. i. of Hildreth's History of the United States.

I am aware that Roger Williams is often complimented as the advocate of freedom of opinion, and of religious toleration; but it is known to all impartial readers of history that he was a religious bigot, and full of that fanaticism so peculiar to Baptists. Even Hildreth, who compliments him as a "zealous minister," states that he "*exercised by way of* PROPHECY," to the "acceptance and edification of his Church." He laid claims to *inspiration*, and actually went about *prophesying*, and blending his predictions with the great idea of what he called "soul-liberty."

It is recorded of Roger Williams, elsewhere, that he got a second great idea into his head, to wit: That as men and women came into this world *naked*, so they ought to come into the Church through the water *without clothes on!* Was such a man, though he may have been pious, qualified to found a Church of Christ?

Elder Graves, like most other Baptist writers and preachers, complains that Methodists receive into their communion and fellowship *irreligious persons*, mere seekers of religion, while Baptists receive none but genuine Christians, who, like the apostles in the days of Christ, are always ready "to give a reason of the hope that is in them!" Methodists take in seekers, say they, and take even these upon *a trial of six months!* But Baptists receive members alone upon "*an experience of grace*," the congregation judging of that experience, and voting accordingly. And when a person is converted, and baptized by *immersion*, they say of him that he can *never fall from grace.* And yet they have among them some men and women of the very worst morals; and not a few are to be found in their communion and fellowship who are *notorious drunkards.* To say the least of it, they have as many bad men and hypocrites in their churches, according to numbers, as are to be found in any of the other orthodox denominations of the country. But once in a while they bring to trial and actually expel from their communion individuals: thus rejecting persons who, according to their creed, God has not rejected! Is there no insincerity in all this?

But Mr. Graves's Church will receive no one into its fellowship who is not *a believing adult;* and still, *one-third*, if not *one-half* of all the persons they do receive, give no other evidence of a genuine conversion to God than that of *a dream*, the *hearing of a voice*, the *sight of a ghost*, or the visitation of an *angel*, or of *God himself!* I could give the names, residences, and loud professions of many of these "bright and shining lights;" but I will content myself with a few cases only, the truth of which I vouch for, and which will serve as *specimens* of Baptist conversions.

CASE NUMBER ONE.

I was present in December, 1841, in the Presbyterian church in Jonesborough, during a celebrated Baptist revival, when a colored woman was received into that Church, as a portion of the fruits of said revival—the Baptists having been kindly tendered the use of the house by the Presbyterians. Among many other foolish things which she mentioned as a part of her religious experience, she stated that "*Christ first appeared to her while she was in bed with a man!*" I remarked to two Presbyterians, with whom I was seated, that I thought the Saviour had selected a singular time and place to impart his grace to that woman! They bowed assent. The next day, this woman was immersed in Green's Mill-pond, in the west end of the town, *upon this identical experience!*

CASE NUMBER TWO.

A lady in the neighborhood of Fall Branch, some fifteen miles north of Jonesborough, a short time previous to that Jonesborough occurrence, gave to the Baptist Church, as her experience, that she had attended the preaching of Elder Riggs, on a certain occasion, and was taken sick at the *stomach*—said she soon learned it was *conviction for sin*—engaged earnestly in prayer to God—soon after *vomited copiously*—thereupon obtained immediate relief, and felt her load of sin removed! Upon this experience, she was received into the Church, and immersed in the name of the Trinity!

This is changing the *seat* of human depravity, which has hitherto been regarded as the *heart.* I would like to have seen the *discharge!* I would likewise be gratified to know whether or not sins of omission and commission, *after* one's conversion, can be got rid of, either by *vomiting* or *purging!* It would greatly relieve the anxieties of the mind, as well as save the labor of much prayer and religious exercise!

CASE NUMBER THREE.

A lady in Carter county, who had been baptized by a Methodist—who left that Church and was immersed by Mr. T., a Campbellite minister—in the spring of 1842, left that Church, and was *reïmmersed* by Elder Edens, of the regular Baptist Church. In her *experience*, upon being received into the Baptist Church, she stated that she had, but a short time previous to that, walked out into the woods, where she met *Christ* and the *apostles*, in open daylight, under a large tree, singing a *Baptist* song! She stated that she united with them in singing—that Christ pardoned her sins—that she could not be mistaken, for she saw the blood running out of *both of his sides*, where he had been pierced! Upon this "experience of grace," she was received into the Church, pronounced a Christian, and immersed, notwithstanding the Saviour was really pierced in but *one side!*

CASE NUMBER FOUR.

During court week in the town of Jonesborough, in the spring of 1841, I heard Elder Bowers preach in the Methodist church, at night; and among the rare disclosures he made, he related his religious experience, and gave the audience what he styled the "evidence of his conversion." He said that he went to bed at night, a distressed and wicked sinner —that when he awoke in the morning, to his utter astonishment, he found his wife and child to be the most handsome human beings he had ever beheld with his eyes; and, continued he, "by this I knew I had passed from death unto life!"

Now, here is an instance in which religion made a *false impression*, because it rendered to the natural eye of the convert, individuals handsome, whom God, in his providence, had actually created otherwise! We know the parties, and they are any thing but handsome!

CASE NUMBER FIVE.

In Lee county, Virginia, but a few years since, a certain man of lawful age appeared before a Baptist church, and asked to be received into fellowship, on the ground that God, for Christ's sake, had pardoned his sins. The pastor of the church, Elder G——, told him to proceed and tell the brethren what the Lord had done for his soul. He stated substantially—"I went last summer for to see a Christian *git* baptized, and ever since I have been a-wandering, and wandering, and wandering: I have been company for nobody, and nobody has been company for me!" Here he came to a dead halt, and all hands looked blank! Elder G—— relieved the audience by requesting the brother to proceed and tell what the Lord had done for his soul. Looking the pastor full in the face, the new convert repeated, word for word, what I have just given above, and halted as before! Elder G—— *feelingly* inquired, "And do you think, brother, the Lord has converted your soul?" With a countenance beaming with the hopes and expectations of one about to be received into full fellowship with the only Scriptural Church on earth, he exclaimed, "Now, old *hoss*, you are a chattin'!" Upon this faith and profession, he was unanimously received, immersed the next day, and admitted to the Lord's table, as spread by that denomination!

CASE NUMBER SIX.

In Bradley county, Tennessee, not long since, there lived a man by the name of P——, close to a Baptist church; and near to which lived Elder B——, who was anxious that P—— should *"jine the Church."* Accordingly, at a protracted meeting, several of the *"breethring"* surrounded him, and asked him to relate his experience. He held forth after this style: "The first bad feelins I ever had on the subject of religion, was when I went with Brother B—— to meetin', at Hurricane Creek. After meetin', several breethren went home with an old brother to stay all night, and they axed me to go too. They sat around the fire talking about religion, until I felt so bad 'coze I had none, I went right to bed, and went fast to sleep. I waked up in the night, and I found that good man, Brother B——, in bed with me; and I never felt as happy before!" This was pronounced a sound conversion. Mr. P—— was received into full fellowship, and forthwith immersed in the name of the Trinity!

Need I multiply cases? Let these suffice, as they are only in keeping with hundreds dispersed throughout the country, a portion of which every reader can call to mind in his own range. Meanwhile, let it not be said that such cases are those of *clear conversion*, while those evidences upon which other Churches have received members, pronouncing them Christians, are *deceptive*. I would as soon credit the juggling pretences of *witchcraft*, as to believe these ludicrous accounts of conversions! And a Church had better by far give countenance to the foolish superstitions and absurd practices of fortune-tellers, diviners, charmers, spirit-rappers, and such like, than to encourage any human soul to believe that these vain conceits are religion.

Those who may be disposed to regard these *cases* of Baptist conversions as severe in their application to that Church, are here reminded that they are designed to *offset* Mr. Graves's "Revival and Camp-meeting Excitements," in his Thirty-ninth Letter, where he gives specimens, and ridicules Methodist conversion! I claim in this, as in every thing connected with this controversy, to be acting on the *defensive;* and if I chance to use a degree of severity unusual in religious controversy, the mantle of enlightened public opinion will shield me from blame!

CHAPTER VI.

Elder Graves copies largely from F. A. Ross, of the Presbyterian Church—An address delivered in Virginia, a reply to Ross—Correspondence between Ross and the author of this work—Ross opposes the Methodist doctrine of the Direct Witness—Distinguished Presbyterians advocate it—Ross charges Methodists with being Tories—Himself proven to be a free negro, and the son of an old Scotch Tory of the Revolution—The Methodist common masses destitute of moral honesty and integrity of character—Methodists fanatical—Presbyterians more so, as shown by the conduct of three of the editors of the Calvinistic Magazine—Witchcraft and conjurors—The congregation complimenting the address—Reply by the author.

THE Thirty-ninth Letter of Mr. Graves, commencing on page 352 of his famous *compilation* of slanders long since refuted, is made up of an article from the "*Calvinistic Magazine*," of which the celebrated *F. A. Ross*, a New School Presbyterian, was the ostensible editor.

His Thirty-second Letter, commencing on page 384, is nearly all taken from the pen of this man Ross, from whom he gathered his idea of the *revolutions of the Iron Wheel.* The last *fifteen* pages of this letter are from the "*Calvinistic Magazine*," abusive of Methodist class and band meetings, comparing them to the *Romish confessional*, and calling in question the *virtue* and *integrity* of the Methodist membership, as well as that of the clergy!

His Thirty-third Letter, commencing on page 403, is abusive of all the peculiar institutions of Methodism, and winds up with showing "how Presbyterians regard it," thus drawing upon the same sources.

Now, to all this abuse of Mr. Ross, copied and approved by Mr. Graves, I replied in an ADDRESS which occupied *four hours* in its delivery, kept up through a period of *two years*, in East Tennessee and Western Virginia. This ADDRESS I delivered ONE HUNDRED TIMES, speaking in all FOUR HUNDRED HOURS—equal to *thirty-three entire days*—often in the open air, and to five, ten, and fifteen hundred persons, generally, on each occasion! In the winter season, I was confined to churches; and the crowds were not so large as in the spring, summer, and fall, when I spoke in the open air. My reply to Mr. Ross I deem a sufficient reply to the same slanders, when copied and endorsed by Mr. Graves; and as the latter has given them an extensive circulation and a permanent form, I deem it proper to end this chapter by copying my ADDRESS entire. This document originally appeared in the JONESBOROUGH MONTHLY REVIEW, of which I was the editor and proprietor—a work which had a circulation of about three thousand, and was got up avowedly to meet the "*Calvinistic Magazine*," which was then published in Abingdon, Virginia. The slanders of Ross and Graves, now in book form, will be preserved in hundreds of families unkind in their feelings towards Methodism. It is therefore proper that this Address should be incorporated into this work, and placed before the public in a form that will be preserved. The Address explains itself, taking in connection therewith the brief correspondence that precedes it.

[From Brownlow's Monthly Review.]

TO THE PUBLIC.

THE following correspondence will show the motives which prompt the editor of this periodical to submit to the world, in pamphlet form, an address recently delivered near Marion, Virginia, upon the subject of the controversy between the

Methodists and Presbyterians, forced upon the former by the abuse, misrepresentations, and slander of that PRINCE of calumniators, *Frederick Augustus Ross*:—

MARION, VIRGINIA, July 11, 1848.

REV. W. G. BROWNLOW:

Dear Sir:—The undersigned, members of the Methodist Church, would respectfully suggest to you the propriety of publishing, in your Review, the address which you delivered on the 9th instant at the camp-ground near this place, together with the *documents* which you introduced upon that occasion;—even upon the charitable supposition that *wilful perversions* of what you there said will not be attempted; however, human memory is so frail, that honest difference of opinion, after the lapse of a few days or weeks, will probably arise about it. Indeed, we already feel the necessity of having the documentary evidence which you then laid before us, embodied in some form to which we may conveniently refer; for we cannot recollect your authorities with sufficient distinctness to make them available to us in ordinary and casual conversations upon the subject. Besides, Sir, we incline to the belief that the subject-matter of that day's address, inclusive of documents, would be as acceptable to the patrons of your Review as any thing else which you could lay before them.

Very respectfully yours, etc.,

JOHN W. SCHOOLFIELD,
FRANCIS NEWMAN,
JAMES BRUMFIELD,
JAMES M. PRUNER,
JOHN T. THURMAN,
BENJAMIN L. WILBERN,
WILLIAM SNAVELY,
JAMES C. DAILY,
JOHN KILLINGER,
WILLIAM W. PRUNER,
JOSEPH ATKINS.

SMYTHE COUNTY, VA., July 15, 1848.

To Messrs. J. W. SCHOOLFIELD, F. NEWMAN,
JAMES BRUMFIELD, and others:

Gentlemen:—Your communication of the 11th instant, requesting me to publish the address I delivered last Sabbath at your camp-ground, together with the documents, was handed to me on yesterday, and I hasten to reply.

I will comply with your request, and publish the address at my earliest convenience. The matter for the Review, now in course of printing, has been furnished, and will be out soon after my return to Tennessee. In the next issue, I will give the address you call for, *verbatim et literatim et punctuatim*, so as to silence those who, I learn, aro already misrepresenting me in various particulars. The address I delivered at your camp-ground on last Sabbath, which occupied four and a half hours, is the same in substance which I have been delivering in Tennessee and Virginia for two years past, and which I am safe in saying I have delivered in the hearing of fifty thousand persons.

I find that very great excitement prevails in your county upon the subject of this controversy, and especially in your town and vicinity. I cannot say that I regret it: I believe good will grow out of the controversy. Let the members and friends of the Methodist Church stand firm, and resist, at all hazards personal to themselves, the slanders of F. A. Ross & Co., and their efforts to demolish our beloved Methodism. If fall we must, let us fall with our faces to the foe: let us fall in defence of the "moral honesty and integrity of character" of our "common masses," and in defence of the *private characters* of our wives, mothers, daughters, sisters, and other female relations, who are held up to public gaze, through the polluted pages of the "Calvinistic Magazine," as a generation of *prostitutes.*

They say that I have "raised the Devil" by my visit to this country. This is a mistake: the Devil was here before I came to the State, and I have only enraged his Satanic Majesty, and caused him to show his hand. He was "raised" at the time the authorities of the Presbyterian church in Marion invited him there, in the person of F. A. Ross, to dedicate their new church; and also when the *sainted* pastor of their church, Mr. Palmer, and every preacher and elder in the infamous Athens Synod, "with absolute unanimity," endorsed the slanders, blackguardism, and abuse of the "Tract" and "Magazine," declaring them all to be true, *according to the Scriptures!*

I am, gentlemen, respectfully, etc.,

W. G. BROWNLOW.

ADDRESS.

LADIES AND GENTLEMEN:—There is nothing more common in this age of polemic warfare than for every combatant who assails the doctrines, motives, or, if you please, the *character* of another, to claim the right to do so, because (as he says) he acts on the *defensive.* The reason of this must be obvious to every reflecting mind. He who acts in the defensive is entitled to the sympathies of the public, because he is supposed to have been unjustly assailed; and these sympathies will justify the *defender,* while the *aggressor* would justly deserve the opprobrium of the intelligent, and the frowns of the candid. But, as both your humble speaker and

F. A. Ross, of the New School Presbyterian Church, and the respective friends of each, claim this ground, it is of the utmost importance that this controversy should be settled, and that the public should be at once enabled to decide to whom this high claim belongs. It seldom occurs, in a family or neighborhood quarrel, that both of the parties to the dispute are acting on the defensive. Some one *commenced* the war; some one is the aggressor; some one is to blame more than another for the existence of said quarrel. So it is in the present controversy which divides, distracts, and agitates all East Tennessee and Western Virginia. Who is it? It is my purpose, before I leave this stand, to show you who is guilty in this case.

To *defend* one's self, presupposes an unwarranted attack from another—not merely an *attack*, but one for which there was no just cause. I may attack an enemy of mine—a sworn and uncompromising foe—with all the violence of which my nature is capable, and still I may act on the defensive, if the *previous* conduct and threats of violence were such as to make my assault necessary to my future safety. You, gentlemen, any of you, may attack an enemy in like manner, and still act on the defensive, if the *previous* threats of that enemy were such, in the eyes of the law, as to make that attack necessary to your future safety. Nay, it is a principle in common law, both here and in England, that if an evil-disposed person threaten your life upon sight, you are justified in shooting him down upon sight. This was the principle the gallant Putnam acted upon when he assailed the *wolf* in his den. He made the attack, but it was in self-defence. The HOWLINGS and PROWLINGS of the "*varmint*" in the neighborhood, to say nothing of his depredations among the live-stock of the farmer, could no longer be tolerated. The vile "wolf in sheep's clothing," upon whom I am visiting a righteous retribution, has "howled" about the borders of Methodism long enough! But how was it when the United States declared war against Great Britain? In the language of the Declaration of Independence, she "kept among us, in time of peace, standing armies, without the consent of our Legislatures," etc., etc.

But, ladies and gentlemen, how stands the case as between Mr. Ross and your humble speaker, or any other Methodist preacher who may have engaged in this controversy? Who commenced this "war of words and fight of quills?" In the language of the time-honored instrument just quoted, "let *facts* be submitted to a candid world." FREDERICK AUGUSTUS ROSS, of the New School Presbyterian Church, commenced this war; nor can he deny it, with any degree of countenance. He began the war, moreover, without any provocation, and at a time that peace reigned in all the Churches, and when God was very powerfully reviving his work in most of the Churches. Yes, at this time it was that the Devil granted this vile miscreant the commission of Lieutenant-General, to put a stop to the work, and to disturb the peace of society!

Mr. Ross, as is his custom, composed an able, argumentative, and slanderous discourse, about four years ago, familiarly known as his "*Turnpike Sermon*," in which he ridiculed, misrepresented, and vilified the whole Methodist Church. This discourse he delivered all round his extensive circuit of East Tennessee and Western Virginia, as bitterly as he seems to be opposed to circuit-riding. When this sermon was worn threadbare, he prepared another on *Church government*, in which he stated that Methodism is worse than Romanism. Next in order came his memorable discourse upon the "*Direct Witness.*" To all this, extending through an entire year, the Methodists made no reply. Their silence was construed into COWARDICE, and our members were everywhere told that our ministers were afraid to meet Mr. Ross. The vain and wicked man gave in to the same delusion himself, and made a publication in which he held up the Methodist clergy, one and all, as a pack of white-livered cowards, who would go among the caves and mountains and misrepresent Presbyterianism, but who, when they came into Abingdon, Jonesborough, Rogersville, Greenville, Knoxville, etc., took care to tread lightly in flannel socks! Hush! Take care! You are in Abingdon now! you are in Knoxville, forsooth, among people of *respectability*—take care how you put your feet down! Well, I am not here to-day for the purpose of representing Methodist preachers in a *bullying* capacity. I will, however, speak of *one* who neither fears F. A. Ross nor all the multitudes that go with him; and for the self-same reason, too, that Hezekiah and his captains of war declared they were not afraid of the King of Assyria nor all the multitudes that were with him; namely, that with them there is but an *arm of flesh*, while they had the Lord our God to help them, and to fight their battles!

Again, Mr. Ross held up this fundamental doctrine of the Methodist Church—I mean the *witness of the Spirit*—as "unscriptural, false, fanatical, and of mischievous tendency." On this issue, he challenged the whole Methodist ministry to meet him, from our bishops down to our local brethren. His challenge was accepted by WILLIAM H. ROGERS, one of the itinerant preachers in this Conference in Sullivan county, and a discussion ensued, which occupied a whole day, at which not less than two thousand persons were in attendance. I was there, a silent spectator; and while I have the highest possible regard for my friend Rogers, it is due to candor to state that he, like every other Methodist preacher I have heard in reply to Ross, labored under the false notion that enlightened public opinion required him to treat his opponent as a dignified Christian minister, and to extend to him all the courtesies of the sacred desk. The result was, that he contradicted

Rogers, interrupted him, and rudely sought to embarrass him every fifteen or twenty minutes. I spit upon such vitiated public taste as this: I bid defiance to any such false conceptions of courtesy as this. I take the slanderer by the throat, and drag him forth from his hiding-place, and shake him naked over hell, in all his deformity! This I intend to do on this occasion.

Did all this public speaking against Methodism satisfy the slanderous appetite of Mr. Ross? No. He followed this up with the publication at the North of the *bantling* I hold in my hand—a "Tract" against Wesley and the Methodists, of one hundred and eight dreadful pages. The vile and slanderous character of this publication, since endorsed by the Synod of Tennessee, and recommended by the ministers of that Church, I shall show up before I leave this stand. Not content with this publication, Mr. Ross, and his associates in blackguardism and lying, commenced the publication in Abingdon of the "CALVINISTIC MAGAZINE," the very first number of which contained an open declaration of war, and announced the determination of its *reverend* editors, ISAAC ANDERSON, FRED. A. ROSS, JAMES KING, and JAMES MCCHAIN, to wage a war of extermination against the entire Methodist Church. And just here, in the presence of this large assembly, and in the fear of God, I proclaim from this sacred stand that, for *low Billingsgate slang, obscene vulgarity, and wholesale abuse of public and private character*, this magazine is without a parallel among all the dirty, rabid, and disgraceful publications of the age. And still this is the vulgar, lying, and dirty publication which Mr. Ross boasts can be found on the centre-tables in all the parlors of Presbyterian families in Marion and elsewhere. Quite a compliment this to the *taste* of Presbyterian ladies in Marion!

I repeat, and I pray you not to forget it, that I do not restrict the responsibility for the contents of this magazine to the four ministers named as its editors. I herewith read to you from the editorial address given in the first number:

> In October, 1845, they (your editors) laid the subject before the Synod of Tennessee; and meeting with their CORDIAL APPROBATION AND CO-OPERATION, began the publication of the present series of the magazine in 1846.

Since then, ladies and gentlemen, the Synod has approved of the course of the magazine in its session at Athens, Tennessee, and earnestly recommended it to all their churches. In this vote of endorsement, Mr. Ross boasts, in an editorial, that every preacher and elder in the Synod voted by formal resolution. He says, to use his own words, that the Synod adopted both his tract and magazine "with *absolute unanimity*"—that is to say, without a dissenting voice! But more about this endorsement before I have done.

Now, when an enemy wages an *unprovoked* war against me, or the Church of my choice, which is the same, I am certainly acting in the defensive when I attempt to repel the invasion. And when my character, and the private and personal character of every female relative I have on earth is assailed with bitterness and malice—not by this degraded free man of color only, but by the whole Synod of Tennessee—I have a right to defend; and at the risk of my life, I will defend. Nay, I am here to-day for that purpose, prepared to meet any consequences. Some of the lying partisans of Mr. Ross have the audacity to say that the Methodists commenced this war, and that he is defending. I have given you this history of the controversy expressly with a view to correct this slander. From the facts which I have submitted—*and facts they are*—you can determine who is the *aggressor*. Mr. Ross commenced the war; but the Synod of Tennessee—like the American Congress in the case of the Mexican war—*adopted* it, and has made it the war of the Presbyterian Church. For two dreadful years, Mr. Ross carried on this war of "conquest" without any opposition. But, with God's help, he shall have opposition from this out, until he prays for a treaty of peace—opposition as untiring and vigorous as he has been vindictive and malevolent.

The captains and lieutenants under this great *guerilla chief* of the Presbyterian Church, now tell you that the magazine was set on foot to meet the "EPISCOPALIAN," a Methodist paper published at Knoxville. This is false; because that paper was started, in part, to meet the *anticipated* slanders of the magazine. The Episcopalian was first agreed upon at the Athens Conference, and I published the prospectus for the Conference. Previous to that, the prospectus for the magazine had been published in the Abingdon papers, in one of the Jonesborough papers, and, I believe, in the Knoxville papers: these itinerant ministers in the stand behind me will attest the truth of these statements.

The friends of F. A. Ross everywhere find it necessary, in order to sustain him, to show that his speeches and publications were not an *attack* upon Methodism, but that they were *provoked*. In many places they apologize for him by declaring that *I*—yes, *I*, a common disturber of the peace, and a man who will let no one escape—first got up the war. Even the *Rev. A. Converse*, the editor of the Christian Observer, the organ of Presbyterianism, published in Philadelphia, gravely asserts in his paper that Mr. Ross has said certain hard things about Methodism, "in answer to what the Rev. Mr. Brownlow had published against him." This is a falsehood as absurd as ever sickened the imagination of a fool. Here, even in this town, you know it is boasted that Mr. Ross has never noticed any thing I have said, and that he does not attend my appointments because he regards me as being beneath his notice!

Ladies and gentlemen! This war had progressed for twc

long and dreadful years, on the part of Mr. Ross, with his indiscreet friends boasting that the Methodist preachers were afraid to meet him, before I opened my mouth in public, or even wrote a paragraph upon the subject. And when I did engage, I did it reluctantly, because I knew that it would injure me in a *pecuniary* point of view, as it has done; but I acted from a sense of duty. I knew that others were engaging, more competent to debate the points at issue than myself; but even they were treating him with too much courtesy. And without incurring the imputation of vanity, I hope you will allow me to say, that he never did receive *justice* at the hands of a Methodist preacher until I took him up. True, he recently caught it at Glade Spring, at the hands of the able and accomplished President of Emory and Henry College. Yes, President Collins, as I am informed, though he did not violate any of the rules of courtesy in debate, nevertheless showed the defects of Ross to be as numerous as were the ingredients which the witches of the dark cave threw into the boiling cauldron. He showed Mr. Ross to have, as I will do to-day, an

> "Eye of newt, toe of frog,
> Wool of bat, and tongue of dog,
> Adder's fork, and blind-worm's sting,
> Lizard's leg, and owlet's wing."

All that now remains to be presented, by way of preliminary, is contained in the following correspondence between myself and Mr. Ross. This correspondence is full of interest, and will amuse you no little. Such *diplomacy* you have not witnessed since Webster and Ashburton concluded their treaty of peace! Mr. Ross outdoes me in expressions of high regard for me, and opinions of my integrity; but this is because he entertained higher opinions of me than I did of him! As a conscientious man, I could not give him a better character in a private letter than I was willing to give him in a public discussion:

JONESBOROUGH, December 14, 1846.

REV. F. A. ROSS:

Dear Sir:—The first of six appointments I have published to reply to your "Tract" against Mr. Wesley and the Methodists, is on Sabbath next, at Blountville, at which time and place I shall be glad to see you, as well, also, as at the remaining five. I propose to give you hour about, on each occasion. Should you not deem it worth the while to attend, I shall of course proceed to fill my engagements.

For a knowledge of the propositions I shall assume, on these occasions, I refer you to the Jonesborough Whig of the 9th inst., a copy of which is herewith forwarded to your address.

Respectfully, etc.,
W. G. BROWNLOW.

The positions I took, and which I published in the newspaper referred to, were the following, and covered the ground of the controversy laid down in the "Tract," except so much of that work as was *personal*, and assailed the characters of our ministers and members:

I. The doctrine of the DIRECT WITNESS OF THE SPIRIT, as taught by JOHN WESLEY, is the doctrine of the Bible, held by all orthodox Christians in Europe and America; and, with the Presbyterian Church, has long been a clearly defined article of religious belief.

II. That FREDERICK AUGUSTUS ROSS solemnly SWORE, before God and the Presbytery at which he was made a minister, that he would preach and defend the doctrine of the Direct Witness of the Spirit; that he did so from the pulpit and press, for several years thereafter, and in a printed sermon, in 1828, before he *abandoned* Presbyterianism, he declared that such as deny this doctrine *have no religion!*

III. That "witchcraft and ghost stories" were *universally* believed in Europe till the 16th century, and maintained their ground with firmness till the middle of the 17th century; that the Presbyterian Church entered extensively into the belief, even *before* the days of WESLEY; that in New England, in North America, in the years 1691–2, there were almost as many imprisonments and executions, on account of *witchcraft*, as there have been Mexicans slain by our army in the present war; and that some of the Presbyterian clergy refused to pray for persons condemned to die on charges of witchcraft, till said persons would acknowledge themselves to be *witches* and *wizards!*

To this brief epistle and these printed items, I received the following answer:

ROTHERWOOD, December 21, 1846.

REV. W. G. BROWNLOW:

Dear Sir:—Your polite communication of the 14th was received Saturday last, on my return from Rogersville.

I have no doubt the discussion to which you invite me would be, on your part, as FAIR and HONORABLE [and of course as gentlemanly!] as you propose *or I could desire;* and there might be occasions when it would be proper for me to accept an invitation. But I decline the meetings you propose, *in the same courtesy which you have been pleased to exhibit toward me,* simply upon the ground that I deem such a meeting uncalled for on my part, for the following reasons:

The question of the Direct Witness of the Spirit, as taught by Mr. Wesley, is a great question, *now abroad* in the land, and it is *now* to be settled by the press. Oral debate *now,* anywhere, and especially within the circle of appointments you propose, would, I think, have little influence in satisfying the public mind. The debate eighteen months ago, invited by me, had the desired result of *arousing attention.* The publications on both sides, and notices from the pulpits, have given the subject deep lodgment in the general mind. I am myself perfectly satisfied with the progressive tendency of things, as to Mr. Wesley's views of the Direct Witness of the Spirit.

In reference to my own views of this point of doctrine, you are mistaken, and do me injustice, in supposing that I differ from the Presbyterian Confession of Faith and Catechisms. I believe the doctrine exactly as there expressed. Moreover, I hold with Henry, Doddridge, Scott, Stuart, Barnes, Chalmers, etc., precisely, and just because I deem these writers correct exponents of the Confession of Faith, and, *as such,* holding views the opposite of that advanced by Mr. Wesley. As decisive of this fact, I quoted the Confession of Richard Watson, whom you will acknowledge to be your ablest theologian. He confesses that Mr. Wesley "*differed from a great part of the evangelical clergy of the day,*" and gives Scott [and the very passage quoted by me in my book] as expressing the view of the "great part of the evangelical clergy" against Mr. Wesley. [See Watson's Institutes, vol. ii. pp. 272 and 284.]

So, then, the fact stands thus: Richard Watson, the ablest of Methodist writers, admits that "a great part of the evangelical clergy of the day" *differ* from Mr. Wesley, and that Scott is a fair sample of this body who differ from Mr. Wesley—that is to say, such writers as Henry, Doddridge, Chalmers, etc., etc. If so, then, do these writers fairly exhibit the views of the Confession of Faith of the Presbyterian Church? If they do, then they and the Confession are against Mr. Wesley, by the concession of Mr. Watson. Very well: I am [if I understand myself and them] with those writers and the Confession of Faith, and am against Mr. Wesley as far as, and no farther, precisely, than Watson admits the great part of the evangelical clergy to be.

I have written this, Mr. Brownlow, *for your own private eye and consideration alone.* If, after this, you think proper to proceed to attempt to show, from the pulpit, that I am violating my ordination vows, [and of course you must mean knowingly and wilfully, or in criminal ignorance,] I have nothing more to say.

Yours, very respectfully,
FRED. A. ROSS.

Ladies and gentlemen! As tedious as I have been in my exordium, you must indulge me while I offer a few brief comments upon this extraordinary letter:

1. And, first, the time for *oral* debate had passed away when this invitation was given to Mr. Ross to meet me, and through the press alone were these disputed questions to be settled. Still, the infatuated man has gone on ever since, in every direction, to discuss these points!

2. Nothing could be effected within the circle I had proposed. I was unfortunate in selecting my points for action. But where were these six appointments to which he was invited? They were in Blountville, Kingsport, Elizabethton, Rheatown, Jonesborough, and the vicinity of Washington College. I supposed these were all important points, and he seems to have thought so since, as he has gone to some of them and opened a brisk fire, "solitary and alone." Indeed, it is perfectly in order to debate these points in dispute anywhere, when he can go in a gang by himself; but when he is to have some one with him who has the moral and physical courage to expose his forgeries, falsehoods, and slanders, the time for *oral debate* has ceased, and the press alone is the medium through which these controverted points are to be settled!

3. He quotes Richard Watson, whom I frankly and thus publicly acknowledge to be one of our ablest theologians. And he gives chapter and verse where *he* says Watson acknowledges that Mr. Wesley taught a different doctrine, upon the subject of the *Direct Witness*, from that taught by the "great part of the evangelical clergy of the day" in which Wesley lived. He cites, as you will perceive, Watson's

Theological Institutes, vol. ii. pages 272 and 284. And will you believe me when I say that those pages prove no such thing? Strange as it may seem to you, those pages prove no such thing! He deliberately lies. He cites the page, supposing that I will take his word for it. Here is the volume of the Institutes, and here are the pages cited. Richard Watson proves the doctrine of the *Direct Witness* to be scriptural; and to show that himself and Mr. Wesley were not singular in the belief, he quotes Hill's Lectures, Bishop Bull, Scott's Commentary, and Bishop Horsley. On page 284, Watson lets down upon *Calvinism,* and declares that controversy, by Calvinists, has always been conducted with great intemperance. On page 275 of this same volume, Mr. Watson declares his belief in the doctrine of the *Direct Witness,* and controverts the Ross view of it, as described by Bishop Bull in an extract he gives, and in another extract he takes from Scott. After stating the views of Bull and Scott, Mr. Watson adds:

> To this statement of the doctrine we object that it makes the testimony of the Holy Spirit, in point of fact, but the testimony of our own spirit; and, by holding but *one* witness, contradicts St. Paul, who, as we have seen, holds *two.* For the testimony is that of our own consciousness of certain moral changes which have taken place—no other is admitted, and therefore it is but one testimony.

4. Mr. Watson does confess, in his Life of Wesley, that Mr. Wesley differed from the greater part of the evangelical clergy of his time, in his plans for evangelizing the world. This no Methodist denies. Rather, we glory in its truth—we boast that his plans of yearly and quarterly conferences, circuit-riding, class-meetings, and love-feasts, were unlike the operation of other Churches.

5. This is a *confidential* letter—strictly so—intended for my eye and consideration alone! Do you hear that, Master Brooks? I have read you the letter, but I enjoin it upon

you, one and all, not to speak of its contents! Especially do I charge you, *ladies*, not to name it; for they say you are more apt to tell what you hear, than are the gentlemen!

But do you wish to know the *secret* of this *injunction of secresy?* I will tell you. Mr. Ross's friends everywhere take the ground that he will not *condescend* to meet me in debate; (Heaven save the mark!) and he favors the same view in his private conversations with them. Well, in this letter to me, he places his refusal upon different grounds: he says the time is passed, and the press is the medium! He does not object because I am beneath his notice—no, not he. He declares here, over his proper signature, that I am a Christian minister—a courteous and a fair debater—an honorable man and a gentleman. But, says he, this is for your own private eye, Mr. Brownlow: do not say any thing about it, because I don't want my friends to know that I talk one way about you behind your back, and then write the very reverse of that to you, in a private letter!

I repeat, that I am here endorsed as a gentleman and a Christian, who cannot and will not do any man injustice. Indeed, more character is given me than I ever had the vanity to claim. When I first perused this love-letter, I was tempted to bite my finger, to see if it were me. But I am sorry that the endorsement is not from a more respectable source. Nay, I shall convince you, before I leave this stand, as heavily as it may bear upon me, that this my eulogist is unworthy of confidence, and that he will not tell the truth when a lie is more convenient!

Ladies and gentlemen! You have listened to the strong and vivid pictures of Mr. Ross and myself, drawn by his *friends* and my *enemies*, in this vicinity. They have set before you, in bold relief, his eminent abilities, his attainments in literature, and his thorough accomplishments in all things pertaining to the ministry. You have heard of his charity, his meekness, his manliness, his piety, his frankness, his gentlemanly bearing, his independence and bravery, his disregard of popular clamor—making no conflicting statements, concealing no opinions! This picture is presented in contrast with that of the humble individual who now addresses you—who is utterly ignorant, having no education, no information: having no character—a common liar—a mere epistolary driveller: having flooded the country with blackguardism and slander—rude and unpolished in manners!

Now, ladies, look on this picture, and then on that. The first is the Presbyterian *Hyperion;* the latter, the Methodist *Satyr.* Now, my first observation is, that when I shall have exhibited the real picture of Mr. Ross to this assembly—which I intend to do, for I am a skilful artist—these Virginia admirers of his will not know their kind, affectionate, and dearly beloved pastor!

But what will become of your speaker? Shall I present a portrait of him? No, ladies; no, gentlemen, no. His address here to-day must speak for itself. Let him pass for a low, vulgar ragamuffin, whose true picture has been given by the artistic skill of the accomplished *Rossites* of Marion! To be serious, ladies and gentlemen, this studied disparagement of your humble servant need not, and ought not, to excite a feeling of indignation. These are the ravings of *despair;* and as such, are objects of *commiseration.* They can do no harm. The wives and sisters of certain gentlemen have taken Mr. Ross by the arms, and marched with him to and from the church, and have sat with him at table; and it is necessary that he should now be sustained as a *gentleman.* The people of this country have sense—they have sagacity—they have judgment. With their judgment of men and worth of men I for one will be satisfied.

Ladies and gentlemen! I will next proceed to read you the extracts from Mr. Wesley's celebrated Tenth and Eleventh

Sermons, out of which this controversy has grown, and upon which Mr. Ross founds the charge of *falsehood, fanaticism,* etc.

Mr. Wesley preaches two sermons on one text, Romans viii. 16: *"The Spirit itself beareth witness with our spirits that we are the children of God."*

In his Tenth Sermon, on this text, Mr. Wesley says:

> Let us first consider what is the witness, or testimony of our spirit. But I cannot here but desire all who are for swallowing up the testimony of the Spirit of God in the rational testimony of our own spirit, to observe, that in this text the apostle is so far from speaking of the testimony of our own spirit *only*, that it may be questioned whether he speaks of it *at all*,—whether he does not speak *only* of the testimony of God's Spirit. It does not appear but the original text may be fairly understood thus. But I contend not, seeing so many other texts, with the experience of all real Christians, sufficiently evince that there is in every believer both the testimony of God's Spirit, and the testimony of his own spirit, that he is the child of God. — *Vol. I., Serm. X., head I. section* 1, *p.* 85.

Again, after speaking at length concerning the witness of "our spirit," he says:

> 7. But what is that testimony of God's Spirit, which is superadded to and conjoined with this? How does he "bear witness with our spirit that we are the children of God?" It is hard to find words in the language of men to explain "the deep things of God." Indeed, there are none that will adequately express what the children of God experience. But perhaps one might say (desiring any who are taught of God to correct, to soften, or strengthen the expression) the testimony of the Spirit is an inward impression on the soul, whereby the Spirit of God directly witnesses to my spirit that I am a child of God; that Jesus Christ hath loved me, and hath given himself for me; and that all my sins are blotted out, and I, even I, am reconciled to God.
>
> 9. Then, and not till then—when the Spirit of God beareth that witness to our spirit, "God hath loved thee, and given his own Son to be the propitiation for thy sins; the Son of God hath loved thee, and hath washed thee from thy sins in his blood"—"we love God, because he first loved us;" and for his sake, we love our brother also. And of this we cannot but be conscious to ourselves: we "know the things that are freely given to us of God." We know that we love God and keep his commandments; and "hereby also we know that we are of God."—*Serm. X., p.* 87.

Again:

But what is the witness of the Spirit? The original word, μαρτυρία, may be rendered either (as it is in several places) *the witness*, or ambiguously, *the testimony*, or *the record:* so it is rendered in our translation, 1 John v. 11, "This is the record," [the testimony, the sum of what God testifies in all the inspired writings,] "that God hath given to us eternal life, and this life is in his Son." The testimony now under consideration is given by the Spirit of God, to and with our spirit: he is the person testifying. What he testifies to us is, "that we are the children of God."

4. Meantime, let it be observed, I do not mean hereby that the Spirit of God testifies this by any *outward voice:* no, nor always by an inward voice, although he may do this sometimes. Neither do I suppose that he always applies to the heart (though he often may) one or more texts of Scripture. But he so works upon the soul by his immediate influence, and by a strong though inexplicable operation, that the stormy wind and troubled waves subside, and there is a sweet calm; the heart resting as in the arms of Jesus, and the sinner being clearly satisfied that God is reconciled—that all his "iniquities are forgiven, and his sins covered."—*Serm. X., head II., sections* 1 *and* 4, *p.* 91.

My next and last quotation is from the Eleventh Sermon, fifth head, first section, and ending on page 95. It is in these significant words:

1. The sum of all is this: the testimony of the Spirit is an inward impression on the souls of believers, whereby the Spirit of God directly testifies to their spirit, that they are children of God. And it is not questioned whether there is a testimony of the Spirit, but whether there is any *direct* testimony—whether there is any other than that which arises from a consciousness of the fruit of the Spirit? We believe there is; because this is the plain, natural meaning of the text, illustrated both by the preceding words, and by the parallel passage in the Epistle to the Galatians; because, in the nature of things, the testimony must precede the fruit which springs from it; and because this plain meaning of the word of God is confirmed by the experience of innumerable children of God; yea, and by the experience of all who are convinced of sin, who can never rest till they have a direct witness; and even of the children of the world, who, not having the witness in themselves, one and all declare none can *know* his sins forgiven.

2. And whereas it is objected, that experience is not sufficient to prove a doctrine unsupported by Scripture; that madmen and enthusiasts of every kind have imagined such a witness; that the design of that witness is to prove our profession genuine, which design it does not answer; that the Scripture says, "The tree is known by its

fruit;" "examine yourselves; prove your ownselves;" and, meantime, the direct witness is never referred to in all the book of God; that it does not secure us from the greatest delusions; and lastly, that the change wrought in us is a sufficient testimony, unless in such trials as Christ alone suffered: we answer, 1. Experience is sufficient to *confirm* a doctrine which is grounded on Scripture. 2. Though many fancy they experience what they do not, this is no prejudice to real experience. 3. The design of that witness is, to assure us we are children of God; and this design it does answer. 4. The true witness of the Spirit is known by its fruit, "love, peace, joy"—not indeed preceding, but following it. 5. It cannot be proved that the direct, as well as the indirect witness, is not referred to in that very text—"Know ye not your ownselves, that Jesus Christ is in you?" 6. The Spirit of God, witnessing with our spirit, does secure us from all delusion. And lastly, we are all liable to trials, wherein the testimony of our own spirit is not sufficient; wherein nothing less than the direct testimony of God's Spirit can assure us that we are his children.

These are the extracts quoted by Mr. Ross, and of which he says, on page 8 of his *immaculate* production—

I hold the common faith, as to the witness of the Spirit, as it stands in the Presbyterian Confession, and as it ever has been held by Presbyterians in all their branches, by Episcopalians in England and America—as it has been taught by evangelical Congregational, by orthodox Baptist and Lutheran Churches.

It is the settled faith of these denominations which I express when I affirm, as I now do, that the doctrine of the Direct Witness of the Spirit, as taught by Mr. Wesley, is UNSCRIPTURAL, FALSE, FANATICAL, AND OF MISCHIEVOUS TENDENCY.

Again, on page 35 of this same Tract, Mr. Ross thus speaks of the doctrine advanced by Mr. Wesley—a doctrine to which every Presbyterian, Methodist, Baptist, Lutheran, etc., in this assembly or elsewhere, who has any religious experience, most heartily subscribes:

I have never seen Mr. Wesley's doctrine of the Direct Witness affirmed by any commentator on Romans or Galatians, or anywhere else in the writings of evangelical men, save in the works of Mr. Wesley, and the teachers who follow him—or in the books of other admitted mystics.

Now, in this connection, I beg leave to read you the resolution of the notorious Athens Synod, adopted in October, 1846, as Mr. Ross boastingly asserts, with "*absolute una-*

nimity"—that is to say, without one dissenting voice. I read from the Calvinistic Magazine. The resolution is in these words:

Resolved, that in the estimation of Synod, a Tract lately published by F. A. Ross, entitled, "The Doctrine of the Direct Witness of the Spirit, as taught by Rev. John Wesley, shown to be *false, unscriptural, fanatical, and of mischievous tendency*," IS AN ABLE PRODUCTION, setting forth that important subject in its true scriptural light, and is earnestly recommended to the perusal of all the members of our Church.

We now have the case fairly before us; and I shall proceed to convict both Mr. Ross and the members of this Synod, either of wilful falsehood or criminal ignorance, or both.

Now, since Mr. Ross and his Synod profess to give the views of the several denominations mentioned, let us examine into the correctness of their pretensions. And first, as to the *Congregationalists*. They are so called from the fact that they reject all church government, except that of a single congregation, under the direction of one pastor, with their elders, assistants, or managers—each congregation enacting its own laws and regulations. They are Calvinists, and they are a denomination of Protestants who are principally confined to the New England States. If I were so disposed, I could adduce various authorities to prove that Mr. Ross and his Synod have grossly misrepresented the Congregationalists upon this important doctrine. I will, however, content myself with giving you a few brief quotations from a small work I hold in my hand, written by the REV. THOMAS C. UPHAM, Professor of Moral and Mental Science in Bowdoin College, in the State of Maine. Professor Upham is an acceptable minister of the Congregational Church, extensively known as the author of works on "The Intellect," "The Sensibilities," "The Will," "The Life of Faith," "Interior Life," and the work I hold in my hand, entitled, "Religious Experience." This last work sets forth the views of the Congregationalists upon the doctrine of the *Direct Witness*. Most of his other productions are now adopted as text-books in many colleges and universities, especially those under the control of his denomination. On page 7, Professor Upham says:

> If I know any thing, *I know certainly* that the true resting-place of my soul is and must be in the Infinite Mind; that it is not and cannot be anywhere else. Perhaps no part of the Scriptures, during the more recent periods of my experience, has affected me more than the prayer of our Saviour for his disciples, "That they *all may be one, as thou, Father, art in me*, and I in thee, that they also may be one in us."

On page 8, the Professor says, in speaking of the necessity of a change of heart, and of a knowledge of that change on our part:—

> WHAT IS PROOF OF THE ATTAINMENT?—1. *The direct witness of the Spirit.* "The Spirit itself beareth witness with our spirit that we are the children of God." "He that *abideth* in me hath the *witness in himself.*"
>
> 2. The witness of *our own spirit* that our tempers and acts are such as the word of God requires.

But, says this Kingsport gladiator, I speak the common faith of all orthodox Congregationalists when I say, as I now do, that this doctrine is "false, unscriptural," etc. And again, he declares, as cited from page 35, that he never has seen this doctrine taught by any evangelical writer, or any commentator on Romans or Galatians, save in the writings of John Wesley and the teachers who follow him! You are right, brother *Fred.*, exclaims every elder and preacher in the Athens Synod: you are right! for we have never seen or heard tell of this thing in all the course of our *eventful* lives!

II. As to the *Episcopalians*, they hold the doctrine of the *Direct Witness* in the same sense in which it is held by Mr. Wesley and the Methodists. This fact no intelligent man can be ignorant of, and this no man will deny, unless he is as unscrupulous a liar as is F. A. Ross, or the members of the

Athens Synod! Hear the following extract from page 363 of Buck's Theological Dictionary, under the caption of "*Methodist Tenets:*" and bear in mind that Buck is a *Calvinist,* and not a follower of Wesley. He says:—

> The doctrines of the Wesleyan Methodists ARE THE SAME as the Church of England, (the Episcopalian Church,) as set forth in her liturgy, articles, and homilies.

What will this audience think when I tell them, as I now do, that the TWENTY-FIVE Articles of Religion set forth in the Methodist Discipline, by Mr. Wesley, were taken from the Creed of the English Episcopalians, and abridged for our convenience? What will you think when I tell you, as I now do, that Mr. Wesley was a minister of the English Episcopal Church, and that he never separated therefrom to the day of his death! Don't be surprised, for these are the facts in the case, and no man knew them better than the *anointed slanderer* to whom I am this day replying. The members of the Synod may not have known these facts, for they seem to have never read any thing but the productions of Ross's pen!

But here is a short extract from a volume of sermons written and published by the Rev. JOHN HURRION in 1729, an able minister of the Episcopal Church:—

> The malignant opposition made to him (the Holy Spirit) by some, and the vile contempt cast upon him by others, are things which have quenched and grieved him, and *caused him to depart* to that degree as hereby almost all vital religion is lost out of our world. Hence it is that the glory of God in Christ, the faith, joy, and zeal of Christians, are under such a cloud at this day. Is it not, then, high time to speak?—*Sermon on the Holy Spirit.*

I repeat, the Methodists and Episcopalians do not differ in doctrine: they never have. We differ upon the subject of *Church government,* the subject of *Episcopacy,* that of *Ordination,* the authority of *Presbyters,* the *Succession,* etc., etc.

But I have no time to dwell upon these topics, or to consume time in fruitless efforts to show that the order of bishops and presbyters is one and the same. I leave such men as Doctors Stillingfleet, Miller, and Whitaker, and Archbishops Cranmer, Grindal, and Tillotson, to settle these controverted points.

III. As to the *Lutherans*, for the very reverse of what Mr. Ross has asserted, and the members of the Athens Synod have sworn to, I refer this assembly to *Mosheim's Ecclesiastical History*, and to Martin Luther's Commentary on *Galatians*, a work, by the way, which Mr. Ross and his synodical under-strappers declared they never heard of!

FORTY-ONE propositions, extracted out of Luther's works, by order of Pope Leo, were condemned as heretical, scandalous, and offensive to pious ears; and all persons were forbidden to read his writings upon pain of death. One of these propositions was that asserting the *direct influence of God's Spirit in converting the soul*, a doctrine to which the Church of Rome never did subscribe. These facts are known to every reading and intelligent man and woman in this assembly. But especially are they known to the members of the Lutheran Church, several of whom I have the pleasure to address on this occasion.

In further proof of what I assert, I could quote the Life of Luther, Hawies' Church History, and the second volume of the History of Charles V. When I see to what extreme meanness this man Ross and his synodical associates have resorted to injure the Methodist Church, I can scarcely avoid an excess of acrimony and vehemence in the delivery of this address.

IV. As it relates to the *Baptists*, they are, of all the denominations named, the farthest from denying the truth of the doctrine of the *Direct Witness*. Are there any *Baptists* in this assembly? I am answered, yes; and I am glad to hear the response. I hope you will listen to me—not that I wish to enlist you on our side of this controversy, but because I wish you to see how you are misrepresented, ay, even *slandered.* You may resent, or you may submit: we Methodists can fight our own battles, and we intend to do it.

The Baptists teach that no man is a Christian, entitled to membership in their Church, or a fit subject for immersion, until he has the direct witness of God's Spirit in the work of regeneration. To prove this, I have the authorities of "Rippon's Baptist Register," "Evans's Sketch of Religious Denominations," and "Adams's View of Religions." But I lay all these aside, and appeal to the sense of this assembly. Does not every one here know that the Baptists carry this matter farther than even the Methodists do? They will not receive a member into their Church until he has this *direct witness*—until he can tell where, when, and *how* God, for Christ's sake, pardoned his sins! And as to plunging one of you into this river here on my back, a Baptist preacher would not touch you with a ten-foot pole, unless you testify your belief in the doctrine. And yet Ross and the Synod say they teach the common faith of all orthodox Baptists when they say the doctrine is "false, fanatical, unscriptural, and of devilish tendency!"

V. But I proceed now to examine the faith of the *Presbyterians* on this important but controverted point. And now for it, ladies! now for it, gentlemen! I hope to have your undivided attention, as I have had thus far, for I propose to make out a stronger case against Mr. Ross and his Synod in this case than I have done in any of the denominational cases just disposed of; and I shall rely alone upon *Presbyterian* authorities—I may say, upon the very authors cited by Mr. Ross in his love-letter to me, and in whom he says he believes, and by whom he says he swears!

The Rev. MATTHEW POOLE, of England, an eminent Presbyterian minister, more than one hundred years ago, wrote and published a Commentary on the Scriptures; and in explanation of this same text in Romans says:—

> The Spirit of adoption doth not only excite us to call upon God as our Father, but it doth ascertain and assure us (as before) that we are his children; and this it doth not by an outward voice, *as God the Father to Jesus Christ*, nor by an angel, as to *Daniel* and the *Virgin Mary*, but by an inward and secret suggestion, whereby he raiseth our hearts to this persuasion, that God is our Father and we are his children. This is *not* the testimony of the *graces* and *operations* of the *Spirit*, but of the *Spirit* itself.

The Rev. John Brown, a Presbyterian divine of Scotland, published a body of divinity just one hundred years ago, and among other works a Dictionary of the Bible, in which, under the head "*Spirit*," he says:—

> The third person in the Godhead is particularly called *Holy Spirit* or Holy Ghost, to express the mode of his relation to the Father and Son, and because he, by spiritual methods, works spiritual qualities and affections in us. He is the Spirit of adoption, that brings us into the family of God, dwells in every one of God's children, and renders them conformable to his image. (Rom. viii. 15.) He is said to be *sent*, because authorized by the Father and Son—(John xvi. 7)—to be given, because freely bestowed in his *person*, gifts, and graces—(John vii. 39)—and *poured out*, because carefully and plentifully bestowed. They that are joined to the Lord are one spirit, *Christ and they* have the *same Holy Ghost dwelling in them*, and they are conformed to him in the gracious temper of their soul.

Rev. John Flavel, of England, a distinguished Presbyterian minister, on page 167 of his Whole Works has a sermon on the text, "*And you hath he quickened, who were dead in trespasses and sins*," in which he says:—

> Then do we begin to live when we begin to have union with Christ, the fountain of life, by *his Spirit communicated to us*.
>
> The Spirit of the Lord is *poured out upon us* to quicken us with the new spiritual life: it gives us an *ease supernatural*, a new *supernatural being*, which is therefore called a new creature.
>
> The Spirit, who is God by nature, *dwells in* and actuates the soul whom he regenerates, and, by sanctifying, causes it to live a divine life.
>
> None can make another by any words to understand what that

pleasure is which the renewed soul *feels diffused* through all its faculties and affections in its communion with the Lord, and in the *sealings* and *witnessings* of his Spirit.

President EDWARDS, the head and front of Presbyterianism in his day, speaking of the great revival in New England in the year 1734, and in defence of the *enthusiasm* of the subjects of that revival, says:—

Such extraordinary external effects of inward impressions have not only been found in here and there a single person, but there have also been times wherein many have been thus affected. So it was in the year 1625, in the west of Scotland, in a time of a great outpouring of the Spirit of God. It was a frequent thing for many to be so extraordinarily seized with terror in hearing of the word, by the Spirit of God convincing them of sin, that they *fell down* and were *carried out of the church*, who afterwards proved most solid and lively Christians. There have been instances of persons crying out in transports of divine joy in New England. There has, before now, been both crying out and falling down in this town, (Northampton,) under awakenings of conscience, and in the pangs of the new birth, and also in some of the neighboring towns. In one of them, more than seven years ago, was a great number together that cried out and fell down under convictions, in most of which, by good information, was a hopeful and abiding issue.—*Edwards on Revivals*, p. 126, and onward.

DR. SCOTT, an Episcopalian, approved by Presbyterians, in commenting upon this very text of Mr. Wesley, says:—

The Holy Spirit, by producing in believers the affections which dutiful children bear to a wise and good father, attests their adoption into his family: while they are examining themselves concerning the reality of their conversion, and find scriptural evidence of it, the Holy Spirit *shines on his own work*, excites their holy affections, and thus puts the matter beyond doubt. *This witness* is borne along with *that* (witness) of our own consciences, not without it, nor against it.

Rev. MATTHEW HENRY, a Presbyterian minister of distinction, referred to by Mr. Ross, in a sermon on this text, says:—

They that are sanctified have God's Spirit, witnessing with their spirits that they are the children of God; and in this they CANNOT *as they* OUGHT NOT *to be deceived.*

DR. DODDRIDGE, one of Mr. Ross's favorites, says, in a sermon on this same text in Romans:—

> *So he, the Spirit himself,* by his INTERNAL AND GRACIOUS OPERATIONS, *beareth witness with the* ANSWER OF OUR SPIRITS, *that we* ARE THE CHILDREN OF GOD.

And still Mr. Ross affirms that he never saw any such sayings as the foregoing in the writings of any commentator on Romans or Galatians, or anywhere else in the writings of any evangelical men, save those of Wesley and the leaders who follow him. The Synod at Athens, "with absolute unanimity," say that they are as ignorant as Ross is—that they never read the *standard authors* of their own Church!

But, ladies and gentlemen, I will trouble you with two other authorities upon this point, before I dismiss the subject; and this I do more for the purpose of showing up the ridiculous position of Ross and his synod, than with a view to instruct or edify you. These two authorities are also Presbyterian, and they are "*evangelical*" to all intents and purposes. The first is the *Presbyterian Confession of Faith*—alias, the "Arabian Nights' Entertainments"—an old-fashioned work, truly abounding with all the extravagance of Eastern hyperbole! Here it is, the old Saybrook platform—a real old Calvinian 74-pounder! Face up, witness, to Ross and his synod, who in your eyes must be worse than infidels, for they have denied *the* faith!

On page 77 of the Confession, chap. xviii., treating of "The Assurance of Grace and Salvation," this venerable old platform says:

> Although *hypocrites* and other *unregenerate men* may vainly deceive themselves with false hopes and carnal presumptions of being in the favor of God and estate of salvation, which hope of theirs shall perish, yet such as truly believe in the Lord Jesus, and love him in sincerity, endeavoring to walk in all good conscience before him, *may, in this life, be certainly assured that they are in a state of grace,* and may

rejoice in the hope of the glory of God, which hope shall never make them ashamed.

II. This certainty is not a bare conjectural and probable persuasion, grounded upon a fallible hope, but an *infallible assurance of faith*, founded upon the divine truth of the promises of salvation, the inward evidence of those graces unto which these promises are made, the *testimony of the Spirit of adoption witnessing with our spirits that we are the children of God*, which Spirit is the earnest of our inheritance, whereby we are sealed to the day of redemption.

Here it will be seen that the Confession, in urging this doctrine of the *Direct Witness*, says that "hypocrites and other unregenerate men"—such as Ross and the members of the Athens synod—may vainly deceive themselves with false hopes, but declares that their hopes shall perish! And in quoting Scripture to prove its position upon the *Direct Witness*, it is remarkable that the Confession cites Mr. Wesley's text: "The Spirit itself beareth witness with our spirits, that we are the children of God!"

The next authority we offer is from the second volume of the Calvinistic Magazine, published in Rogersville, in 1828. It is from a printed sermon on "The Proofs of our Religion," in which it is declared and proven that a man denying this doctrine of the *Direct Witness* is a hypocrite, or has no religion. Who do you suppose delivered this sermon, and superintended its publication? *Frederick Augustus Ross!* Yes, Mr. Ross thus preached twenty years ago. I will only trouble you with the following extract, found on page 360 of the volume I hold in my hand:

And the doctrine of the Trinity [or Direct Witness] is wonderfully adapted to affect the heart; for in the Scriptures it is never mentioned as a mere fact, in which our affections are not concerned, but is always brought before us in connection with the glorious work of redemption. There we are told of the Father's unspeakable love in the gift of his Son; of the Son's obedience even unto the death of the cross; of the *Holy Spirit, coming in love, sent by the Father and the Son, to regenerate the sinner, and to purify, to enlighten, to give peace and joy to the believer.* There is, therefore, a moral meaning in the Trinity. A man then must FEEL his heart overflowing with love to God the Father for the gift of his Son. He must FEEL that the HOLY GHOST IS PRESENT, APPLYING THESE TRUTHS TO HIS HEART, before he can know the meaning of the Trinity, [or Direct Witness.] No man ever did believe in the meaning of this doctrine who was a stranger to the feelings I have described, AND NO MAN EVER DENIED THE DOCTRINE WHOSE SOUL WAS FILLED WITH THESE AFFECTIONS.

This was the doctrine Mr. Ross preached twenty years ago. And why? Because he *solemnly swore*, when he was ordained a minister, that he would preach and defend this, and every other doctrine taught in the Confession. And these ministers seated behind me know, and will tell you, that they regard the ordination vow of a clergyman as more solomn, and even more binding, than any oath administered by a justice of the peace. Twenty years ago, then, Mr. Ross *swore* that he believed this doctrine of the *Direct Witness*, and would preach and defend it. But two years ago, in this same town of Rogersville, on the Lord's day, before a large assembly, in a sermon *against* this doctrine, he held up his right hand, and bringing it down to the board, *swore*, "This doctrine of the Direct Witness is false, fanatical, unscriptural, and of mischievous tendency, SO HELP ME GOD!" And in October of the same year he induced an entire synod to swear the same false oath, and to *perjure themselves in the sight of high Heaven!*

Ladies and gentlemen! You now begin to see, even if it be "through a glass, darkly," *why* it is that Mr. Ross has not met me at this place to-day, as was expected, and even desired, by his friends, if they were sincere in their professions. Before I am through I intend you to see—if not "face to face," which cannot be in his absence—but I intend you to see as clear as a sunbeam, the reason of his non-appearance. It is not because I am beneath his notice—no, he tells me otherwise in this *beautiful* letter of his, just read in your hearing. Besides, he knows, and his friends know, that I stand fair in my own Church; that I am recognized by the Church to which I belong as a local elder in good standing. He knows, and so do his friends, that although I commenced my review of the man and his writings upon my own hook, still my Church recognizes me as a true exponent of her principles in a controversy with Mr. Ross. And you all know that if the Methodist Church is worthy of being *put down*, she ought to be demolished through her *acknowledged organs*, and in no other way can she be demolished.

I am, no doubt, safe in saying that President Collins never would have *condescended* to meet F. A. Ross in discussion, but for the fact that he was, and still is, the acknowledged organ of the New School Presbyterian Church in all this country. Mr. Ross, of himself, is a low-bred, false-hearted, adulterous, and unprincipled *free negro*, unworthy of the notice of the high standing and literary rank of the President of Emory and Henry College; but on account of the Church which puts him forth, and backs him, he is entitled to notice.

Now, in the very worst aspect of the case, I am not more degraded than is the *sable* leader of the Presbyterian Church; and on account of my relation to the Methodist Church, I too am entitled to notice. So you all think, by nodding your assent. Why, then, is your champion not here? Because he dared not attend. He would stick his head in the fire before he would meet me in the presence of such a crowd as this, and have me brand him with falsehood, forgery, slander, and adultery, as I would do, and make him submit to it! Yes, if he were in this stand behind me, I would turn upon him, as Nathan did upon David, and staring him full in the face, I would tell him, Sir, THOU ART THE MAN!

THE DEPRAVITY OF THE MAN!—Under this head, ladies and gentlemen, I propose, in a very brief manner, to exhibit some proofs of the deep, dark, and damning depravity of this man Ross. The following passage *against the doctrine of the Direct Witness* occurs in the writings of DR. CHALMERS, one of the most pious, eloquent, and celebrated Presbyterian divines of Scotland—a gentleman who departed this life twelve months ago, at the advanced age of 70 years. In this passage, Dr. Chalmers presents the argument of the *infidel objector* to this doctrine, *and so states the case himself*, but Ross has neither the manliness nor the moral honesty to tell this. Chalmers says:

> Does not this doctrine of a *revelation* of the Spirit, it may be asked, additional to the revelation of the Word, open a door to the most unbridled variety? May it not give a sanction to any conceptions of any visionary pretenders, and clothe in all the authority of inspiration a set of doctrines not to be found within the compass of the written record? Does it not set aside the usefulness of the Bible, and break in upon the unity and consistency of revealed truth, by letting loose upon the world a succession of *fancies* as endless and as variable as are the caprices of the human imagination?

☞ In *reply*, DR. CHALMERS says:

> All very true, did we pretend that the office of the Spirit was to reveal any thing additional to the information, whether in the way of *doctrine* or of *duty*, which the Bible sets before us. But his office, as defined by the Bible itself, is not to make known to us *any truths* which are not contained in the Bible, but *to make clear to our understandings* the truths which *are* contained in it. He opens our understandings to understand the Scriptures. The word of God is called the Sword of the Spirit. It is the instrument by which the Spirit worketh. He does not tell us any thing that is out of the record, but all that is within it *he sends home with clearness and effect upon the mind.*—Chalmers's Works, p. 126.

Again:

> It is surely not necessary that the Spirit add any thing to the truth of God's omniscience, as it is put down in the written record. It will be enough that he gives to the mind upon which he operates a steady and enduring *impression* of this truth.—Ibid, p. 127.

Again, speaking of an unregenerate man, he says:

> Only grant us the undeniable truth, that he may understand how he *cannot* discern the things of the Spirit unless the Spirit *reveal* them to him; and yet with this understanding, he may not be one of those in behalf of whom the Spirit hath *actually* interposed with his peculiar office of *revelation.*—Ibid, p. 125.

In these last repeated extracts, Dr. Chalmers goes on to teach and vindicate the *Direct Witness*—not only so, but he overturns the arguments of these *infidel objectors*. All this Ross understood perfectly. But the *fraud*, nay, the *forgery* he perpetrates with malice aforethought, and, as I believe, being instigated by the Devil, and not having the fear of God before his eyes!

My audience! the man who would do this thing is not too good to forge a note of hand upon his neighbor for $100, one day after date! He is not too good to utter a lie, too! He is prepared for "treason, stratagem, and spoils;"—and that man is *F. A. Ross*, the leader and champion of New School Presbyterianism!

Mr. Wesley, in his Works, declares that at the time he began to raise up his societies in London, "*vital religion was well-nigh lost and forgotten.*" This statement Mr. Ross declares to be one of *boasting and lying*, and in saying that, the Synod of East Tennessee affirms that he told the truth, according to the Scriptures!

Here is what Dr. Watts says in his "*Preface to An Humble Attempt to revive Vital Religion,*" in 1735:

Among the papers published last year, there hath been some inquiry made whether there be any decay in the "dissenting" interest, and what may have been supposed to have been the occasion of it. So far as I have searched into that matter, I have been informed that whatsoever decrease may have appeared in some places, there have been sensible advances in others. And without entering into any debate about the particular reason of its declension in any town whatsoever, I am well satisfied that the great and general reason is THE DECAY OF VITAL RELIGION IN THE HEARTS AND LIVES OF MEN; and the little success which the ministrations of the gospel have had of late for the conversion of sinners to holiness, and the recovery of them from the state of corrupt nature and the course of this world, to the life of God by Jesus Christ.—Nor is the complaint of the declension of virtue and piety made only by the Protestant dissenters. It is a general matter of mournful observation among all that lay the cause of God to heart, and therefore it cannot be thought amiss for every one to use all just and proper efforts for *the recovery of dying religion* in the world.

From Buck's Theological Dictionary, page 369, under the head "Methodists," I take the following:

> At the time this society was formed, it was said that the whole kingdom of England was tending fast to infidelity. "It is come," says Bishop Butler, "I know not how, to be taken for granted by many persons, that Christianity is not so much as a subject of inquiry, but that it is now at length discovered to be fictitious; and accordingly they treat it as if, in the present age, this were an agreement among all people of discernment, and nothing remained but to set it up as a principal subject of mirth and ridicule, as it were, by way of reprisal for its having so long interrupted the pleasures of the world." There is every reason to believe that the Methodists were the instruments in stemming this torrent. The sick and the poor also tasted the fruits of their labors and benevolence: Mr. Wesley abridged himself of all his superfluities, and proposed a fund for the relief of the indigent; and so prosperous was the scheme, that they quickly increased their fund to eighty pounds per annum.

In Watson's Life of Wesley, an author quoted by Mr. Ross, page 62, I find the following:

> A more striking instance of the rapid deterioration of religious light and influence in a country scarcely occurs, than in our own, from the Restoration till the rise of Methodism. It affected not only the Church, but the dissenting sects, in no ordinary degree. The *Presbyterians* had commenced their course through Arianism down to Socinianism; and those who held the doctrines of Calvin had, in too many instances, by a course of *hot-house planting, luxuriated them into the fatal and disgusting errors of Antinomianism,* There were, indeed, many happy exceptions; but this was the GENERAL STATE of religion and morals in the country, when the Wesleys, Whitefield, and a few kindred spirits came forth, ready to sacrifice ease, reputation, and even life itself, to produce a reformation.

And now, my audience, in further proof of what Mr. Wesley has said about the morals of Europe, and by way of certificate for the morality of Presbyterianism, I beg leave to cite the testimony—not of a Methodist, or a Baptist, or a Lutheran, or an Episcopalian, but of the whole Presbyterian Church of Scotland, met in General Assembly. Let not this audience, and the few *spies* sent here to take notes of what I say, charge that I am slandering the Presbyterians of Scotland—the witnesses are the united Fathers of their

Church. In the preamble to an act of their Assembly, passed in the year 1578, it is openly set forth that

> The General Assembly of the Kirk finding universal corruption of the whole estates of the body of the realm, the great coldness and slackness in religion in the greatest part of the professors of the same, with the daily increase of all kind of fearful sins and enormities, as incests, adulteries, murders, (committed in Edinburgh and Stirling,) cursed sacrilege, ungodly sedition and division within the bowels of the realm, with all manner of disordered and ungodly living, etc. etc.

In 1648, just two hundred years ago, and coming down more nearly to Mr. Wesley's time, the General Assembly again testifies to the state of Presbyterian morality in Scotland. I read from "Breckenridge and Hughes's Discussion," page 397. The Assembly says:

> Ignorance of God, and of his Son Jesus Christ, prevailed exceedingly in the land: that it were impossible to reckon up all the abominations that were in the land; and that the blaspheming of the name of God, swearing by the creatures, profanation of the Lord's day, uncleanliness, excess and rioting, vanity of apparel, lying and deceit, railing and cursing, arbitrary and uncontrolled oppression, and grinding the faces of the poor by landlords, and others in places of power, were become ordinary and common sins.

The testimony of the Associate Synod of Scotland, as late as the year 1778, and coming down to Mr. Wesley's time, is of the following import:

> A general unbelief of revealed religion (prevails) among the higher orders of our countrymen, which hath, by a necessary consequence, produced, in vast numbers, an absolute indifference as to what they believe, either concerning truth or duty, any further than it may comport with their worldly views.

But the question under consideration here is not whether Presbyterians were, or were not, in those days, less moral than other denominations, which seems to have been the fact, themselves being witnesses—but is whether or not Mr. Wesley *lied*, as charged by Ross and the Athens synod, when he said, as he did, that "*vital religion*" was becoming extinct in the whole kingdom of England, when he began to raise up his societies. I have shown, by testimony that no court or jury can reject, that Mr. Ross is the *liar*, and that his synodical associates are the SLANDERERS. Among these is your pastor, *Mr. Palmer*, as painful as it may be to some of you to have his name used in this connection. The only apology I can offer for the synod is, that its sayings and doings were eternally, omnipotently, and immutably "*foreordained*."

Mr. Ross and his synod, by partisan blaspheming, and by their malignant abuse, have compelled me to enter into this oral disputation, as well as the one we are carrying on through the medium of the press. I have already taught them a few facts respecting their religion, as well as mine, with which they seem to have been unacquainted before. And before I am done with these shameless traducers, I will make them ashamed of themselves, if their foreheads are not *petrified*, and *impervious to a blush!*

On page 87 of Mr. Ross's slanderous "Tract," you will find the extract I now read you, commencing after a *full stop*, and winding up with a *period*. I wish you to listen to it attentively, and recollect its *charge* and *sentiment*, as upon this paragraph I found the charge of *wilful lying* and *malignant slander*, both against Mr. Ross and the synod. Listen to the base and infamous LIBEL:

> I beg, in this connection, to say that all my Swedenborgian quotations are from Mr. Wesley's "Thoughts on the Writings of Baron Swedenborg." (Vol. vii. p. 426, etc.) And that it is remarkable MR. WESLEY NOWHERE CHALLENGES SWEDENBORG'S CLAIM TO VISION, BUT RATHER SEEMS TO ADMIT IT!!

Now, ladies—you too, gentlemen—hear the testimony which shall convict these *reverend LIARS!* They give chapter, and verse, and volume of Wesley's Works—the very book I hold in my hand! And well they may; because this book contains the only tract or article by Mr. Wesley, in existence, against the writings of Baron Swedenborg, as every intelligent Methodist knows. Here it is, headed as Mr. Ross says, covering eight leaves or sixteen pages in this book, vol. vii. of Wesley's Works, pages 426—440. Mr. Wesley says:

Many years ago the Baron came over to England, and lodged at one Mr. Brockmer's, who informed me, and the same information was given me by Mr. Mathesius, a very serious Swedish clergyman, (both of whom were alive when I left London, and, I suppose, are so still,) that while he was in his house he had a violent fever; in the height of which, being totally delirious, he broke from Mr. Brockmer, ran into the street stark naked, proclaimed himself the Messiah, and rolled himself into the mire. I suppose he dates from this time his admission into the society of angels. From this time we are undoubtedly to date that peculiar species of insanity which attended him, with scarce any intermission, to the day of his death.

In all history I find but one instance of an insanity parallel to this. I mean that related by the Roman poet of the gentleman at Argos, in other respects a sensible man.

I make no scruples to affirm this is as arrant nonsense as was ever pronounced by any man in Bedlam.

Be this a specimen of the Baron's skill in expounding the Scriptures. Come we now to his memorable visions and revelations.

Any serious man may observe that many of these are silly and childish to the last degree; that many others are amazingly odd and whimsical; many palpably absurd, contrary to all sound reason; and many more contrary, not only to particular texts, but to the whole tenor of Scripture.

Who illuminated either Jacob Behmen or Baron Swedenborg flatly to contradict these things? It could not be the God of the holy prophets, for he is always consistent with himself. Certainly it was the spirit of darkness. And indeed "the light which was in them was darkness," while they labor to kill the never-dying worm, and to put out the unquenchable fire! And with what face can any professing to believe in the Bible give any countenance to these dreamers?—that filthy dreamer in particular, who takes care to provide harlots, instead of fire and brimstone, for the devils and damned spirits in hell! O my brethren! let none of you that fear God recommend such a writer any more! much less labor to make the deadly poison palatable, by sweetening it with all care! All his folly and nonsense we may excuse, but not his making God a liar—not his contradicting, in so flagrant a manner, the whole oracles of God! True, his tales are often exceedingly lively, and as entertaining as the tales of the fairies, but I dare not give up my Bible for them; and I must give up one or the other. If the preceding extracts are from God, then the Bible is only a fable; but if "all Scriptures are given by inspiration of God," then let these dreamers sink into the pit from whence they came.

Wakefield, May 9, 1782. JOHN WESLEY.

THE SLANDERS COMPLAINED OF.—Ladies and gentlemen: under this head I propose to present you other and different views of this controversy from those upon which I have dwelt thus far. Having said a good deal to-day of a severe character against Mr. Ross and the Athens synod, and intending, before I leave this stand, to say a good deal more, I will briefly present our ground of *complaint*, as Methodists, in justification of my course, and of my abuse. In other words, I will, for the information of such in this large assembly as have not had access to the "Calvinistic Magazine," in which, under various heads, within the last three years, this man Ross, and the pliant tools of the synod—who go at his bidding and come at his call—have taken occasion to express themselves most freely as to the *ignorance, degradation, hypocrisy, corruption*, and even *infamy*, of the *membership* and *ministry* of the Methodist Episcopal Church in the United States. They talk about abuse! The disciples of Ross, Palmer, Morrison & Co., are the last people on earth who should complain of my abuse, or the abuse of any Methodist who attempts a refutation of the slanders of Ross. That vile man and his associates have attempted to immolate the whole Methodist Church upon the brazen altar of *personal abuse!* The language of bitter reproach and burning invective has been exhausted upon our members, ministers, doctrines, and discipline, by this anointed band of calumniators. And as to Ross himself, St. Giles has been put to the blush in the filthiness of the epithets which he has bestowed upon the living and the dead of our Church! And yet, as if in mockery of all human sincerity, as if intending to add insult to injury, the vile advocates of this man, and the dirty little whippers-in, cry out that we substitute *abuse* for *argument!*

I will bring together, in this part of my address, a *few* only of the published opinions of these slanderers, and of the hard speeches which these ungodly sinners have uttered against our Church. I beseech every lady and gentleman under the sound of my voice to hear these sayings patiently and impartially. I will read to you from the Magazines themselves, giving chapter and verse; and invite any gentleman present, who may feel free to do so, to stand at my side and see that I read correctly.

In the Magazine for August, 1846, the *Rev. Slanderer* says:

> But the broad fact remains, after all concessions, that Methodism is a *debauched pietism*, in which the imagination has run wild, and passion, bodily sympathy, and mysticism are supreme, while true moral character is subordinate and degraded. We speak out and challenge examination. We speak out and say that rottenness is in the very bones of the moral system created by Methodism, to an awful extent.

In the Magazine for November, 1846, he says:

> It is sometimes asked, with great greenness, what business have we, the editors of the Calvinistic Magazine, with the Methodist system? We answer—just the same business we would have if a man living in the same house with us had a barrel of gunpowder in his room. We think we should have the right to try to get that powder out of the house. So we have the right to expose popery, and prelacy, and Methodism, as dangerous to the civil and religious liberty of our country.
>
> We said in the outset that this article is No. 1. We have materials for at least twelve numbers of the *Great Iron Wheel*, in which, if spared, we will show the beginnings of Romanism in as many particulars in the Methodist Episcopal Church. And as proof of what is to come, we feel sure no candid man will rise from the reading of this number without saying, with a long breath, "Well, Methodism is worse than I thought it was."

In the Magazine for April, 1847, in the second number of his "Iron Wheel," he says:

> We have often remarked a peculiar insensibility, as a characteristic of the Methodist common mass, *a peculiar insensibility to moral honor and integrity of character*. We have not dropped this sentence in hasty writing. We say *deliberately* it is so—it is so—WIDE AND DEEP.

Upon this last extract indulge me in offering a word of comment. He says the Methodist common masses are insensible to moral honor and integrity of character—that is to say, they are destitute of both! Has it then come to this, that a Christian people will sustain a minister who openly comes out and charges that the *common masses* of one of the most numerous sects in this country, a highly respectable and evangelical denomination, are destitute of moral honesty and integrity of character? What constitutes a gentleman and a Christian, in this community? I answer, moral honesty and integrity of character. This is all any man possesses that renders him worthy of the esteem of his fellow-men. He who has neither is a mockery of a man—a burlesque of our noble species—a beast in human form!

But who are our common masses? On my right, they are those young men, sons of honest farmers and mechanics, who eat bread by the sweat of their brows! On my left, they are those Methodist mothers and daughters, the wives and children of the farmers and mechanics of this country—the better part of society—who wash their own clothes, sweep their own houses, spin and weave their own garments, and cook their own victuals! You—yes, *you*, young ladies and young gentlemen whom I address—are charged, by this vile slanderer and dirty blackguard, with being destitute of moral honesty and integrity of character; and the Athens Synod, to a man, swore upon their oaths that he told the truth when he made the charge. Yes, this big, two-fisted ditch-digger and grass-cutter, the *Rev. Mr. Palmer*, who sometimes preaches to you in this village, declared by his vote in this Synod, that you, his neighbors, were just this degraded set of poor wretches that Ross has charged!

Again: on page 135 of the same number, he says:

> It hardens the conscience to moral obligations. It prostrates body and soul under the feet of an irresponsible ministry. It injures the piety of the good man. It encourages hypocrisy. It must, if fully developed, *demoralize society*.

Once more he says, in his article styled "Iron Wheel:"

It is astounding that any set of men, after the American Revolution, should have dared to fabricate, and set in motion, this great Iron Wheel of the Itinerancy! Just look at it, and you see it is a perfect system of passive obedience and non-resistance.

The thing is a naked despotism—imperial power, in an ecclesiastical aristocracy, unblushingly avowed and gloried in.

The system is dangerous to our liberties, civil and religious. It ought to be understood and done away, by public opinion, enlightened by the spirit of the Bible; and the movement to do it away cannot be too soon.

The Methodist system is death to all the institutions for which Washington fought and freemen died!

Besides these, in the Magazine for April, 1847, he introduces certain *Latin Questions* and *Answers*, liable to be asked of "*married women and single girls*," in our band and class-meetings, which he asserts they "*aré bound to answer*," and which bring these females "*under priestly control*"—charging, in substance and in fact, that Methodist females who frequent these meetings are STRUMPETS, and that our ministers are a set of FORNICATORS! We will not interpret or add the *Latin* in question, because of its REVOLTING OBSCENITY.

During the sitting of the Supreme Court in Knoxville, in September last, a distinguished lawyer, an elder in Mr. Ross's church, wrote him frankly, that the Methodists regarded him as charging the Methodist females as aforesaid, and requested him to *disavow* such charges or intention, in his next Magazine. To this he replied with great warmth, on page 332 of the October number:

Is it all pure and proper to tell in Latin what Rome does? But is it all filthy, if we tell in the same Latin what Methodism would do "if the class confessional was enforced as Mr. Wesley planned it, and as it is in the discipline?" Obscenity! Why, every thinking man knows that this cry of modesty is hypocritical cant, to hide the class and band. Obscenity! WE HAVE NOTHING TO RECALL. Rather the more earnestly we desire that Methodist mothers may read that very page in the Calvinistic Magazine. Respectfully we urge her to read it alone with her husband, and to ask him the English of the Latin. Then let her remember that the priest has a right to ask of ladies these questions. After this, will she compare the Latin questions to be put by the priests, with the questions required to be asked in the band at every meeting? Then may she pray God to shield her and her daughters from the horrid consummation of the class confessional, "if enforced as Mr. Wesley planned it, and as it is in the discipline."

Thus, it will be seen he takes nothing back. Rather, he says, let the Methodist mother "pray God to shield her and her daughter from the *horrid consummation* of the class confessional!" *Consummation* Webster defines thus: "the most *intimate union of the sexes!*"

Now, in reference to this Magazine, and all its slanders, the Athens Synod, on the 12th of October, 1846, WITHOUT A DISSENTING VOICE, as Mr. Ross boasts, adopted the following resolution, and published it in the Magazine for November of that year:

Resolved, That synod recommend the Calvinistic Magazine, published under the editorial care of Rev. Isaac Anderson, D. D., F. A. Ross, James King, and James McChain,* AS A MOST EXCELLENT PERIODICAL!!!

To show this audience that I do not err in saying that all this slander of the "Tract" and "Magazine" is but the language of the Synod—*of the Church*—I herewith read what *Mr. Blackburn,*† a Presbyterian preacher of Maryville, said in the Knoxville Register of the 5th of January, 1848. This reverend gentleman, reflecting the sentiments of Dr. Anderson, the senior editor of the Magazine, and of the Synod of which he is a member, or liable to be in turn, says:

Mr. Ross has, in association with three other ministers and coeditors, enunciated our views on Methodist Church government. *The Calvinistic Magazine is our regularly constituted organ; and until its teachings are disavowed, is properly taken as our true exponent.* We subscribe to "The Great Iron Wheel" our cordial assent. We are to be held accountable *as a Church,* because the Magazine was called into existence,

* It is proper to say, that while the other gentlemen were associate editors, Mr. Ross wrote all these violent articles.

† Mr. Blackburn is now the editor of the "Presbyterian Witness," at Knoxville, 1856.

and the editors appointed *by solemn vote of our synod.*—To the Cæsar of public judgment shall we go. Many have been the tirades published against the Magazine: *they fall on us.* We have, however, never complained; and, by the grace of God, never shall. We believe there are errors in Arminianism—corruption and tyranny in Methodist Church government; and this belief we will proclaim to the world, though we were assured that the powers of earth, and all the *foreign aid* they could get, were combined against us."

Here is a frank and open confession, in one of the political journals of East Tennessee, by a Presbyterian preacher, that Mr. Ross is the great boa-constrictor of the New School Church, and the *shark* of the Athens Synod, (whose life is a perfect romance of calumny!) who has used the names of the members of the Synod as *saddle-bags,* in which to deposit his slanders! Here is a confession to the effect that the members of the Synod were the *pilot-fishes* to this great *shark;* but neither Mr. Blackburn, nor naturalists, have informed us what portion of the *spoils* the pilot-fish is entitled to!

In addition to what is said in the Magazine, we subjoin a few extracts from a book published by Mr. Ross, entitled, "The Direct Witness," etc. On page 92, he says:

The doctrine of the direct witness of the Spirit, as taught by Mr. Wesley, is mischievous in its tendency. Mischief to the soul of man is upon its very face; and mischief has followed its propagation, and that continually, everywhere!

On page 97, he concludes a chapter in these words:

I appeal, wherever this address may go, whether mischief is not upon the face of Mr. Wesley's doctrine, and mischief has not followed its propagation, AND THAT CONTINUALLY, IN EVERY PLACE: whether it is not *everywhere* the ALCOHOL of pretended religious experience, producing nothing better than fanatical intoxication.

Again, on page 106, Mr. Ross thus denounces the whole Methodist ministry as a pack of lying, slanderous hypocrites, who go about the dirty work of the Devil, and making the naturally depraved hearts of sinners worse than they are wont to be:

Go among the inhabitants of the obscurest dell, or highest peak, or farthest limit of prairie, visited by the Methodist itinerant, and there you find the Presbyterian has been already misrepresented. Whose hands have scattered these arrows? *Methodist preachers.* Whose lips have taught these wild or simple people to hate God's sovereignty, his electing love, and preserving grace, with a hatred beyond that of the natural heart? METHODIST PREACHERS.

On page 108, after denouncing Methodists as "novices, deceivers, hypocrites, fools, and fanatics," Mr. Ross proceeds to inquire—

May I not show Methodism to be Methodism? May I not show its government and discipline to be planted with the germs of Romanism? May I not show that Methodism, having these degrading elements, is utterly feeble to exert high moral power on man?

In reference to the "Tract" containing all this slander, and even more and worse, this same Synod, with a recklessness and malice not even excelled by the *"New York Empire Club,"* adopted the following resolution "WITH ABSOLUTE UNANIMITY"—that is to say, WITHOUT ONE DISSENTING VOICE!

Resolved, That in the estimation of synod, a Tract lately published by F. A. Ross, entitled, "The Doctrine of the Direct Witness of the Spirit, as taught by Rev. John Wesley, shown to be *false, unscriptural, fanatical, and of mischievous tendency,"* IS AN ABLE PRODUCTION, setting forth that important subject in its true scriptural light, and is earnestly recommended to the perusal of all the members of our Church.

To all this we add the following from Mr. Ross's Glade Spring discourse:

No. 2.—It is a degradation to any one to join the Methodist Church, unless he set his face as a flint to reform it.

In conclusion, these are *some* of the slanders the Methodists complain of. And when gentlemen speak of *abuse* heaped upon Mr. Ross, let them consider WHAT it is we are replying to—not merely this *degraded and slanderous blackguard—this illegitimate son of an old negro wench—this adulterous descendant of an old Scotch Tory*—but all the RULING ELDERS AND MINISTERS OF THE LATE SYNOD OF TENNESSEE!

And what Mr. Blackburn has here said of the coöperation of the Synod with Mr. Ross, in this great work of detraction, I can with safety say of *nine-tenths* of their membership in East Tennessee. It is a mistaken notion into which many of the Methodists have fallen, that Mr. Ross's course is not approved by his members. A FEW individuals desire him to cease his abuse of the Methodists, and *half* of these few desire peace because they dread the final result of the controversy. The great mass of the New School party, steeped to the nose and chin in devotion to the writings of Ross, drink down what he says, with most disgusting complacency. Hence, any pretension of friendship and esteem is but adding insult to injury. They pretend to invite Methodist preachers to their pulpits, to their sacramental boards, and to their houses, while they are hurling all this scorn at them through their highest ecclesiastical courts, and in this dogmatic spirit! The controversy with them, is held, not for *truth*, but for *victory*. These are the Scylla and Charybdis with the Rossites; while they are making the Church a mere thoroughfare to Rome or Geneva!

There are many kind-hearted Methodists in the country who are opposed to all this angry controversy, and who oppose it from correct motives. Their kindness feeds on *reflection* rather than *impulse:* they know that Christians cannot add to their graces by this busy, bustling spirit of controversy—this struggle to be seen and heard. They recollect that Elijah found not the Lord in the *tempest*, but in the quiet and calm —"*Be still, and know that I am God.*" Many hypocritical Rossites take advantage of this goodness of heart, and condemn, in no measured terms, the controversy, when in the company of such persons. Nay, more—they speak feelingly of *union*, and profess great friendship for their Methodist brethren. Beware of all such! Like the fabled bat of Madagascar, they will suck all the blood out of your veins, while they fan you to sleep with their wide-spreading wings of union!

But *who* is it that makes this powerful appeal to the Revolutionary sires, in this country, to rise up in their might and put down the monster Methodism, before it destroys our civil and religious liberties? Is it the son of George Washington, who served his country so faithfully? No. Is it the son of Andrew Jackson, who led our armies to victory upon the plains of New Orleans? No. Is it the son of Zach. Taylor, or Winfield Scott, who, at the head of the American army, recently triumphed on so many fields in Mexico? No: these distinguished generals had no sons; or if they had, they have expressed no such fears of the ruinous tendency of Methodism. Who is it, then? Echo answers, WHO? I reply, it is the adulterous, slanderous, unprincipled, and degraded son of an old Virginia *negro wench*—the illegitimate son of an old *Scotch Tory* of the war of the Revolution, who did all that lay in his power to destroy those liberties "for which Washington fought and freemen died." In other words, it is *Frederick Augustus Ross*—the last man living that ought to open his mouth about opposition to civil and religious liberties, or even hint at the war of the Revolution!

I will read you an extract or two from the "JOURNAL OF THE CONVENTION OF VIRGINIA, for June, 1776," a venerable old document, giving the proceedings of a patriotic band of men one month prior to the Declaration of American Independence. On page 66, June 27, we find the following intelligence:—

Mr. Cary, from the committee appointed, presented to the Convention, according to order, an ordinance to enable the present magistrates and officers to continue the administration of justice, and for settling the general mode of proceedings in *criminal* and other cases till the same can be more amply provided for; which was read the first time, and ordered to be read a second time.

Resolved, That this Convention will to-morrow again resolve itself into the said committee.

Among the *criminals* arraigned at the bar of the Convention, under arrest for "*giving aid and comfort to the enemy,*" was *DAVID ROSS,* the father of the ostensible editor of the Calvinistic Magazine, a Scotchman by birth, a foreigner in feeling, and a *Tory* in practice. On page 78 of the Journal, under date of "Friday, June 28, 1776," this authentic old document proceeds:—

Mr. Archibald Cary, from the Committee of Privileges and Elections, reported that the committee had, according to order, had under their consideration the information respecting *David Ross,* and had come to the following resolution thereupon, which he read in his place, and afterwards delivered in at the clerk's table, where the same was again read and agreed to:

Resolved, That the information against the said David Ross be heard before this committee on the second Monday after the meeting of the next Convention or Assembly; and that the said Ross be discharged out of custody, *on giving bond and security in the sum of* £5,000 to appear at the next meeting of Convention or Assembly, to answer the said information on the day fixed for hearing the same; *and that he doth not in the meantime give intelligence to or in any manner aid or assist the enemy.*

Upon the laying over of Ross's case to a future day, his *accomplices in Toryism* petitioned the Assembly to let them leave the country for England; whereupon the following resolution was adopted, and is found on page 77 of said Journal:

Resolved, That the said petition is reasonable, and that the petitioners have leave to depart this country *after taking an oath not to bear arms against America, nor give intelligence to the enemy* during the present war.

The most important item in the history of this old Tory will be found on page 35 of said Journal, dated June 6, 1776, where the Convention had DAVID ROSS before them as a prisoner, on a charge of having delivered a *Colonel's commission* to a certain person to bring the *Indians against this country to coöperate with the British*, and they were in motion accordingly; and for that he was publicly tried, and of the crime convicted, and came within one of being put to death!

Surely F. A. Ross is the last man in Tennessee who ought to speak of "illustrious predecessors," or the "*liberties for which Washington fought and freemen died!*" His old father was a most recreant Tory, the partner of old *Hook*, furnishing the British army with the very *beef* and *meal* they were employed to furnish the American army, and then, in turn, informing the British officers of the movements of the American army!

Did ever John Wesley, Francis Asbury, or any other Methodist preacher, go this length against the war of the Revolution? *No*, NO, NO! But the *Rev. Mr. Bile*, of Boston, a distinguished Presbyterian preacher, a native of New Jersey, did openly take sides with the British in that memorable struggle, and was dismissed from his congregation, and fled to England to save his neck from the halter!

Since Ross and his Synod have arraigned the Methodists upon their opposition to "civil and religious liberties," I wish to show what ground they occupy themselves. THOMAS JEFFERSON, the father of American democracy, understood the genius of Presbyterianism, not in its theological deformity, but as a *statesman*, in its bearing upon the "liberties for which Washington fought and freemen died." In volume fourth, page 358, of his works, Mr. Jefferson says:—

The atmosphere of our country is unquestionably charged with a threatening cloud of fanaticism, lighter in some parts, denser in others, but too heavy in all. I had no idea, however, that in Pennsylvania, the cradle of toleration and freedom of religion, it could have risen to the height you describe. This must be owing to the growth of Presbyterianism. Here, Episcopalian and Presbyterian, Methodist and Baptist, join together in hymning their Maker, listen with attention and devotion to each other's preachers, and all mix in society with perfect harmony. It is not so in the districts where Presbyterianism prevails undividedly. Their ambition and tyranny would tolerate no rival, if they had power. Systematical at grasping at an ascendency over *all* other sects, they aim at engrossing the education of the country; are hostile to every institution they do not direct; are jealous at seeing others begin to attend at all to that object.

On the same subject, he says, in his letter to William Short, page 322:—

The Presbyterian clergy are the loudest, the most intolerant of all sects—the most tyrannical and ambitious: ready at the word of the lawgiver, if such a word could now be obtained, to put the torch to the pile, and to rekindle in this virgin hemisphere the flames in which their oracle, Calvin, consumed the poor Servetus, because he could not subscribe the proposition of Calvin, that magistrates have a right to exterminate all heretics to the Calvinistic creed. They pant to re-establish by law that holy inquisition which they can now only infuse into public opinion.

And to show that Mr. Jefferson wrote even *prophecy*, listen to DR. ELY, the great expounder of American Presbyterianism, in a Fourth of July sermon delivered in Philadelphia in 1827:—

We have assembled, fellow-citizens, on the anniversary of our nation's birthday, in a RATIONAL AND RELIGIOUS manner, to celebrate our independence of all foreign dominion, and the goodness of God in making us a free people. On what subject can I, on the present occasion, insist with more propriety than on the duty of all the rulers and citizens of these United States, in the exercise and enjoyment of all their political rights, to honor the Lord Jesus Christ? Let it, then, be distinctly stated and fearlessly maintained, *in the first place*, that EVERY MEMBER OF THIS CHRISTIAN NATION, FROM THE HIGHEST TO THE LOWEST, ought to serve the Lord with fear, and yield his sincere homage to the Son of God. Every RULER should be an avowed and sincere friend of Christianity. He should *know* and *believe* the doctrines of *our* holy religion, and *act* in conformity with its precepts.

This he ought to do; because as a *man* he is required to serve the Lord, and as a PUBLIC RULER he is called upon by Divine authority to "kiss the Son." The commandment contained in Proverbs iii. 6, "*in all thy ways acknowledge him,*" including *public* as well as private ways, and POLITICAL no less than domestic ways!

Let all, then, admit that our civil rulers ought to act a religious part in all the relations they sustain.

If a ruler is not a Christian, he ought to be one, in this land of evangelical light, without delay, and he ought, being a follower of Jesus, to honor him even as he honors the Father. In this land of religious freedom, what should hinder a civil magistrate from believing the gospel and professing faith in Christ any more than any other man? If the chief magistrate of a nation may be an irreligious man with impunity, who may not?

Our rulers, like any other members of the community who are under law to God as rational beings, and under law to Christ, since they have the light of Divine revelation, ought to search the Scriptures, assent to the truth, profess faith in Christ, keep the Sabbath holy to God, pray in private and in the domestic circle, attend on the public ministry of the word, be baptized, and celebrate the Lord's supper. None of our rulers have the consent of their Maker that they should be Pagans, Socinians, Mussulmen, Deists, the opponents of Christianity; and a religious people should never think of giving them permission as public officers to be and do what they might not lawfully be and do as private individuals.

☞ In other words, our presidents, secretaries of the government, senators, and other representatives in Congress, governors of States, judges, State legislators, justices of the peace, and city magistrates, are just as much bound as any other persons in the United States to be *orthodox in their faith*, and virtuous and religious in their whole deportment. ☜

Since it is the duty of all our rulers to serve the Lord and kiss the Son of God, it must be most manifestly the duty of all Christian fellow-citizens to honor the Lord Jesus Christ, and promote Christianity, by electing and supporting as public officers the friends of our blessed Saviour.

In all thy ways acknowledge him, is a maxim which should dwell in a Christian's mind on the day of a public election as much as on the Sabbath, and which should govern him when conspiring with others to honor Christ, either at the Lord's table or in the election of *chief magistrate.*

If the wise, the prudent, the temperate, the friends of God and of their country, do not endeavor to *control our elections*, they will be controlled by others; and if *one* good man may, without any reasonable excuse, absent himself, then *all* may.

If all the truly religious men of our nation would be punctual and persevering in their endeavors to have good men chosen to fill all our national and State offices of honor, power and trust, *their weight* would soon be felt by politicians, and those who care little for the religion of the Bible would, *for their own interest*, consult the reasonable wishes of the great mass of Christians throughout the land.

I could wish to see every professing Christian in attendance on elections; but rather let him never give a vote than receive a *treat* for his suffrage. ☞ *I propose, fellow-citizens, a* NEW SORT OF UNION, *or, if you please, A CHRISTIAN PARTY IN POLITICS, which I am exceedingly desirous all good men in our country should join.* ☚

All who profess to be Christians of any denomination ought to agree that they will support no man as a candidate for any office who is not professedly friendly to Christianity, and a believer in Divine revelation.

☞ THE PRESBYTERIANS ALONE COULD BRING HALF A MILLION OF ELECTORS INTO FIELD. ☚

Let a man be of good moral character, and let him profess to believe in and advocate the Christian religion, and we can all support him!!! At one time he will be a Baptist, at another an Episcopalian, at another a Methodist, at another a Presbyterian of the American, Scotch, Irish, Dutch, or German stamp, and always a friend to our common Christianity.

I am free to avow that, other things being equal, I would prefer for my chief magistrate, and judge, and ruler, A SOUND PRESBYTERIAN; and every candid religionist will make the same declaration concerning his own persuasion.

WITCHES AND WIZARDS—GHOSTS AND GHOST-SEERS!

LADIES AND GENTLEMEN:—I will conclude this address, already extended beyond what I could desire, by giving you a touch upon *witchcraft!* Mr. Ross and his Synod attribute to Mr. Wesley and the Methodists the honor of having led off in the belief of *witchcraft* and *sorcery*, and they charge that this doctrine of the *Direct Witness* led them into this delusion! If I can get your attention for thirty-five or forty minutes, I will convince you that the *Presbyterians* are the last people on this continent who should object to any one believing in the reality of *witchcraft*, or even practicing *sorcery!*

But as I wish to *assert* nothing but what I have *proof* for, I will read you the following short extract from Mr. Ross's "Tract," page 73:—

The doctrine of the Direct Witness is FANATICAL, because, according to it, *we may claim that there is now* CONNECTION WITH THE DEVIL IN *WITCHCRAFT;* AND THIS MR. WESLEY BELIEVED.

Now, I could multiply extracts of this kind to an indefinite extent from the recent writings of this *Rev. Slanderer*, en dorsed by the slanderous Synod at Athens, but I forbear.

By *witchcraft* is generally understood a supernatural power, of which persons are supposed to obtain the possession by entering into a compact with the Devil. They give themselves up to Satan, body and soul, and he engages that they shall want for nothing, and that he will avenge them upon all their enemies. As soon as this bargain is concluded, the Devil delivers to the witch an *imp*, or familiar spirit, which, like the imp of Sin, in Milton, "yelps all around," ready at a call to do whatever is directed! By the assistance of this *imp* and of the *Devil* together, the witch, who is almost always an old woman, (ladies, keep a look-out!) is enabled to transport herself through the air on a broomstick to distant places, to attend the regular meetings of the witches!*

To show that I am correct in my definition of this art, I read the following extract from Buck's Theological Dictionary, a Calvinistic work:—

> WITCHCRAFT, a supernatural power which persons were formerly supposed to obtain the possession of by entering into a compact with the Devil. Witchcraft was universally believed in Europe till the sixteenth century, and even maintained its ground with tolerable firmness till the middle of the seventeenth. The latest witchcraft frenzy was in New England in 1692, when the execution of witches became a calamity more dreadful than the sword or the pestilence. Some have denied the existence of witchcraft altogether. That such persons have been found among men seems, however, evident from the Scriptures.

---

* At this moment, the eyes of the audience were turned up to the inner comb of the roof of the shed. I looked up, and discovered a huge *scorpion* creeping from board to board, and told them it was a *Rossite*, and that as they were most imbittered against our *women*, the Methodist females in the assembly had better keep an eye on the impostor! Instantly the reptile let all holds go, and landed in the lap of a young lady, but it was not long until, among hands, they had it under foot! Ross himself is fast getting beneath the feet of an indignant and insulted community!

According to this definition of witchcraft, there never were but TWO regular-built WIZARDS in all this country—the one is *F. A. Ross*, and the other *James Gallagher*, both Presbyterian clergymen. These men published to the world, in the Calvinistic Magazine, (old series,) which I hold in my hand, that they entered into a compact with devils, great and small —little devils and big devils, horned devils and *muly* devils —in a cave in Bay's Mountain, in East Tennessee, in September, 1829. There they held their first synod, and adopted their first resolutions against Methodism — resolving that Bishop Asbury was a tory, and hid himself in a garret-loft in New York during the war of the Revolution! There they learned, in person, from devils, (good authority!) that Methodist preachers are tyrants in religion, and tyrants in politics! And there, too, they learned that "Methodism is death to all the liberties for which Washington fought and freemen died!" Here it is, in the Book of the Chronicles of Hell, in which are registered the memorable exploits of these *rev. subalterns* of his *Satanic Majesty*, one of whom "pealed the banner-cry of hell" in this village, not long since, and was cheered with reiterated shouts of applause and enthusiastic admiration! The other *son of Belial*, Gallagher, is now lying, swindling, and preaching in the West, having left this country with several thousand dollars, which he lied and begged the public out of, as some of you know, by going with his knees and elbows out, and living on cold potatoes and buttermilk when strangers visited him! When his *Tartarian Highness* adjourned this synod in the cave, it was to meet again in Athens, on "Mars' Hill!"

The REV. JOHN BROWN, a Presbyterian divine, already quoted, says, in his Dictionary of the Bible, under the head "Witchcraft"—a work, by the way, to be found in almost every Presbyterian family in the country:

WITCH is a woman, and WIZARD is a man, that has dealings with Satan, if not actually entered into compact with him. That such persons are among men, is abundantly plain from Scripture, and that they *ought to be put to death.*—Great caution is necessary in the detection of the guilty, and in punishing them, lest the innocent suffer, as many instances in New England and other places show.

To attempt a serious refutation of the doctrines of witchcraft is no part of my business. That there ever were witches, that is, persons endowed with such powers as are usually ascribed to them, is what I do not believe for one moment. The whole matter is absurd and impossible. To suppose an ignorant old woman (or indeed any human being) capable of transforming herself into a *cat,* or an *old field hare,* is to suppose her capable of counteracting the laws of nature, which is competent to none but God alone. Yet, absurd as the doctrine of witchcraft is, it is a notorious fact that the *Presbyterian Church,* both in our own country and other lands, is still annoyed with it, and is likely to be for a century to come.

I hold in my hand a "History of the Salem Witchcraft," compiled by a Presbyterian, as the writer says, "from the best authorities"—in which it is declared that "so many are the cases of persons convicted of witchcraft in New England, in the years sixteen hundred and ninety-one and two, that it would require a larger volume than this to record them all;" and this contains, as you may see, 365 pages!

Hear the following extract, found on page 15:

Mr. Parris had an Indian servant in his house. This man, with his wife, set about discovering the authors of these evils. With this intent, they made *a rye-cake,* which they compounded with the *urine* of the persons afflicted, and gave it to a dog to eat. By this proceeding they hoped to clear the eyes of the bewitched of the gross films of mortality, and enable them to see their invisible tormentors. The incantation took effect, and the first person accused by the sufferers was the Indian woman herself. She was committed to prison immediately, and persecuted with blows and otherwise, in order to extort confession, and to compel her to criminate other witches, her supposed accomplices. Under this discipline it is not wonderful that the poor squaw acknowledged an intercourse with the Devil; after which she was publicly sold for her prison fees.

This Mr. Parris was a resident Presbyterian clergyman of Salem, in whose family these witchcrafts seem to have originated. And this "rye-cake" was a regularly built Presbyterian *johnny-cake!*

Here, on page 21, is a plate representing poor Proctor pulling hemp without a foothold, and the Rev. Mr. Noyes, a Presbyterian clergyman, refusing to pray for him, though requested, because Proctor would not own himself a wizard, and then go out of the world with a lie in his mouth!

Here is, also, another work, entitled "Wonders of the Invisible World," written by ROBERT CALEF, a Presbyterian merchant of Boston, and printed in 1828—just at the time this man Ross began to figure in the ministry! This is a work of 333 pages. On page 4 it is said, in reference to these New England witchcrafts:

Were it, as we are told in *Wonders of the Invisible World,* "that devils were walking about our streets with lengthened chains, making a dreadful noise in our ears, and brimstone (even without a metaphor) was making a horrid and a hellish stench in our nostrils;" and "that the Devil, exhibiting himself ordinarily as a *black man,* had decoyed a fearful knot of proud, froward, ignorant, envious, and malicious creatures to enlist themselves in his horrid service, by entering their names in a book tendered unto them, and that they have had their *meetings and sacraments, and associated themselves to destroy the kingdom of our Lord Jesus Christ,* in these parts of the world."

What a remarkable *coincidence* is here brought to light! When the Devil came into New England, near two centuries ago, to try and destroy the kingdom of our Lord Jesus Christ, he came in the person of a "*black man.*" When he revived the work in Tennessee and Virginia, in 1846, he came in the person of a "*nigger*" again.

I now hold in my hands the second of two sermons delivered in Cincinnati in March, 1846, in the First Presbyterian

Church, by JOSEPH L. WILSON, D.D., the head and front of the Old School party in the United States, up to the day of his recent death. This is the second sermon, and Dr. Wilson says, in the opening paragraph:

> Having before proved the *reality of witchcraft*, and given examples of its *practical effects-as an art*, among pagans, infidels, and several sorts of nominal Christians, I shall now attempt to show more fully the operation of this art in the fulfilment of the prophecy expressed in our text.

And as a part of this Presbyterian game of *sorcery*, *necromancy*, *etc.*, I will introduce the case of DOCTOR ASHBEL GREEN, a distinguished Presbyterian clergyman who recently departed this life in Philadelphia, and, I hope, has gone to heaven, notwithstanding his familiarity with *evil spirits* in this life! Dr. Green was once the editor of the organ of his Church, in Philadelphia; at another time he was the President of the Princeton Theological Seminary; and he has been the Moderator of the General Assembly. He reflected upon the subject of *necromancy* and *sorcery* until he finally concluded that he was a veritable *teapot*, and so declared himself from the pulpit. He would place one hand on his hip, so as to form the *handle*—the other arm he would elevate to an angle of 45 degrees, and declare it to be the *spout*. The opposite leg from the spout he would give a *tilt*, and make an effort to pour out the tea!

But let us come still nearer home. Who are the editors of the Calvinistic Magazine? Here are the names—ISAAC ANDERSON, FRED. A. ROSS, JAMES KING, and JAMES M'CHAIN. Listen to me while I take them up, one by one, and show how they stand related to witchcraft, sorcery, necromancy, and other "*peculiarities*" of Presbyterianism!

And, first, as to Doctor Anderson: he is known to be the master-*conjuror* in East Tennessee, excepting always old Geo

Wright, of Mossy Creek. I hold in my hands two of the Doctor's letters to old George, in his own handwriting, in which he presses him to visit Maryville, and take with him his favorite *divining-rod*—a peach-tree rod—and assist him in finding some stolen money, taken from the house of a Mr. Thompson, of that place, whilst at church on Sabbath! He urges old George, because he says he is known to be "*a master-hand in the art,*" and because it is a part of their creed of *sorceries*, that if the money be removed from where it was first deposited after it was stolen, it would be impossible to find it! These letters bear date May 26th, 1847, and June 7th, 1847. They have both been published in my "Review," and their genuineness not denied. Here they are —any gentleman is welcome to inspect them! In addition to these letters, the Doctor wrote to Anderson Mathes, a Presbyterian clergyman who died in Rogersville, of consumption, and sent to heaven, by the dying man, a whole batch of *local news* relative to *Blount county*—as if the inhabitants of heaven cared more about Blount than any other county in the Lord's moral vineyard! And yet Ross and his party talk about Wesley's not doubting Swedenborg's claim to visions, and intercourse with departed spirits!

This same Dr. Anderson undertook to find a stolen horse at a Presbyterian camp-meeting, a few years ago, by divining with his peach-tree rod, asking the rod the direction which the thief went, and whether he was black or white—the rod meantime giving *affirmative* or *negative* answers! About the same time he visited the house of an *old sorcerer* in Knox county, and took with him the *plot* of some land he owned in the Chilhowee mountains, to get the *rod-diviner* to tell him *where* he might dig on that land for gold or silver—the land being at least thirty miles distant! And when I was in Maryville last winter, the old Doctor had commenced trying to *mesmerize!* How far he has progressed in that art, I am not able to say. These are the facts; and I *dare* a denial of them, in a public way, by a responsible man.

The next editor in order is *F. A. Ross.* But do you intend to charge that he is a *sorcerer?* exclaim you. Yes, I do—or that he believes in witchcraft and necromancy. He has long been a *mesmerizer;* and *Louisa Dickinson* and *Eliza Neal,* not to say *Polly Guthery,* of Scott county, in this State, could tell of his *faith* and *works* upon this subject. But last Wednesday, I believe it was, *Miss Coghill,* a beautiful Presbyterian girl of Kingsport, and a *pious* member of Ross's congregation, had an heir, which was murdered, and attempted to be buried in one corner of a smoke-house. When I left Tennessee, a coroner's jury was sitting on the case. All I have to say about it now is, that this young lady visited Ross's house a great deal, and rode in his carriage. I will add, however—and let Mr. Ross deny the fact if he dare—that NINE MONTHS before this child was born, Miss Coghill lay at Ross's home, pretending to be sick!!!

But the Presbyterians of Jonesborough had a fair or a supper, or whatever you please to call it, the proceeds of which were to be applied to improvements then contemplated on their house of worship. The supper was *one dollar* per man and lady. I saw Frederick in the procession, marching into the town-hall with a lady swinging to each arm. They all paid their money. Next to the supper, the arrival of a mail was announced, and letters were handed out, and postage demanded. Then came a *fortune-teller,* in the person of a *dead doll*—a large eastern doll of wax—placed upon a stand, telling gentlemen and ladies *fortunes* for FIFTY CENTS, cash in hand. I was told that Frederick planked up an eagle half dollar, and had his fortune told by a *dead doll,* holding his ear down to receive the news! I have tried hard to learn what this little glass-eyed sister told him, but he refuses to tell. I believe she whispered these words in his ear: "*Fred-*

erick Augustus! in 1847 *and '48, Brownlow is to get after you with a sharp stick, and such another time you never had in this life!"*

But is JAMES KING a sorcerer, or does he work with a *diviner's rod?* He does! I know Mr. King, and know him to be a clever man personally. The meanest act I ever knew him guilty of, was to be associated with an unprincipled *free negro* in the editorial management of the dirty Magazine I hold in my hand!

Mr. King once found a *silver mine,* near where he lives, by working a peach-tree rod; and sold an interest in it to a Mr. Preston, of Abingdon, and another to Colonel White, of the same place; and although his *silver* turned out to be *iron,* he demanded his pay, and, as I am informed, received about TWO THOUSAND DOLLARS for his discoveries made with a *diviner's rod!* This is more than all the Methodists on earth ever made by *sorcery!* Now, are they not a pretty pack to talk about Mr. Wesley believing in witchcraft?

To conclude, what shall I say of JAMES MCCHAIN? I confess to you frankly, that I know nothing about the man, only that he is a WEAK BROTHER, having scarcely sense enough to practice the enchanted frauds of the marvellous believers in witchcraft. That he too, is a believer, I have no doubt, or he could not be a sound Presbyterian. I don't suppose he serves as an editor, but is thrown in to make up the number; and is required to *sneeze* every time Mr. Ross takes *snuff!*

I have now concluded my Address; and although my voice has held up, as it usually does, yet I am greatly exhausted, as you perceive. The heat has been oppressive; and the labor of speaking in the open air so long and so loud, very severe. But the cause is a good one, worthy suffering in; and I make no complaint. I thank you, ladies and gentlemen, one and all, for the patient and attentive hearing you have given me on this occasion.

☞ At the close of this Address, the following resolutions were offered for adoption by J. W. Schoolfield; and being seconded, Rev. G. K. Snapp took the vote of the audience:

Resolved, That the thanks of the Methodists, and the friends of Methodism, now assembled at this camp-ground, be and they are hereby tendered to Rev. W. G. Brownlow, for his able defence of our much-loved doctrines, and of the venerated memory of our sainted founder, and of our yet more cherished and highly-prized characters, against the vile and ribald aspersions of Frederick A. Ross, and his endorsers—the members of the East Tennessee Synod—who have willingly become the tools or partners in the slanders of their more sable, yet still more able and accomplished leader, in sophistry, falsehood, and detraction.

Resolved, That the editors of the Methodist Episcopalian, the Jonesborough Whig, and Jonesborough Review, be requested to give the foregoing resolution an insertion in their respective publications.

Staley's Creek C. G., Smythe co., Va., July 9th, 1848.

REPLY.

I thank the gentlemen who have moved and seconded the adoption of the resolution just read, and for the compliment paid me therein—all of which has been without agency of mine, or previous knowledge of such an intention. But I thank this large assemblage of ladies and gentlemen still more sincerely, for the unanimity and alacrity with which they have adopted them. Their adoption has been like that of the endorsement of what I have this day made war upon, by the Athens Synod—it has been "*with absolute unanimity!*" I will not disguise the fact, although I am not a very vain man, that this compliment is acceptable to me; and the more gratifying, coming, as it does, from so many ladies and gentlemen of the first respectability in our county.

I beg, however, to state to the members and friends of the Methodist Church present, that they are under no sort of obligations to me for any services they may have supposed me to render the Church, here or elsewhere. I have done nothing more than my *duty*—nothing more than I am prepared to do at all times, in all places, and at all hazards, under like circumstances of offence, and against any combination of wicked men and devils! What I have said and done, it is the duty of every Methodist preacher to do—a duty they owe to the ashes of the venerable dead—a Wesley, an Asbury, and a host of others—whose souls are at peace with God, while their reputations are assailed by these hell-hounds of sectarian malice! Were I to sit quietly by my fireside, at home, or look tamely on at all this abuse of my female relatives and acquaintances, I should be ashamed to look one of them in the face when I might chance to meet with them!

The speech you have just responded to, is substantially the same which I have been delivering for the last two years, to so many thousand persons, in Tennessee and Virginia. And I remark, with gratitude to God, that during all that time I have been but once interrupted by rain, (at Greenville, Tenn.,) and never have had so much as a bad cold to prevent my speaking.

You have alluded, classically enough, to the "*sable leader*" of the Athens Synod, in this work of falsehood and detraction. The fact of the *copper color*, the *woolly head*, and other similar appendages of the *negro*, which cling to this *Rev. Malungeon*, notwithstanding his *Caucasian* features, in the general, should be kept prominently before the proud, spirited, and high-minded Virginian. Let the distinction of *color* be kept up, and let our identity as a race of white men be preserved. Let the Presbyterians of Marion trample upon marriage relations, despise the distinction between white and colored people, and bid defiance to the powers of enlightened society, if they choose; but let us, my friends, have more self-respect than to imitate their example.

Peace is desirable; and if our Presbyterian friends want it, let them choke off, and choke down, this "sable leader" of theirs, and cease to uphold him in his outrageous course

Then, and not till then, can they have peace, unless they *conquer* a peace, which they can never do! You will hear much said about my *abuse* on this occasion. I have been severe, and I *intended* to be severe; because I have been replying to publications which teem with the most vulgar and abusive language, and with the vilest and meanest insinuations against our entire ministry and membership. I have been replying to a slanderer, who delights in fishing up from the *sewers* of all the corrupt writers against Methodism, every vile slander and false insinuation that they have set afloat. This is the natural aliment on which Ross lives. His language is that of a peculiar dialect, used by the bar-room bully and street loafer. He is the embodied personification of all my conceptions of a villain. He is the *living* picture of moral death—a travelling monument of the wrath of an offended God, and a fearful witness to the truth of the words of inspiration, which assert that the heart of man is *desperately wicked!* Yes! his heart, like his complexion, is bronzed and burnt to blackness by crime; and can now be seen in his wild and fierce black eye, glowing with a fire approaching to ferocity! His voice, everywhere raised to a pitch of deadly passion, is constantly heard, like the hoarse croaking of some bird of ill-omen!

CHAPTER VII.

State of human society calls for controversy—The Methodist creed not Calvinistic, as falsely alleged by Graves—Methodist Articles of Religion—What Calvinism is, and with whom it originated—American Baptists are generally Calvinistic—Testimony of Elder Howell—The Philadelphia Baptist Confession of Faith—Thomas Jefferson and the Five Points of Calvinism—Testimony of Buck and Watson to the effect that Baptists are Calvinists—Further proof from the "Baptist Watchman"—Ranting about Baptism—Abusive spirit of Calvinism—A sound system of theology offered to the Baptists!

WERE the state of human society such as to unite all hearts in one common bond of love—that Divine love which creates an entire union of sentiment, affection, and design—religious disputes would be at an end, and those halcyon days so long predicted, and so earnestly desired, would be realized; but so long as error and bigotry, sin and its attendant miseries, are in the world, and so long as such violent, ill-tempered men as Graves are put forward as leaders of sects, so long will there be a call for controversy; and moreover, he who conducts it in accordance with truth and righteousness, renders an important service to the Church and to the world.

I am not among those, however, who consider all religious controversy, in the present state of society, detrimental to the cause of Christ. In addition to its eliciting truth by the exposure of error, it has a tendency to exercise the human faculties—to make mankind think deeply and accurately, and to dive *cautiously* and *understandingly* into the great sea of theological truth. No one can read the Sacred Scriptures with care, and fail to perceive that the inspired writers carried on a perpetual warfare against such abettors of error as this man Graves: that they were commissioned especially to denounce all false gods, false doctrines and systems of religion, and bad men, who were going about "teaching the doctrines of devils." Nor was Jesus Christ himself, the adorable author of Christianity, less engaged in controverting the erroneous systems of religion adopted by the Pharisees and Sadducees, and other heretical sects which had sprung up among the Jews; and never were blended together more wisdom and meekness than were exemplified in the sharp controversies which He carried on with such vile adversaries as this man Graves! Moreover, his chosen instrument, St. Paul, the apostle extraordinary to the Gentiles, imbued with the spirit of his Divine Master, carried on a deeply argumentative and strenuous controversy with both Jews and Gentiles. Nor were the immediate successors of the apostles less assiduous in defending the truth against the malevolent attacks of Jewish and Pagan adversaries. Look next at the memorable era of the Reformation! The greater proportion of the writings of Luther and Calvin are not only strictly controversial, but absolutely *severe.* Nor was there a less urgent call for wielding the sword of controversy in the days of John Wesley, than there was in the days of Martin Luther. The temple of error and superstition was rebuilt in England in Wesley's day, and with his controversial arm he demolished it. And now, in America, in the glorious nineteenth century, the doctrine of justification by the atoning blood, the Direct Witness of the Spirit, and holiness of heart and life, are openly and violently assailed by such unregenerate adversaries as Graves, Ross, and others, who are pouring forth floods of calumny against Wesley, and all who dare to lift their warning voices in favor of these great cardinal doctrines of the Bible.

But recalling myself from this digression, which has been

by way of preliminary, I will notice the attack of Mr. Graves upon the *doctrines* of the Methodist Church. The heading of his twenty-sixth chapter, found on page 327, sufficiently indicates its contents. It is in these words: "The peculiar *doctrines* and usages of Methodism—a *Calvinistic* creed, a Popish liturgy, and an *Arminian* clergy!" Not content with this slanderous representation of Methodist *doctrines*, he renews the assault, and multiplies his misrepresentations, in his thirty-ninth chapter, commencing on page 500. To show his points, and convict him of gross falsehoods, it is only necessary, with the intelligent reader, to give the heading of this chapter, which is as follows:

THE "CALVINISM" OF THE CREED AND THE ARMINIANISM OF THE CLERGY.

The "Articles of Religion" Calvinistic—They preclude the idea of the ultimate apostasy of the believer—The ground of Justification examined—The scriptural argument—The Methodist clergy preach against their own creed as well as the teachings of Holy Scripture—Revival and camp-meeting excitements—The doctrine of apostasy made necessary—The tendency of such teaching and doctrine is to make infidels.

Now, it is remarkable that any man should rise up, at this late day, and charge directly upon the Methodist Church that she teaches a *Calvinistic creed;* that her Articles of Religion are Calvinistic; and that the tendency of her doctrines is to make infidels! I say this is strange, because it is known to every intelligent man in the nation, that every Protestant denomination in Europe and America has, to a greater or less extent, made war upon Methodism because Methodism is directly at war with all the distinctive features of Calvinism! All well-informed men know that the *doctrines* of the Wesleyan Methodists are the same as the Church of England, as set forth in her liturgy, articles, and homilies, and that these are all at war with Calvinism proper.

The title-page of every Methodist Discipline in America

runs thus: "The *Doctrines* and Discipline of the Methodist Episcopal Church." And after a very brief account of the *origin* of the Church, the *first* section, covering ten pages, sets forth, in unmistakable terms, her "*Articles of Religion*," numbering twenty-five articles. They are there to be seen and consulted by all who desire to know what her faith is. Not a few of these "Articles" make war, either directly or indirectly, upon some peculiarity of *Calvinism*. And for the information of such as may not be able, for the moment, to lay their hands on this little book of Discipline, I will state the heading of each Article, as laid down in the book:

1. Of Faith in the Holy Trinity.
2. Of the Word, or Son of God, who was made very Man.
3. Of the Resurrection of Christ.
4. Of the Holy Ghost.
5. Of the Sufficiency of the Holy Scriptures for Salvation.
6. Of the Old Testament.
7. Of Original or Birth Sin.
8. Of Free Will.
9. Of the Justification of Man.
10. Of Good Works.
11. Of Works of Supererogation.
12. Of Sin after Justification.
13. Of the Church.
14. Of Purgatory.
15. Of speaking in the Congregation in such a Tongue as the People understand.
16. Of the Sacraments.
17. Of Baptism—(*not acceptable to Baptists, by any means!*)
18. Of the Lord's Supper.
19. Of Both Kinds.
20. Of the one Oblation of Christ, finished upon the Cross.
21. Of the Marriage of Ministers.
22. Of the Rites and Ceremonies of Churches.
23. Of the Rulers of the United States of America.
24. Of Christian Men's Goods.
25. Of a Christian Man's Oath.

Reader, procure this book of Discipline, as published by the General Conference, either North or South; examine these "Articles of Religion," and see if they, or any one of them, in the remotest degree favors, much less *teaches* Calvinism. Examine our standard works, such as Wesley's Sermons, Notes on the New Testament, and other miscellaneous works, Watson's Theological Institutes, Benson's Sermons, Fletcher's Checks, Clarke's Commentary on the Bible, and see if they do not all war upon Calvinism, showing the system up as unscriptural, absurd, and iniquitous!

Methodism a Calvinistic creed! Does Elder Graves know what constitutes a man a *Calvinist?* The name of *Calvinists* was first given to those who embraced the doctrines established at Geneva by JOHN CALVIN, the celebrated reformer of the sixteenth century. More especially, since the meeting of the Synod of Dort, the name has been applied to all who embrace Calvin's leading views of the gospel.

Calvinists belonging to different sects complain much of being misunderstood and misrepresented, and, strange to say, they generally seek to conceal their real sentiments! However, it is not to be wondered at that those who resolve all the wicked motives and conduct of both men and devils into the *efficient* decrees of God, should labor to conceal their sentiments, or hide the deformities of such a system. Now, as *John Calvin* will be allowed by all to be a competent teacher of Calvinism, I shall contend that his exposition of the doctrines which take his name may be consulted as the most satisfactory. Therefore I shall commence with an extract or two from his own Institutes. He teaches Calvinism after the following most approved style:

> Predestination we call the eternal decree of God, by which he hath determined in himself what he would have to become of *every individual of mankind.* For they are not *created* with a similar destiny; but eternal life is ordained for some, and eternal damnation for others.—CALVIN'S INSTITUTES, vol. ii. page 420.
>
> We affirm that this counsel, as far as concerns the *elect,* is founded on his gratuitous mercy, *totally irrespective of human merit;* but that, to those whom he devotes to condemnation, the gate of life is closed by a just and irreprehensible, but incomprehensible, judgment. In the elect, we consider calling as an evidence of election, and justifica-

tion as another token of its manifestation, till they arrive in glory, which constitutes its completion. As God seals the *elect* by vocation and justification, so, by excluding the *reprobate* from the knowledge of his name and the sanctification of his Spirit, he affords an indication of the judgment that awaits them.—Page 425.

When the human mind hears these things, its petulance breaks all restraint, and it discovers as serious and violent agitation as if alarmed by the sound of a martial trumpet. Many, indeed—as if they wished to avert odium from God—admit election in such a way as to deny that any one is reprobated. But this is puerile and absurd; because election itself could not exist without being opposed to reprobation. God is said to separate those whom he adopts to salvation. To say that others obtain by chance, or acquire by their own efforts, that which election alone confers on a few, will be worse than absurd. Whom God passes by, therefore, he reprobates, and from no other cause than his determination to exclude them from the inheritance which he predestines for his children.—Page 442.

Observe: all things being at God's disposal, and the decision of salvation or death belonging to him, he orders all things by his counsel or decree in such a manner, that some men are *born* devoted from the *womb* to certain death, that his name may be glorified in their destruction.—Page 449.

The perplexity and hesitation discovered at trifles by these pious defenders of the justice of God, and their facility in overcoming great difficulties, are truly absurd. I inquire again how it came to pass that the fall of Adam, independent of any remedy, should involve so many nations, with their infant children, in *eternal death*, but because such was the will of God?—Page 450.

Now it will be seen, from the foregoing extracts, that whatever has or shall come to pass in this world, whether it be good or bad, proceeds from the Divine will entirely, and is irrevocably fixed from all eternity: God having *secretly predetermined*, not only the adverse and prosperous fortune of every person in the world, but also his *faith* and *infidelity*, his *obedience* and *disobedience*, and, consequently, his everlasting happiness or misery after death; which fate or predestination it is not possible, by any foresight or wisdom, to avoid! Methodism recognizes no such God as this, believes in none such, and, consequently, teaches no such doctrines.

But Elder Graves wishes to impress the minds of his numerous readers with a belief that the Baptist Church does not favor the doctrine of *Calvinian reprobation*. I had a controversy with the Baptists of East Tennessee in 1841, in which Elders HOWELL and BUCK took part. Mr. Howell used these words in that controversy:

Every man who *knows any thing at all* about our *Church is fully apprised* that the Baptists, *old or young*, never did believe in the doctrine of Calvinian reprobation.

In that controversy I well recollect to have thrown Elder Howell, a Baptist minister of some celebrity, and at that time the "illustrious predecessor" of Mr. Graves at Nashville, into *spasms* of ill-humor, ay, paroxysms of rage, by the authorities I adduced to prove that the Baptist churches in England and America held *occasional* fellowship with Calvinism. The first authority I adduced was Dr. Waller, writing in the same "Baptist Banner" at Louisville, only three weeks before Elder Howell's denial, given above. Dr. Waller is a Baptist minister of celebrity, and one who, I shall show before this work is completed, has been at war with Elder Graves! Dr. Waller employed this language:

The Baptists have only to adhere to *their true sentiments*, as drawn up from the Bible, as set forth in the *Philadelphia Baptist Confession of Faith*, and they will be invulnerable.

Dr. Waller says that the "true sentiments" of the Baptist denomination are "set forth in the Philadelphia Confession of Faith," and that, in order to become "invulnerable" as a denomination, they have only to "adhere" to those sentiments! This Confession of Faith I have examined with much care, and from beginning to ending I find it to be *Calvinistic*. It is an ancient book. It was first adopted in London, by a convention of ministers and messengers, in the year 1689. It was reädopted by the Philadelphia Association in 1742, more than one hundred years ago, and took the name of the Philadelphia Baptist Confession of Faith. So late as 1829–30, new editions of it were issued, and the work reëndorsed. I could give copious extracts from this work, but the following will be as much as the admirers of Mr. Graves's book will care to see:

OF GOD'S DECREE.

By the *decree* of God for the manifestation of his glory, some men and angels are *predestinated* or *foreordained* to eternal life through Jesus Christ, to the praise of his glorious grace; others being left to act in their sin to their condemnation, to the praise of his glorious justice.

These angels and men thus predestinated and foreordained are *particularly and unchangeably designed;* and their *number so certain and definite that it cannot be either increased or diminished.*

As obnoxious in its nature, and ruinous in its tendency, as is this doctrine of the Baptist Confession of Faith, it is the standard of Faith in that Church; and, as a doctrinal system, it has yet to be abandoned by that Church. I have never met with an avowal more decidedly *Calvinistic* than the one just quoted. It is strange, therefore, that Baptists, believing the number of the *elect* is "so certain and definite that it cannot be either increased or diminished," should want to send *missionaries* among the heathen, or elsewhere! What good can missionaries do, if this doctrine be correct? They cannot *increase* the number of the ELECT, nor can they *diminish* the number of the REPROBATES! Of what service can even the labors of ministers be, either in preaching, *baptizing*, or administering the Lord's Supper, if the destinies of all men are already unchangeably fixed in heaven or hell?

See what MR. JEFFERSON says about this Baptist doctrine! In a letter to the elder Adams, dated April 11th, 1823, he writes as follows:

The wish expressed in your last favor, that I may continue in life and health until I become a Calvinist, at least in his exclamation of "*Mon Dieu! jusqu'à quand!*" [My God! how long! is the French signification] would make me immortal. I can never join Calvin in addressing *his god.* He was indeed an atheist, which I can never be; or, rather, his religion was *dæmonism.* If ever man worshipped a false god, he did. The being described in his five points is not the God whom you and I acknowledge and adore, the Creator and benevolent governor of the world, but a dæmon of malignant spirit. It would be more pardonable to believe in no God at all, than to blaspheme him by the atrocious attributes of Calvin.

Some of my readers may not know what MR. JEFFERSON means by the "Five Points of Calvinism." I will state them; but before doing so, I will premise that they are all five taught in the Baptist Confession of Faith, already quoted from. The following are the five points:

1. Unconditional election and reprobation.
2. Christ died only for a part, viz., the elect.
3. Total depravity of man.
4. Irresistible grace to bring in the elect.
5. The impossibility of falling from grace.

Lest, however, Mr. Graves and his belligerent associates may assert that I *misrepresent* them, I will bring forth further authority to prove this Church *Calvinistic*. I submit the following extract from Buck's Theological Dictionary; and Buck, like Jefferson, was any thing rather than a Methodist:

The Baptists subsist under two denominations, viz., the *Calvinistical* and the Arminian. The Baptists in America, and East and West Indies, are *chiefly* CALVINISTS, and hold occasional fellowship with the Particular Baptist churches in England.

My next authority is *Watson's Theological Dictionary*, an author quoted by Mr. Graves in his crusade against Methodism. It is a settled principle in the legal practice of the country, that a client cannot avoid the force of the testimony of *his own witness*. Mr. Watson says:

The Baptists in England form one of the three denominations of Protestant dissenters. The Baptists subsist chiefly under two denominations—the Particular, or Calvinistical, and the General, or Arminian. The former is by far the most numerous. The Baptists in *America*, and in the East and West Indies, are *chiefly* CALVINISTS.

My *closing* authority is of more modern date: it is from

the "BAPTIST WATCHMAN," of Knoxville, Tennessee, for December, 1855, edited by the Rev. MR. HILLSMAN, a Baptist minister of more celebrity than any one in East Tennessee. He publishes in the "Watchman," with approbation, the communications of a *Calvinistic Baptist writer,* who laments over the apostasy of many of his Baptist brethren in the ministry, in departing from the good old doctrine of *election,* as taught by the Philadelphia Confession of Faith. This writer says:

> I hold—and I think I have irrefutably sustained my positions—to the doctrine of *unconditional, personal, and eternal election.*—There are MANY OF OUR BRETHREN THIS DAY who, as seriously as myself, deplore the *Arminian* tendency of many of our preachers and churches. Well do they remember the former temple in the days of a Mulkey and his faithful coadjutors; and when they compare the present *milk-and-cider theology* with theirs, they are like the ancient Jews at the remembrance of their former temple—weep bitterly. Alas! alas! how has the fine gold become dim in many places of our hill-country! so that it is difficult to tell when a Baptist minister preaches, except he gets to ranting about Baptism. I say this with no disrespect to Baptism: it is a doctrine of the Bible, and ought to be preached; but we should not forget, at the same time, that our people need *indoctrinating* upon more subjects than baptism.

Yes, my Baptist brother, your people need "indoctrinating" upon the beauties of *unconditional election and reprobation,* as set forth in your Philadelphia Confession of Faith—your *standard* of doctrines! I have no doubt that a *hit* at Graves was here intended, for his dishonesty in seeking to *dodge* the Calvinism of his creed, and even denying the faith! I would that all Baptist preachers were honest like this writer, who is himself understood to be a preacher, and would state their odious doctrine as they hold it! He even charges them with hypocrisy, in holding one creed and preaching another. He gives them as a specimen of blunt, honest Calvinistic preaching, the discourses of old JONATHAN MULKEY and his "faithful coadjutors" in the work of preaching and defending "*uncon-*

ditional, personal, and eternal election!" I knew Mr. Mulkey, and many of his "faithful coadjutors," and I will bear them witness that they did stand square up to this "fine gold," and warred like men against the "milk-and-cider theology" of those who offered Christ to all, and held that men were accountable for their base acts of crime, such as stealing, lying, drunkenness, perjury, and murder!

As to all this "*ranting* about Baptism," it is certainly uncalled for, even if Arminianism be true; but in the event that Calvinism be true, it is ridiculous to baptize at all, either by immersion or any other mode. If men are "unconditionally, personally, and eternally elected," they will be saved if they never see water, and die drunk in the bargain! If unconditionally elected—eternally elected—personally and individually elected, the baptism of old *Zeke Holliman* was just as valid as that of the old preacher in the wilderness whose meat was locusts and wild honey! On the other hand, if "unconditionally, personally, and eternally" reprobated, to immerse a man seventy times seven in the veritable *Jordan* would be of no avail.

Alas! how much more manly and Christian-like it would have been for Elder Graves to have stated, with the candor of this writer in the "Watchman," that some of his brethren had become ashamed of the doctrine of "unconditional, personal, and eternal election," and that they wished to repudiate their Philadelphia Confession of Faith—that *he* had himself renounced the doctrine, if such had been the fact, than falsely to accuse the Methodists of holding it, when, as he knew, of all men living, Methodist preachers, from Wesley down, are the most zealous opposers of the doctrine! The only interruption of years of Christian love and fellowship between Wesley and Whitefield was on account of Calvinism—the former opposing, and the latter advocating the abominable doctrine! That Mr. Graves is at heart a Calvinist is evident from the *spirit* diffused throughout all that he says or writes. Hear what MR. JEFFERSON says on this point, in a letter to Dr. Cooper, bearing date November 2, 1822 :—

> The blasphemy and absurdity of the five points of Calvin, and the impossibility of defending them, render their advocates impatient of reasoning, irritable, and prone to denunciation of character.

But if Mr. Graves and his *pious* coadjutors, who are engaged in circulating this slander of Methodism, will not regard it as arrogant in me, I will give them, in a nutshell, what Methodists do hold and teach; and in so doing, I will give them a system of theology which they may rely upon as scriptural, and which they may venture to preach on all occasions, as it will secure to them, one and all, "a conscience void of offence toward God and toward man."

First, then, "go teach all nations," without any sort of disguise or concealment, that God the Father *loved* all men—that the Son *atoned* for all men—that the Holy Ghost enlightens, quickens, and strives with all—and that all *who will* may be saved. In other words, teach the people that the *moving cause* of the salvation of men, in all ages and countries, is the love of God—that the *meritorious cause* of their salvation is the atonement of our Lord Jesus Christ—that the *instrumental cause* is the Spirit and providence of God, with the appointed means of grace, such as water baptism, the sacrament of the Lord's Supper, prayer, etc.; and, finally, that the *conditional cause* is—not *immersion*, but their obedience to the prescribed rules of faith and practice which God has given them to walk by, and which are laid down in the Scriptures, in the Methodist Discipline, and the standard works of Methodism. This is a brief but orthodox system of theology, and it is one in the maintenance of which God will bless the laborer and prosper the cause in his hands. And it is alone under the preaching of these doctrines—summarily contained and comprehensively expressed in the foregoing sentences—that God does revive his work. God never commissioned any man to preach *a limited atonement*—he never sanctioned the doctrine by a revival of his work—he never taught the doctrine, nor did any one of his inspired apostles; and, finally, no young convert ever believed the doctrine!

CHAPTER VIII.

Close Communion considered—Baptists more unscripturally close than others—Derivation of the term Sacrament—Proselyting practice of Baptists—Robert Hall, a distinguished Baptist preacher, opposed to Close Communion—A case of outrageous bigotry and Close Communion—Elders Graves, Buck, and Howell, for Close Communion—Baptism essential to salvation, both with Baptists and Roman Catholics—Close Communion leads to treason against God—Christ's kingdom eternal—John's kingdom temporary—Terms of Methodist communion reasonable and scriptural—They exclude no orthodox Christians in good standing in their own Churches.

In this chapter I propose to say all that I deem necessary to be said on the subject of *Close Communion*, and the practice of both the Baptist and Methodist Churches in America. No preachers of any denomination are so clamorous upon the subject of "communion" as those of the Baptist denomination. On all occasions, during their communion seasons, publicly and privately, with a view to creating an impression favorable to their illiberal and bigoted practice, they regret, in one breath, that they cannot invite their brethren of other denominations to the Lord's table, "because they have never obeyed the command;" and, in the next breath, they justify their niggardly proscription of better men than themselves by quoting that scripture which teaches that "it is not meet to take the children's bread and give it to *dogs!*"

On page 470 of the "Iron Wheel," Mr. Graves heads his thirty-eighth chapter, which covers thirty pages of his work, in part, with these remarkable words—remarkable, as I shall hereafter show, because *utterly false*, and uttered with a perfect knowledge of their having no foundation in truth, because he has seen the Discipline, where the lie is given direct to his assertions:—

The Methodists' terms of communion—None so close, or so unscripturally close—They invert the ordinances and violate the Divine order—The Discipline forbids Methodist preachers to invite members of other denominations—All who commune with Methodists must not only believe, but dress like them.

This chapter Mr. Graves concludes after this fashion, on page 496:—

In conclusion, let me ask, in all earnestness, why will Methodist preachers continue to give general invitations to all professed Christians, and sinners too, and especially urge Baptists to come to their tables, and when they respectfully decline, charge them with an unchristian spirit, and bigotry; and when Baptists do not invite them, abuse them for uncharitableness and want of liberality? Methodist ministers have their rules and directions, as we have seen, and they are bound to their strict observance by all the sanctities of oaths and promises; and why do they not keep them touching the administration of the Supper, as they are known to do in other matters?

Do they not invite Baptists to their table with the intent to insult us, to outrage our feelings, and to prejudice our views and practice in the eyes of the world? For me to ask and urge a man or woman to do that—to participate in some act which I well knew his or her principles of honor or virtue would not allow, and which I well knew that man or woman considered criminal, would I not be offering a gross insult to that person? And suppose I had been repelled and rebuked again and again, in what light must my third and fifth and twentieth invitation be regarded!! Do not Methodist preachers know full well that Baptists can no more go to their tables, or commune with them, without a surrender of all their principles and a violation of the word of God, etc.

The word *sacrament* is derived from the Latin word *sacramentum,* which signifies an obligation or oath. The word was adopted by the writers of the Latin Church to denote those ordinances of religion by which Christians come under an obligation of obedience to God, and which obligation, they supposed, was equally sacred with that of an oath. It was also applied by the early writers of the Western Church to any ceremony of our holy religion, especially if it were figurative or mystical. But a more definite signification of this word by degrees prevailed, and by divines of modern times it is used in a strict sense.

Of sacraments, in a strict sense of the word, Protestant Churches admit of but two; and a greater number cannot well be made out from Scripture. These are BAPTISM and the LORD'S SUPPER. This latter, it is admitted by all denominations of Christians, with the exception of *one*, is of perpetual obligation, and that it was designed by its Founder to be one of the visible expressions of our faith in his blood, and of our fraternal love to his followers. Do Baptists—I mean *Close Communion* Baptists—regard it in this light? Does Elder Graves so regard it, who, by his writings and oral instructions, seeks to widen the breach between Baptists and others? Let his illiberal writings, and his bigotry and abuse of all who are not of his "faith and order," answer these searching interrogatories!

When the table is spread, by any one denomination, and the bread and wine placed thereon, it is emphatically *the table of the Lord*, and not the table of *that particular denomination*. The duty of the administrator is to invite all orthodox Christians who are in good standing in their respective Churches—as the Methodists *invariably* do—to join in the commemoration of the death and sufferings of Christ; and he is not at liberty to withhold the sacred elements from such, or to order them to stand aside, as the Baptists do on all occasions. If a Baptist commune with the members of any one of our evangelical denominations, acknowledged by Baptists themselves to be orthodox upon all questions of faith, (excepting only *immersion*,) he is arraigned before his Church upon a charge of *immorality;* and if he refuse to acknowledge publicly that he has sinned against God and his brethren, promising to do so no more, he is publicly expelled, his name is at once erased from the Church book, and he is told that he is no longer a member, entitled to the privileges of God's people! And why? Because he had communed with—say, Methodist, Presbyterian, or Lutheran *Christians!* Nor would this be done in an isolated case, but thousands would be expelled, if thousands dared thus to commune, and refused to make these *humiliating* confessions—acknowledging really, to appease the wrath of a bigoted membership, what they neither felt nor believed!

Mr. Graves speaks frequently of "the *proselyting* features of Methodism," and denounces such a spirit, as though his own Church is not more deeply imbued with this hateful spirit than that of any other denomination in the United States! In East Tennessee, it is within my own certain knowledge that men have joined the Baptist Church with an express stipulation that they were to be allowed the privilege of communing with other Christian denominations, and afterwards, when the flimsy arguments of their pastors failed to convince them that such acts of fellowship were *sinful,* for doing so they have been turned out, publicly expelled, by the very congregations who thus received them! The truth is, that the Baptists in East Tennessee, where I am best acquainted, frequently hold out inducements of this kind to get persons of liberal and charitable views to join them, believing that they can strengthen them in the faith of their narrow-mindedness; and when some have proved refractory, and contended for "open communion," as stated before, they have dismissed them from their ranks!

Let me, just at this point, ask the advocates of a restricted communion, including the "North Carolina Publishing Society of the Baptist Church," a few plain questions, demanding of them categorical answers. What *real* difference is there between attending this communion-service with Pedobaptists, and other exercises of devotion, such as preaching, singing, and prayer? What difference is there between attending at the Lord's table with a respectable and pious Methodist or Presbyterian, and uniting with him in a prayer-meeting, or at a throne of grace, in a revival, in behalf of a few penitent seekers of religion? Why preach, exhort, sing, pray, shout, shake hands, and rejoice with Methodists and Presbyterians, at one of their protracted meetings, and then utterly refuse to commune with them, or let them commune with you? I leave the REV. ROBERT HALL, an educated and pious gentleman, and evidently the most talented minister the Baptist Church ever laid claim to, to answer these questions; for it is plain to be seen that our Tennessee Baptists will not *condescend* to answer them. And let every Baptist "read, mark, learn, and inwardly digest" the following sensible, ay, and liberal Christian views of Mr. Hall:—

I must beg leave to notice a striking inconsistence in the advocates of strict communion. Nothing is more certain than that the communion of saints is by no means confined to one particular occasion, or limited to one transaction, such as that of assembling around the Lord's table: it extends to all the modes by which believers recognize each other as the members of a common Head. Every expression of fraternal regard, every participation in the enjoyments of social worship, every instance of the unity of the Spirit exerted in prayer and supplication, or in acts of Christian sympathy and friendship, as truly belongs to the communion of saints as the celebration of the eucharist. In truth, if we are strangers to communion with our fellow-Christians on other occasions, it is impossible for us to enjoy it there; for the mind is not a piece of mechanism which can be set agoing at pleasure, whose movements are obedient to the call of time and place. Nothing short of an habitual sympathy of spirit, springing from the cultivation of benevolent feeling and the interchange of kind offices, will secure that reciprocal delight, that social pleasure, which is the soul of Christian communion. Its richest fruits are frequently reserved for private conference, like that in which the two disciples were engaged in their way to Emmaus, when their hearts burned within them, while the Lord opened to them the Scriptures. When they take sweet counsel together as they go to the house of God in company, when they bear each other's burdens, weep with those that weep, and rejoice with them that rejoice, say, have Christians no mutual fellowship? Is it not surprising that, losing sight of such obvious facts, our opponents always reason on the subject of communion as though it related merely to the sacrament? In every other particular they act just as we do.

However our opponents may deviate from Scripture, let them at least be consistent with themselves, and either follow out their own principles to their just consequence, by withholding from the members of other denominations every token of fraternal regard, or freely admit them to the Lord's table. As the case stands at present, their mode of proceeding is utterly untenable. In a variety of instances, they indulge themselves in those acts of communion with Pedobaptists which are peculiar to Christians: they frequently make them their mouth in addressing the Deity: they exchange pulpits, and even engage their assistance in exercises intended as a preparation for the eucharist; and after lighting the flame of devotion at their torch, they most preposterously turn round to inform them that they are not worthy to participate. It would be difficult to convince a stranger to our practice that it were possible to be guilty of such an absurdity. Is the observance of an external rite, let me ask, a more solemn part of religion than addressing the Majesty of heaven and earth? And shall we depute *him* to present our prayers at his footstool who would defile a sacrament by his presence? Suppose them to relax from their rigor, and to admit pious Pedobaptists to their fellowship: to what would it amount? To nothing more than a public acknowledgment of their union to Christ, and their interests in his benefits; and as they fully acknowledge both, why scruple to do it at the table of their common Lord? Why select an ordinance designed for the commemoration of the dying love of the Redeemer as the signal for displaying the banners of party; and, by reviving the remembrance of differences elsewhere consigned to oblivion, give the utmost publicity to dissensions which are the reproach of the Church and the triumph of the world?

I have charged the Baptists of this country with selfishness, bigotry, intolerance, and a shameful want of Christian liberality; but *I* am regarded as an enemy, and hence full credit is not given to what I say. To satisfy others that Baptists are chargeable with bigotry, I will give one more quotation from the illustrious author before mentioned, Mr. Hall:*

* By consulting Parke Godwin's Universal Biography, the reader will see that Mr. Hall was not only an eminent Baptist preacher and distinguished theological writer, but his *father* before him was a Baptist preacher. Robert was educated in a *Baptist* college at Bristol. He was once a Professor in King's College at Aberdeen, where he took the degree of Master of Arts. He was pastor of the Baptist congregation at Leicester for twenty years. In 1826 he became the President of Bristol Academy, and the pastor of Broadmead Chapel. He carried his congregations with him in favor of open or free communion. He died in 1831, aged 67. (See page 474 of Godwin.)

The very appellation of Baptist, together with the tenets by which it is designated, become associated with the idea of *bigotry*. With mingled surprise and indignation others behold us making pretensions which no other denomination of Protestants assumes—placing ourselves in an attitude of HOSTILITY towards the whole Christian world, *and virtually claiming to be the* ONLY *Church of Christ upon earth*. Fortified as it is by its claims to antiquity and universality, and combining in its exterior whatever is adapted to dazzle the imagination and captivate the senses, there is yet nothing in the *Church of Rome* that has excited more indignation and disgust than this very pretension. What then must be the sensation produced when, in the absence of all these advantages, a sect comparatively small and insignificant erects itself on a solitary eminence, from whence it repels the approach of all other Christians!

I will here give an instance of the combined bigotry and despotism of Baptists, which occurred within eight miles of where I was then living, and which will serve to illustrate their *feelings* and *practice* throughout the South and West, moderated in their outward appearances in proportion to the refined state of society, and the strength and influence of other denominations. At a Baptist protracted meeting at Sinking Creek church, in Carter county, and only about eight miles west of Elizabethton, the Methodists and Presbyterians were invited to attend, from the village of Elizabethton, which they did, and aided in the labors of the meeting. Towards the close of the meeting the sacrament of the Lord's Supper was administered, and the pastor of the church, ELDER BAYLESS, after detailing the reasons why they could not suffer others to commune with them, determined to convince them that they were not wanting either in Christian love or affectionate regards for them. Accordingly, he notified the congregation that "*all who were in good standing in their own Churches might occupy the front seats, and see the Lord's people partake of his shed blood and broken body!*" What amazing condescension! What a display of Christian charity! How calmly resplendent must have been the glory of this scene—this ebullition of a haughty dogmatism! Ye murky clouds of superstition from the Scandinavian forests, do permit yourselves to be eclipsed by the smoke of the bigotry displayed on this occasion! Stand fast, ye inhabitants of earth and heaven, and see the light of Christian charity, in its full-orbed glory, burst at once upon the congregation of *saints* at Sinking Creek, while "all who are in good standing" in other Churches are permitted to occupy seats near to the *throne*, and witness the glorious sight! Look on, ye unpolished barbarians of the Methodist order, and ye unbaptized heathens of the Presbyterian persuasion, totally ignorant of the fashionable etiquette of Christian courtesy, and learn what religion is!

But, to be serious, those who were "in good standing in their own Churches" had no right to complain at this treatment, for they were, at that time, living in the neglect of *a known duty*. And they must have known, nay, did know, from what Elder Bayless taught them, that they could no more get to heaven without being *immersed by a Baptist preacher*, than they could arrest the sun in his course, or check the impetuous cataract of Niagara in its onward and terrible progress!

Messrs. Graves and Bayless are by no means alone in their *exclusive* views upon these points. In an editorial headed "*Invalid Baptism,*" in the Louisville Baptist "Banner and Pioneer" of February 24, 1842, a paper I have been careful to preserve—an article from the pen of ELDER BUCK, the then resident editor, an erudite Gothamite indeed, only excelled by the jackdaw strut of his co-laborer, the immortal Howell—I find the same proscriptive spirit displayed. I give the article *verbatim, et literatim, et punctuatim, et spellatim:*

We regard nothing as gospel baptism but the immersion in water, of a believer, in the name of the Father, Son, and Holy Ghost.

How frequently do Baptist ministers, if but a hand or a part of the subject be uncovered in the water, immerse again? And whoever thought that this was *Anibaptism?* And yet we risk nothing in saying, that it is as decidedly re-baptism, as it would be to re-immerse an individual who had been immersed by a Pedo-baptist minister, [a Methodist, Presbyterian, etc.,] OR ANY OTHER UNAUTHORIZED ADMINISTRATOR!

A second extract from the same article is in these words:

Now we take the ground that no baptism is valid, whatever be its conformity to the New Testament model in other respects, unless administered by a SCRIPTURALLY AUTHORIZED ADMINISTRATOR. Again: we take the ground that no body or community of men, can confer this authority or right, upon an individual, to administer the ordinances of the gospel, BUT THE CHURCH OF JESUS CHRIST ALONE, [i. e. the Baptist Church!] Once more: we take the ground, that the church of Jesus Christ is a body of baptized believers, (*of immersed Baptists!*) duly organized and embodied upon the principles of the gospel; AND THAT NO OTHER IS THE CHURCH OF JESUS CHRIST!!

I want the reader to bear in mind this fact, that this mammoth sheet, published weekly, is the organ of the Baptist Church in the South and West, edited at that date by *five preachers* of that denomination, the ablest they could muster.

But Elder Howell has published a work of 300 pages upon this and other subjects. He was appointed to write this work by the Baptist State Convention held in Nashville in 1840; and, true to the trust confided in him, he *dedicated* his book to "The Baptist Convention of the State of Tennessee!" Here is a specimen of the insulting pretensions of this Church, as laid down by Mr. Howell:

These facts and considerations demonstrate that *the Baptist is the only Church which can claim the apostolic origin*, and that in its organization and objects it is conformed in all respects to the word of God; THAT THE APOSTOLIC CHURCH WAS BAPTIST, *and that through several channels* it may be readily and surely traced, in a state of comparative purity, down to our own times.*—P. 286.

Ours is the only denomination who place this ordinance (baptism) in its true position, where it was left by Christ and his apostles: who refuse, on the one hand, to despoil it of its solemn and appropriate forms, and who do not, on the other, unduly exalt its importance and efficacy.—P. 204.

* One of these "channels," and a most important one, too, is that of *Zeke Holliman*, at Providence, *immersing* Williams, and Williams *in return* plunging Holliman "*and the other ten!*" That was a "channel" with a vengeance! Ay, and that was claiming "apostolic origin" for you!

We cannot commune with Pedobaptists, because, NOT HAVING BEEN IMMERSED, THEY ARE NOT BAPTIZED.—P. 185.

We cannot unite with Pedobaptists in sacramental communion WITHOUT AN ACTUAL ABANDONMENT OR PRACTICAL FALSIFICATION OF ALL OUR PRINCIPLES, ON BOTH BAPTISM AND THE LORD'S SUPPER.—P. 134.

In regard, however, to the object especially before us, I shall sustain the proposition that baptism (immersion) has ever been regarded *as an essential preparation for the Lord's Supper*, by component proof. —P. 65.

And as IN BAPTISM we profess to have received SPIRITUAL LIFE, so, in communicating at the Lord's table, we have the emblems of that heavenly food by which we grow, and in virtue of which we hope to live for ever. And as we are born of God *but once*, so we are *baptized but once*, etc.—P. 59.

Now, Mr. Graves takes occasion, throughout his work, to compare Methodists, who sprinkle and pour water in baptism, to *Roman Catholics*. For his benefit, I propose to show that himself, Buck, Howell, and all who endorse their views, are not unlike the *Catholics*, by any means. The Catholic Catechism, and the Canons of the Council of Trent, teach precisely this language:

If any one shall say that baptism is not ESSENTIAL TO SALVATION, *let him be accursed.* Sin, whether contracted by birth from our first parents, or committed ourselves, is, *by the admirable virtue of this sacrament*, REMITTED AND PARDONED!

Verily, if Catholics go to any greater lengths on the subject of baptism than Graves, Buck, and Howell have gone, I have not the capacity to make the discovery. I have given the doctrines of both in their own words, referring to chapter and verse. The hypothesis of these close-communion Baptists nullifies the Abrahamic covenant, dispenses really with the sacred office of the gospel ministry, and the important relations of Church membership. In further consideration of these points, I have some four or five reflections to offer:

1. The Close Baptists lay such a stress upon baptism by *immersion*, as to make it the sole condition of admittance to

the Lord's table—a table which they say can only be spread by ministers who have been *immersed*—no others being invested with ministerial functions—none others being even members of the Church of Christ!

2. The Close Baptists hold and teach that there is no Church militant but THEIRS, and that there is no ministry but such as is constituted by churches of their "*faith and order;*" but they will call on Pedobaptists, at their revivals, to pray for their seekers, and to preach the word—thus making them their "mouth in addressing the Deity," as Mr. Hall expresses it, to ask God's blessings to be poured upon them, or to declare His will concerning them, which is vastly more important and sacred than to prepare and offer the bread and wine!

3. The Close Baptists believe and teach that *immersion* is the only door into the Church; but they will not receive into their communion persons who have been regularly immersed by others, unless they *repudiate* their baptism, and the ministerial functions of all other ministers—therefore, the repudiation of the ministerial functions of all other ministers is *the* door into the Baptist Church!

4. The Close Baptists are influenced by a spirit which is opposed to the kingdom of Christ—a spirit which would *set up another kingdom* in opposition, and nullify the covenant of God, and at the same time wear the name of Christian! God has never had but one spiritual kingdom in the world. This kingdom was set up in the family of Abraham. It was with God's people in the wilderness, and was planted with them in the land of promise. In this kingdom Christ was born. Over this kingdom Christ reigns.

5. And, finally, the Close Baptists have set up a kingdom in opposition to Christ; therefore, the Close Baptists are guilty of TREASON AGAINST GOD!

In the outset of this chapter I quoted from Mr. Graves the

broad assertion, that no denomination laid down terms of communion "so close, or so unscripturally close" as those of the Methodists, with the additional and more monstrous assertion, that "the Discipline forbids Methodist preachers to invite members of other denominations." Both assertions are *false;* and all who have ever witnessed the administration of the Lord's Supper among Methodists, know that the preachers distinctly say: "*This is not the table of the Methodists, but of the Lord, and we invite all orthodox Christians who are in good standing in their own Churches to commune with us.*"

As to the *closeness* of the terms, these are laid down in the Discipline, and invariably stated by the administrator at the table, being a part of the ceremony required on the occasion. They ought not to be made *looser* by any denomination, and such as do not come up to this standard should not approach the table. They are found under the head of "Sacramental Services," etc., and are in these words:

> Ye that do truly and earnestly repent of your sins, and are in love and charity with your neighbors, and intend to lead a new life, following the commandments of God, and walking from henceforth in his holy ways, draw near with faith, and take this holy sacrament to your comfort; and make your humble confession to Almighty God, meekly kneeling upon your knees.

CHAPTER IX.

False assertions by Elder Graves—Nature and use of baptism—The Abrahamic covenant considered—Baptism in lieu of circumcision—The rights of infants secured in both cases—Scriptural evidence of the soundness of these positions—Baptism the door into the Church—Baptists enter the Church backwards!—Dunkers practice trine immersion, but go it face foremost!—Methodists, Presbyterians, Episcopalians, and others, enter the Church of God faces foremost, conscious of rectitude of intention, and of being engaged in acts they are not ashamed of!

On page 415, Mr. Graves properly commences his *tirade* upon Baptism, and continues it through *four* entire chapters of his work. In addition to his misrepresenting every feature of Methodism, as connected with the ordinance of baptism, he teaches heresies as abominable, throughout, as those contended for by the corrupt Church of Rome. He takes the ground that baptism by *immersion* is the only true and scriptural mode; and that a *Baptist preacher* is the only divinely authorized expounder of God's word, and the only legal administrator of the ordinances and sacraments of his Church!

These broad and unqualified assertions, uttered by Mr. Graves and by *ultra* Baptists almost daily, both in *word* and *deed*, are utterly unauthorized and unfounded—do utterly disfranchise the entire ministry of several large and respectable denominations, indeed, of nearly the whole Christian world, and annihilate the clerical character of almost every evangelical minister belonging to those denominations, as well also as the validity of every ceremony performed by them. It is no vindication to say that the Baptists do not intend to go thus far —it is sufficient for the public to know that they *do go thus far.* I have already shown, in the preceding chapter, that with the Baptists, qualifications for admission—not to the *Lord's* table, but to the table of the *Baptists,* with bread and wine spread thereon—are, that the communicants must have been *baptized by immersion,* and that baptism must have been performed by a *Baptist preacher,* who was himself IMMERSED by a man of the same "faith and order." Because, with the Baptist denomination, a man is made a *minister of the gospel,* not by the *Holy Ghost,* but by IMMERSION! Why do I say this? I say it because a Baptist is not a minister of Christ until he is immersed, either in his own estimation or in the estimation of his Church.

The Pharisees, and others, did not oppose the truths uttered by our Lord and his disciples with more vehemence, than do the Baptists oppose all other modes of baptism save the one practiced by themselves. The Sadducees did not advocate the doctrine that there is neither angel nor spirit with more zeal, than do the Baptists that their forms and ceremonies are right, and that those of all other sects are wrong.

I intend this chapter shall be devoted to the nature and use of baptism, and other points connected therewith; but as my custom is, before entering upon the argument, I will submit a few of Mr. Graves's assertions and positions, which shall serve for me as a text. He heads his thirty-fourth chapter, commencing on page 415, with these words—clearly indicating the course of the argument throughout this chapter:

Methodists have two distinct "baptisms," one for infants and one for adults—A distinct and different office for each—A distinct and altogether different design for each—The regeneration of infants in baptism in all cases, plainly taught in the Discipline and standard works of the Book Concern.

He conducts the argument, on page 419, after this truly convincing style:

> Does not the infant of a day differ as much from an adult of twenty-two or fifty, as non-intelligence from intelligence—as irrationality from rationality? and, so far as being the subject of gospel address and gospel motives, as a bell differs from a believer? Then certainly the command to baptize a believer in Christ—and we have a command to baptize no other character—can no more be construed by Methodists into the liberty to baptize unconscious infants and non-believing children of a dozen years, than it can by the Papists into a permission to baptize bells, asses, and locomotives—which they do.

His next, and by far most unanswerable argument, continued on the same page, is this:

> 1. Are not words put into the mouth of the Saviour that he never used, in order to teach the doctrine that no infant or unbaptized person can be saved?! "Born anew of water and of the Holy Ghost," Christ never said; but, "Except one be born of water and *wind* he cannot enter into the kingdom of heaven," *he did say*. This is what he said—these were the *identical* words he used.

I pause only to remark, that this substitution of *wind* for *Spirit*, I take to be according to the *new version* Graves and others are so zealous to have adopted! That such men should be anxious to substitute *wind* for the *Holy Ghost*, is quite natural. Indeed, I have no doubt Graves himself was "born of *water* and *wind*" exclusively! Of course this change of *wind* for *Spirit* is intended to run through the whole translation; and in many respects such changes are peculiarly adapted to Baptists of Mr. Graves's character and sentiments. But let us see how it will work.

"The *wind* itself beareth witness with our *wind*, that we are the children of God." Again: "God is *wind*," ay, and such as "worship him must worship him in *wind* and in truth." And again, in 2 Corinthians iii. 17: "Now the Lord is that *wind;* and where the *wind* of the Lord is, there is liberty."

This last verse, thus translated and changed, is peculiarly

adapted to most of the Baptist preachers in this country, who oppose the use of any and all books except the Bible—publicly boast that they have no *"edecation"* or *"human larnin"*—claim to be inspired—and only announce to an audience such texts of Scripture as God *reveals* to them for special purposes and occasions, either after their arrival at the place of worship, or on their way thither! These men usually profess to *open* their mouths, and to speak as the Lord *fills* them, or, to use their precise language, as He "shall give light and liberty." Truly the Lord fills them with *air*, which, when put in motion by the stentorian lungs of a Baptist preacher, is "*wind;*" and then, if a congregation will take *words* for *ideas*, and *sound* for *sense*, they will have "another gospel;" as "the *wind* bloweth where it listeth, and thou hearest the *sound thereof*, but canst not tell whence it cometh, and whither it goeth: so is every one that is born of the *wind!*"

> "Blow rock and mountain rampart round,
> Till glory echoes back the sound!"

His thirty-fifth chapter, commencing on page 428, has this heading, indicating the points both discussed and *misrepresented:*

> Adult baptism distinct from infant—Its design, with the exception—No faith required of the adult, save that required by the Romish Church—And no profession of regeneration as a condition of baptism—Regeneration ordinarily the same with baptism.

And this chapter he concludes in these words:

> In consideration of these teachings, can Baptists, with any kind of reason, be called upon to recognize the Methodist Episcopal society *as a Christian or gospel Church?* Is it a congregation of believers, according to the definition of the Discipline, in which the word of God is faithfully preached, and the ordinances duly administered?

The pastor of the Baptist church in Nashville has been employed in publishing an essay on "the Church," the positions of which are thus summed up by Elder Graves, in an editorial notice in the "Tennessee Baptist," which I find in that paper for December 22, 1855.

> He takes the true position that Pedobaptist societies are *not gospel Churches in any true sense,* and that Pedobaptist preachers are *not members of gospel Churches,* and consequently *not baptized or ordained,* and therefore *not ministers of Christian Churches.* Why then should Baptists recognize them as such by *associating with them as such*—recognizing them as official ministers by inviting them into our pulpits, or to seats in our deliberative bodies? We do not believe that Baptist churches generally will always act inconsistently.

This is not all Mr. Graves has said recently in his paper, bearing upon this subject. He has boasted that these sentiments, of which his paper is the strenuous advocate, are rapidly gaining ground among the Baptists of the South-west, which I have no doubt is the fact, seeing their endorsement by the "North Carolina Baptist Publishing Society." Revolting as such conclusions must be to liberal minds and truly pious hearts, I do not see how those who hold that *baptism is the door into the Church,* and that nothing but *immersion* is baptism, can hold back from the same conclusions. They are the plain, logical, and unavoidable sequences of such premises, if I have not forgotten what logic is. The only way for pious and charitable Baptists—of whom there are many—to avoid such conclusions, is to *retrace their steps,* and give up their favorite dogma, that *immersion alone is baptism,* which is the *logical thunderbolt,* in their chain of reasoning, which drives them to this revolting conclusion!

Now, what is baptism? It is a sacrament which has occasioned endless controversies during the last two or three hundred years, the *obligation* of which, it is affirmed, rests upon the example of our Lord, who—not in *person,* but by his disciples—baptized such as, by his discourses and miracles, were brought to a knowledge of the truth. Does the obligation of baptism rest upon any thing else? It further rests upon the solemn command of Christ to his apostles, after his resurrection—"Go and teach all nations, baptizing them in the name of the Father, and of the Son, and of the Holy Ghost;" (not of the "*wind*," as Graves would have it!) and upon the *practice* of the apostles, who went forth and did as they were commanded.

But is any thing further to be understood by baptism? I answer, it is a rite or ceremony by which individuals are initiated into the profession of the Christian religion; or, if the reader please, it is the appointed mode by which an individual assumes the profession of Christianity; or, to be still more explicit, it IS THE DOOR BY WHICH PERSONS ENTER THE CHURCH OF GOD ON EARTH, and are admitted to a participation of the privileges belonging to the followers of Christ. In other words, it is by the ordinance of baptism that those who believe the gospel, or profess faith in Christ, are to be separated from the wicked, and joined to the visible Church; and the application of water, or the rite accompanying it, is, as it ever has been, intended to *represent* the washing away, or openly renouncing, the impurities of our natural state—our numerous and grievous offences; and, consequently, it must be understood that at least a profession of repentance must always accompany a profession of faith in Christ Jesus. However, as I shall have occasion to speak of baptism as the *door* into the Church, it is proper here that I qualify this expression. Baptism is properly a sacrament of the gospel—was instituted by Christ himself as the *initiating* rite into the Church; and in this sense I claim to be understood when I speak of it as *the door.* In a strict sense, Christ is *himself* the door into his Church; but water baptism entitles the person to the privileges of the Church on earth, while the baptism of the Holy Ghost is that which qualifies the individual for the Church triumphant. Water baptism alone does not qualify a person for admission into Christ's holy Church; but baptism by "water and the Holy Ghost" will qualify one for the Church on earth and in heaven. And while the former is not essential to salvation itself, of itself, the latter is; and the two united must not be neglected. For the Word says, "Except a man be born of water and of the Spirit, he cannot enter into the kingdom of God."

This is the view that Methodists take of this subject, and it is a view in which almost every evangelical denomination concurs. The Baptists, like the Roman Catholics, carry their opinions far beyond this view of the subject. The Romanists, in their opinions as to the *efficacy* of this sacrament, consider baptism, administered by a priest, as *of itself* applying the merits of Christ to the individual baptized. The Baptists and Romanists differ as to the *mode* and *subjects* of baptism, but not as it regards the *efficacy* of the sacrament of baptism. According to the Romanists, baptism is absolutely necessary to salvation; and they therefore admit its validity when administered to a *dying child* by any person present, should there be no priest at hand! In this they are much more liberal than our Baptist brethren. The Baptists hold that baptism by *immersion* is absolutely necessary to salvation, but deny its validity when administered by any one but a *Baptist preacher*, who has himself been *immersed* by some one who was *immersed before him*, and believed in that as the only true and scriptural mode of baptism. They also deny that children have any right to the ordinance.

But I have something more to say respecting the nature and use of baptism. That baptism is a sacrament of the gospel, that it is an ordinance of great importance, and that it was designed by Christ to be perpetuated in his Church, are propositions which may be sustained by such evidence as will satisfy every honest inquirer after truth, and which nothing but an unreasonable prejudice, spiced with something of the stubbornness of the *mule*, will induce any man to reject.

I shall not stop to inquire in this chapter what is the philological sense of the term *baptizo*, but what is the theological import of the sacrament of Christian baptism. In my arrangement of the examination of this subject, this does not belong to this chapter, though it is necessary to be considered in order to a proper development of the whole subject, and will be brought forward in the course of my argument on the *mode* of baptism.

First, then, in a general sense, Christian baptism confers the mark upon the person baptized of *religious distinction*. All baptized persons are, by that mark of distinction, separated from the common masses of irreligious persons—from the numerous citizens of a wicked world, sometimes known as "the Big Survey." It is the external and visible badge of Christianity. Baptism is a pledge of Divine grace which Christ has given to us, to assure us that all the benefits of salvation shall be secured to us on the conditions of the gospel. A mark of discrimination, then, is hereby applied to the Christian, and he is known as being devoted to Christ, just as a Jew by circumcision was distinguished from a Gentile, and was known to be devoted to the law of Moses. Baptism is, therefore, a seal which Christ puts upon us as his own pledge of our salvation, on the condition of our fulfilling our covenant obligations to him. See Mark xvi. 16, where the promise of salvation is secured to baptized believers: "He that believeth and is baptized shall be saved." Also, Acts ii. 38: "Then Peter said unto them, Repent and be baptized, every one of you, in the name of Jesus Christ, for the remission of sins, and ye shall receive the gift of the Holy Ghost." This is further evident from 1 Peter iii. 21. The apostle in this passage, after noticing the preservation of Noah and his family in the ark, observes: "The like figure whereunto even baptism doth also now save us." But then he says that it is "not the putting away of the filth of the flesh," that is, not merely the *outward ceremony* of baptism, "but the answer of a good conscience toward God"—the fulfilling of the covenant obligations which we take upon ourselves by baptism.

Touching upon the mark of discrimination made known by the rite of baptism, some Baptist writers, holding to immersion as the *only mode*—as does Elder Graves throughout his entire book—have indulged in an amusing degree of fancy. In Robinson's History of Baptism, page 17, it is said:—

> Baptize is a dyer's word, and signifies to dip so as to *color*. The word, then, conveys two ideas—the one literal, *dipping*, the other figurative, *coloring:* a figure, however, expressive of a real fact—meaning that John, by bathing persons in the river Jordan, conferred a character, *a moral hue*, as dyers, by dipping into a dyeing-vat, set a tinct or color.

I think it likely that Elder Graves subscribes to this view of the subject, from various passages in his book! I do not believe one word of it, and for this reason—the theory is not founded in evidence. If baptism, by any mode, confer a *moral hue*, it is essential to salvation, because it is a *regenerating* rite. This kind of *spiritual* baptism the Mormons believe in, who also *immerse*, and at the time of immersing they profess to baptize with the Holy Ghost. This is a revival of the exploded theory of old *Simon Magus!* That the Baptist ministry claim to have had such a prerogative delegated to them, I will not now undertake to say; but, from the importance they attach to immersion *at their own hands*, as well as from the *strange feelings* of many subjects at the time of their immersion, as expressed by them afterwards, I am certainly authorized to infer such a thing.

But in considering the nature and use of Christian baptism, we are not only to regard it as one of the *sacraments* of the Church, and as a *sign* of spiritual blessings, but we are likewise to regard it as the seal of the new covenant. It is God's *mark*, if the reader please, or *signature*, affixed to the volume of inspiration, containing rules for human conduct, promises of eternal life to the faithful, and declarations concerning the future happiness and misery of men.

Just here, I will insert several pages of a small work I published in 1842, which I *compiled* from the most approved authorities of the age in which I wrote:—

In regard to the use of *seals* in general, it will not be irrelevant to premise that it is a custom of immemorial usage, resorted to as a convenient mode of attesting the genuineness or authenticity of the sealed. Anciently, and when the art of writing was unknown, the practice of *sealing* contracts was extensively adopted. Every man had his own *seal*, or *mark*, which he affixed to an instrument instead of signing his own proper name, which he could not do. The practice originated in necessity, at a time when men could not write; but having once obtained as a general custom, it continued long after the necessity which gave it birth had ceased to exist. The Bible abounds with allusions to this custom of *sealing* contracts, covenants, agreements, etc., which need not here be noticed.

Suffice it to say, that God has always affixed his *seal*, or *mark*, or *signature*—whatever we may please to call it—to his several dispensations; and in doing this, he has accommodated the simplicity of the sign to the circumstances of man. Of this nature was the tree of life in the garden of Eden. It was to Adam a token or pledge of the life which was promised him in case of obedience. Besides, when God covenanted with Noah, after the catastrophe of the flood, promising "not to smite any more every living thing," he "set his bow in the cloud;" and "God said, this is the TOKEN of the covenant which I make between me and you and every living creature. And it shall come to pass, that when I bring a cloud over the earth, that the bow shall be seen in the cloud; and I will REMEMBER my covenant which is between me and you and every living creature of all flesh," etc.—See Genesis ix. 2, etc.

We then remark that the *token* or sign thus exhibited was to be as a *remembrance* of the obligation, and a perpetual pledge of the fidelity of the Almighty in the performance of the covenant with Noah.

Well, now, circumcision was the SEAL of the Abrahamic covenant under the Mosaic law. When it was instituted, Abraham was informed that it should "be A TOKEN of the covenant" between God and him.—Genesis xvii. 2. In further proof of this, Paul, in the Epistle to the Romans, iv. 2, says, "And he [Abraham] received the SIGN of circumcision, a SEAL of the righteousness of faith which he had," etc. Circumcision, therefore, among the lineal descendants of Abraham, was the visible mark which God annexed to his covenant—ay, it was the impress of God's SEAL, whereby he attested the validity and binding nature of the covenant, and offered assurance to the Jews of his own faithfulness; just as a man would bind himself in a contract by affixing his SIGNATURE to an article of agreement. In like manner, the Jews assumed the obligations that circumcision devolved on them, by voluntarily becoming a party in the covenant.

It is not necessary to multiply quotations from the Scriptures to prove the position we have assumed; namely, that circumcision was the sign and seal of the covenant made with Abraham, or that the covenant between Jehovah and Abraham, thus sealed and attested, was the evangelical covenant. But we will give one or two other passages, in order to establish, beyond the possibility of cavil, one other important point. It is this: that God instituted a visible Church in the family of Abraham, and that this Church was composed of adults and *infants*, though denied by all regular Baptists, because its denial is necessary to the support of their own theory. This Church was founded on the evangelical covenant, and was the same as the Church which now exists under the gospel dispensation. In proof of these propositions, we direct the reader's attention to the passages heretofore quoted, and to the following from Genesis xvii. 19, 20: "And God said, Sarah shall bear thee a son indeed, and thou shalt call his name Isaac; and I will establish my covenant with him for an *everlasting covenant*, and with his seed *after him*. And as for Ishmael, I have heard thee; but my covenant will I establish with Isaac."

From these passages we learn that God took Abraham and his family, including both adults and *infants*, into a visible covenant-relation to himself, by circumcision; and that this covenant was confirmed unto Isaac and his descendants. This covenant is so repeatedly declared to be *an everlasting covenant*, that we have reason to think, from the very face of the texts themselves, without looking for further evidence, that it was designed to be of endless duration. The terms of this covenant do also show that it was designed to extend to other nations beside those who should be the *natural* descendants of Abraham. And this view of the subject is fully confirmed by collating these passages with those in the book of Genesis, in which God declares to Abraham that all the nations of the earth shall be blessed in him or in his seed. Now the covenant thus explained directs us necessarily to Christ as that seed of Abraham in whom all the families of the earth were to be blessed; and confirms the foregoing propositions—namely, that God instituted a visible Church in the family of Abraham which was composed of adults and *infants*, and that this Church was founded on the evangelical covenant, and the same as the Church now existing under the gospel dispensation. Those propositions are clearly established by the scriptures we have quoted, and by numerous others, and cannot be overthrown by any antipedobaptist in the country.

We now proceed to the consideration of a most important point—a point upon which "hang all the law and the prophets." We proceed to show *baptism* stands in the place of *circumcision*, and seals the same blessings now that once were sealed with blood. If we can sustain this proposition, by Scripture and argument, we have gained all we desire, so far as the nature and use of baptism is concerned, and shall have left our Baptist friends the bag to hold, with both ends open. This proposition will appear from the following considerations:

1st. Circumcision designates a member of the visible Church, for this was to Abraham and his descendants the seal of the righteousness of faith, and none could enjoy the privileges of the Church among the Jews without being circumcised. In proof we offer the following scriptures:—

And the Scripture, foreseeing that God would justify the heathen through faith, preached before the gospel unto Abraham, saying, In thee shall all nations be blessed.—GALATIANS iii. 8.

And he received the sign of circumcision, a seal of the righteousness of the faith which he had yet being uncircumcised: that he might be the father of all them that believe, though they be not circumcised: that righteousness might be imputed to them also.—ROMANS iv. 11.

And when Abram was ninety years old and nine, the Lord appeared to Abram, and said unto him, I am the Almighty God: walk before me, and be thou perfect.

And the uncircumcised man-child whose flesh of his foreskin is not circumcised, that soul shall be cut off from his people: he hath broken my covenant.—GENESIS xvii. 1, 14.

And when a stranger shall sojourn with thee, and will keep the passover to the Lord, let all his males be circumcised, and then let him come near and keep it; and he shall be as one that is born in the land; for no uncircumcised person shall eat thereof.—EXODUS xii. 48.

And if a stranger shall sojourn among you, and will keep the passover unto the Lord; according to the ordinance of the passover, and according to the manner thereof, so shall he do: ye shall have one ordinance, both for the stranger, and for him that was born in the land.—NUMBERS ix. 14.

Baptism now recognizes a member of the visible Church of Christ, and none are entitled to its privileges under the Christian dispensation without being baptized. In proof of this we offer the following scriptures:—

Go ye therefore and teach all nations, baptizing them in the name of the Father, and of the Son, and of the Holy Ghost.—MATTHEW xxviii. 19.

And he said unto them, Go ye into all the world, and preach the gospel to every creature.

He that believeth and is baptized, shall be saved; but he that believeth not, shall be damned.—MARK xvi. 15, 16.

Then Peter said unto them, Repent, and be baptized every one of you in the name of Jesus Christ, for the remission of sins; and ye shall receive the gift of the Holy Ghost:

For the promise is unto you, and to your children, and to all that are afar off, even as many as the Lord our God shall call.—ACTS ii. 38, 39.

2d. Circumcision was the visible seal of the covenant of grace, and of the righteousness of faith. For the proof of this, see the foregoing passages from Genesis, Romans, and Galatians.

Baptism is now the outward seal of the covenant of grace and of the righteousness of faith. In proof of this, we give, beside the passages already quoted, the following:—

Jesus answered, Verily, verily, I say unto thee, Except a man be born of water and of the Spirit, he cannot enter into the kingdom of God.—JOHN iii. 5.

And Philip said, If thou believest with all thine heart, thou mayest. And he answered and said, I believe that Jesus Christ is the Son of God.

And he commanded the chariot to stand still; and they went down both into the water, both Philip and the eunuch; and he baptized him.—ACTS viii. 37, 38.

3d. Circumcision was a sign of the grace of regeneration, or the renewing of the soul in righteousness. In proof of this position, we give the following scriptures:—

But he is a Jew, which is one inwardly; and circumcision is that of the heart, in the spirit, and not in the letter; whose praise is not of men, but of God.—ROM. ii. 29.

For we are the circumcision, which worship God in the spirit, and rejoice in Christ Jesus, and have no confidence in the flesh.—PHILIPPIANS iii. 3.

In whom also ye are circumcised with the circumcision made without hands, in putting off the body of the sins of the flesh by the circumcision of Christ.—COLOSSIANS ii. 11.

Baptism by water is now a sign of the grace of regeneration, or the renewing of the soul in righteousness. The evidence of this we find in the following passages:—

And now, why tarriest thou? arise, and be baptized, and wash away thy sins, calling on the name of the Lord.—ACTS xxii. 16.

Not by works of righteousness which we have done, but according to his mercy he saved us, by the washing of regeneration, and renewing of the Holy Ghost.—TITUS iii. 5.

Husbands, love your wives, even as Christ also loved the Church, and gave himself for it;

That he might sanctify and cleanse it with the washing of water by the word.—EPHESIANS v. 25, 26.

Let us draw near with a true heart, in full assurance of faith, having our hearts sprinkled from an evil conscience, and our bodies washed with pure water.—HEBREWS x. 22.

4th. Circumcision was an ordinance that constantly attended the gospel under the former dispensation. See the following scriptures in proof of this, as well as others already quoted:—

And when eight days were accomplished for the circumcising of the child, his name was called JESUS, which was so named of the angel before he was conceived in the womb.

And when the days of her purification according to the law of Moses were accomplished, they brought him to Jerusalem, to present him to the Lord:

(As it is written in the law of the Lord, Every male that openeth the womb shall be called holy to the Lord;)

And to offer a sacrifice according to that which is said in the law of the Lord, A pair of turtledoves, or two young pigeons.—LUKE ii. 21-24.

Moses therefore gave unto you circumcision; not because it is of Moses, but of the fathers; and ye on the Sabbath day circumcise a man.—JOHN vii. 22.

Baptism by water is an ordinance that constantly attends the gospel under the present dispensation. In proof of this, we might adduce many passages, but will only quote the following:—

Go ye therefore and teach all nations, baptizing them in the name of the Father, and of the Son, and of the Holy Ghost;

Teaching them to observe all things whatsoever I have commanded you; and, lo, I am with you alway, even unto the end of the world. Amen.—MATTHEW xxviii. 19, 20.

From the foregoing facts, circumstances, and considerations, the conclusion is inevitable that baptism is to the Church now what circumcision was under the former dispensation; namely, the outward seal of the covenant, and of the righteousness of faith. In other words, of whatever nature was circumcision under the Old Testament dispensation, of this same nature is baptism under the New Testament dispensation. As the former was the seal which God graciously entered into with man, so also is the latter. And the gospel is nothing more than the complete development of the Abrahamic covenant. This covenant stretches through all time, and comprehends all nations, sexes, colors, and sizes of human beings in its liberal provisions. It was in days of yore a covenant of grace and mercy, of pardon and eternal life, *conditionally*, to universal man. It is now what it was then; and as such, it is not merely of secular good to a few. Hence, says Paul, "*If ye be Christ's*, THEN are ye Abraham's seed, *and heirs* ACCORDING TO THE PROMISE." The gospel was preached to Abraham when the promise was made. And the blessings of that covenant were partially revealed and bestowed under the law of Moses. At that time it bore the mark or seal of circumcision. But in these gospel days, God has appointed baptism as the sign or seal.

The right of *infants* to this seal with all its blessings has once been secured to them by Divine authority: the law securing this right has never been repealed—of necessity, therefore, the right still remains. And it is the bounden duty of all believers in Christ to imitate the illustrious father of the faithful, by stamping upon their infant offspring the seal of the covenant of their God. True, the outward sign and seal of the gospel doctrine and privileges has been changed so as to suit the genius of the present dispensation; but the right of infant children to all the privileges of God's gracious covenant has never been affected thereby—it remains the very same; and he who asserts otherwise, proves to all who are at all acquainted with the theology of the Bible that he is ignorant of the doctrines of that book, and deserves himself to be instructed in the science of salvation.

I am aware that immersionists object to the idea of baptism coming in place of circumcision, from the circumstance of its not being applied to females. This objection is not valid. For, first, nature has rendered it impracticable; and, next, WOMAN, especially under the Patriarchal and Jewish dispensations, was identified with, and in every thing represented by MAN. Hence, as believers are said by St. Paul to be circumcised by the circumcision of Christ, so were women circumcised by the circumcision of man. That this was the case is evident, because none were admitted to eat the Jewish passover except the circumcised; and yet females were entitled to eat the passover, and did so.—See Exodus xii. 48.

But the passover was in the Jewish Church what the Lord's supper is among Christians.—See 1 Cor. v. 7, 8. Will any Baptist deny women the right to the Lord's supper? The Scriptures allow them the right, although there is just as little plain and direct Scripture to prove that females should now partake of the Lord's supper. But circumcision was necessary in all who partook of the passover, as baptism is now necessary in all who partake of the Lord's supper. The conclusion then is irresistible, that the right of females to the privileges of the Church under the former dispensation was secured

9*

to them by the *relation* they sustained to the male part of Abraham's descendants, who bore in their flesh the external *seal* of God's gracious covenant. Hence it is that they are now admitted to the Lord's supper, without any positive precept showing their right thereto.

One other idea, and I close this chapter. I have proven beyond the reach of cavil that *baptism* stands in lieu of *circumcision*, sealing the same blessing now that once was sealed with blood. I have also shown that *baptism*, no matter how administered, or by whom, under the Christian dispensation, is the *door* into the Church. That it is the *door* by which persons enter the Church, even Baptists admit, provided we agree to *immersion* as the mode. For their sakes, and for the sake of the argument, I will allow that *baptism by immersion* is the *door* into the Church. What a ridiculous light this admission places the Baptists of this country in before a refined and civilized world! How do they enter the Church of God? They come in *backwards*, or, if the reader please, *wrong end foremost!* They *back into the Church*, as a goat retreats from his adversary, which, if not an insult to God, is not in accordance with good-breeding. Suppose you knock at my door or ring my door-bell for entrance: I appear, open my door, and politely invite you to a seat in my parlor. You bow, but wheel about, and *back into my house:* have I not cause to feel insulted? God sends forth his ministers to invite men into his Church: they accept the invitation, and, with their consent, suffer Baptist preachers to *push them in backwards*, as though they feel that they are doing something so mean, that they are unwilling to *face up* to the act! What must the Almighty think of such an approach to his Majesty?

Now, the *Dunkers*, a denomination founded by a German in 1724, are *immersionists:* they, too, hold that baptism is the *door* into the Church, and they act consistently by plunging their subjects *faces foremost.* They are *trine immersionists*, and plunge their subjects three times, *faces foremost*, with laying on the hands and prayer—thus entering the Church of God like men conscious of rectitude of purpose, and engage in taking upon themselves obligations of which they are not ashamed! When Presbyterians, Methodists, Episcopalians, and others, baptize either infants or adults, they introduce their subjects *faces foremost!* Our Baptist brethren are almost alone in their vulgarity in *backing into the Church of God!*

CHAPTER X.

Elder Graves against the Methodist views of Baptism—John's baptism considered, both as to its nature and design, its origin and mode—John's was not the Christian baptism—He did not practice immersion—Christ's baptism considered—The design that of complying with the requirements of the law of Moses—The mode not that of immersion—Indecent exhibition of females when immersed!

On page 366 Elder Graves commences his thirtieth chapter; and with his misrepresentations of Methodism, and his ultra, not to say dogmatical views upon the subject of *Baptism*, he covers *twelve* pages. That the reader may see the drift of his arguments, which are more after the order of *bold assertions* than of *logical reasonings*, and that too much of my space may not be occupied with his slang, I will give only the heading of his chapter. This heading indicates not only what he has said in this chapter, but is an index to most of what follows, in several other chapters, upon the subject of Baptism. It is as follows:

Inconsistencies—*Admitting acknowledged sinners into the Church, and debarring for six months an acknowledged Christian from entering!—Giving baptism by force to non-believing children and unconscious infants, and refusing baptism to the professed Christian for six months!*

I will here premise that, throughout Mr. Graves's book, he mixes up the subject of Baptism with what he says about Church government, doctrines, and discipline; and John's baptism—the *mode* and *subjects* thereof; Christ's baptism—its *mode* and *subjects*, and its *design*, all come in for a share of his attention. I will notice these somewhat in detail; and, in doing so, place before the numerous readers of this work such facts and arguments, and scriptural quotations, as I desire them to read and reflect upon.

A variety of views are entertained in relation both to the *nature* and *mode* of John's baptism. Mr. Graves and his ultra Baptist associates regard it as identical with Christian baptism; while others, myself among the number, believe that John's was not the Christian baptism. It is not at all to be wondered that the advocates of exclusive immersion should take the ground that John's baptism was the Christian baptism, but it is truly unaccountable that liberal-minded men of intelligence, who have attentively perused and studied the Bible, should, in any instance, have come to such an erroneous conclusion. I have no idea that John's was the Christian baptism; and, therefore, let the *mode* have been what it may, it can have no sort of tendency to fix the evangelical mode of Christian baptism. But I intend to take the bold ground that John did not immerse, and I defy any immersionist to prove that he did. My first object, however, shall be to show that John's was not the Christian baptism. And in order to demonstrate this fact, I remark, first, that the immediate institutor of John's baptism was God the Father. Here I will again introduce copious extracts from a small work I published upon *Baptism*, in 1842, when I had access to all the best authorities extant; and although I have now had *fourteen* years for reflection, my views upon the points discussed have undergone no change:

"He that sent me to baptize, the same said unto me, Upon whom thou shalt see the Spirit descending and remaining on him, the same is he which baptizeth with the Holy Ghost."—John i. 23. Here God the Father commissioned John to administer baptism, and pointed out to him Christ, not as the *institutor*, but as a *subject* of his baptism—Christ the Son of God the Father. "Go ye, therefore, and teach all nations, baptizing them in the name of the Father, and of the Son, and of the Holy Ghost, teaching them to observe all things, whatsoever I have commanded you."—Matt. xxviii. 19, 20. Here, we say, Christ institutes a baptism, and points to his disciples, the inhabitants of "*all nations*," as his subjects. In this case Christ is the *institutor*, but not the *subject*—in the former case he was *a subject*, but not *the institutor*. Can any thing be more plain? Certainly not. How then can these two baptisms be the same? They are no more the same than are the Mosaic and Christian dispensations the same. They are no more the same than are the Old and New Testaments one and the same.

2d. John's baptism was strictly confined to the Jews, but the Christian baptism was directed to be administered to all nations. John's baptism was, to all intents and purposes, *a Jewish ordinance*. For that is a Jewish ordinance which is confined to the Jews. John's baptism was confined to the Jewish Church; therefore, it was a Jewish ordinance.

3d. John's baptism was the concluding scene of the legal dispensation, and one of those divers washings in use among the Jews, mentioned in Hebrews: "Which stood only in meats and drinks, and *divers washings*, and carnal ordinances, imposed on them (the Jews) until the time of reformation."—Heb. ix. 10.

4th. John's baptism introduced persons into the Jewish Church without any attempt to alter Jewish forms of worship; nor is there any account in the New Testament that his disciples ceased to be members of the Jewish Church, during his lifetime, on account of their baptism. They continued subject to all those ordinances; but the subjects of Christ's baptism are not subject to Jewish ordinances.

5th. John's baptism was unto repentance, and taught its subjects to believe in a Saviour *to come*, while it was without any regular form: the Christian baptism is different, and is in the name of the Father, Son, and Holy Ghost.

6th. John's baptism was not only a token of penitence, but it sealed the faith of its subjects in a Messiah to come, and to suffer for the sins of the world; but the baptism instituted by Christ could not seal such a faith without sealing a LIE, because Christ has come, suffered, and died, and entered into the place of his glory, angels and principalities being subject unto him.

7th. John's baptism commenced being administered six months before the establishment of Christianity itself, or before our Lord entered upon his public ministry! And according to the doctrine of the Baptists on this subject, Christ did not institute Christian baptism unless he instituted it before he entered upon his public ministry; which no man in his proper mind will affirm.

8th. John's baptism was distinctive in its name. It was justly called "*John's baptism.*" And this distinctive appellation is given to it, in part, to distinguish it from the báptism of Christ, or of the Holy Ghost. Why was it never called any thing in the Bible but *John's* baptism? The Bible calls things by their proper names. The baptism which Christ instituted could not be called *John's baptism*, for this would be as egregious a *nickname* as it would be to call it *Peter's baptism*, the baptism of Paul, Timothy, or Philip—as these men baptized—and so on, *ad infinitum*.

9th. John's baptism was not regarded by the apostles, and hence they rebaptized his disciples. Twelve of them were baptized over again by St. Paul, at Ephesus. See Acts xix. 1–7. These persons were Hellenist Jews, who had heard John preach in Judea twenty-six years before they were taken into the Christian Church by St. Paul. They had heard John's doctrine and embraced it, and had received his baptism; but, after returning to their own country, they heard that this evangelical dispensation of the Holy Ghost had taken place, received their first intelligence of the fact from St. Paul, and, upon a profession of their faith in Christ, were baptized into that faith. This rebaptism these persons never would have submitted to, if they had believed the dogma that John's was the Christian baptism—much less would the holy apostles have *profaned* the ordinance by rebaptizing.

10th. John's baptism could not have been the Christian baptism; for, if it were, then most unquestionably his disciples were *christianized*. If so, then the greater part of the Jewish nation were Christians at the very point of time in which Christ opened his ministry, and established Christianity! John baptized, in all, *three millions of persons*. If this mighty nation were christianized *before* Christ entered upon his ministry, they afterwards *backslid;* for it is notorious that they became the most imbittered and malignant foes of the Christian name. And our Baptist friends would be as unwilling to admit their *apostasy*, as they are to allow that John's was not the Christian baptism!

I will now proceed to speak of John's *mode* of baptism. I have regularly read the Bible through *fifteen* times during the last twenty years, and the New Testament *twenty* times, besides the commentaries, sermons, and other theological works of many distinguished divines, both in Europe and America, and, hitherto, I have been wholly unable, as I still am, to make the discovery that John practiced *immersion.* And in attempting to show that he did not immerse, I shall not extend my remarks in this chapter, as the subject will again come up under the general head of THE MODE OF CHRISTIAN BAPTISM. My argument on this point, for the time being, at least, will be rather novel than otherwise, as I propose to found it on the *population* of Palestine, the probable proportion of that population baptized by John, and the *length of time* he was employed in his public ministry. Here, again, I introduce my arguments of 1842, which, outside of my own views, are an epitome, summary, or abstract, of the views of *Hibbard* and other distinguished authors on Christian Baptism:

1. The population of the country in which John's labors were performed. Many of our readers will be surprised to learn that at the commencement of the Christian era the population of Palestine was much greater, in proportion to its extent of territory, than that of the mining districts in England, or any section of the United States. Various circumstances contributed to the formation of a dense mass of inhabitants, a few only of which are necessary to be noticed. Among these few were the religious predilection of the Jews for their own native soil, and their great aversion to the manners and customs of all other nations. Besides, their religion was national, and peculiarly their own—a circumstance which at once cut off all intercourse with other nations. These three considerations alone prevented emigration, and confined the Jews within their own narrow limits—their own territory. Hence, the Jews never thought of planting themselves on heathen soil till the disastrous results of the Assyrian and Babylonian invasions had routed them from the land of their nativity, and the graves of their fathers. Hence, also, we are not astonished to find, in the days of King David, a million and a half of "valiant men that drew the sword," exclusive of the tribes of Levi and Benjamin. And in this census was not reckoned any persons under twenty years of age, nor yet any females. Now, if we reckon five persons to every warrior—which, including the young, the aged, the infirm, and the females, to say nothing of the tribes of Levi and Benjamin, is not an extravagant estimate—we shall make the entire population of Palestine at that day to amount to SEVEN MILLIONS AND A HALF.*

Whoever, therefore, considers the foregoing reasons why the number of Jews should be so great in the days of David, their great aversion to other nations, their own love of country, their universal passion for a numerous offspring, their remaining strictly within the limits of Palestine, and the immense population of even other ancient nations, will not deem the estimate of Josephus an exaggerated one. Josephus says that *one million one hundred thousand* Jews even perished in the siege of Jerusalem, A. D. 70!

2. We are next to inquire what proportion of the vast population of Palestine attended John's ministry, and were baptized by him. On this subject a lengthy detail of arithmetical calculation is not called for. A few general facts, founded on certain express declarations of Scripture, is all that a man of sense will require; and a fool we have no disposition to contend with.

John was not commissioned to go to any sect or party, but to the

* For the correctness of this statement, see Josephus's account of the population of Palestine, A. D. 66.

entire Jewish nation resident in Palestine, to "prepare the way of the Lord." He was *unanimously* received by the Jewish nation; there being no division of sentiment in regard to him, as prevailed in reference to Christ. Even the Pharisees and Sadducees submitted to his baptism. So popular was the sentiment that John was a divine prophet, that the whole Jewish nation was ambitious of the distinction conferred by his baptism. These facts alone prove most conclusively that the greater part of the Jewish people were baptized by John. In the first chapter of Mark, and at the 5th verse, we find these remarkable words, corroborating our statement: "And there went out unto him (John) ALL THE LAND OF JUDEA, and they of Jerusalem, and were ALL baptized of him in the river of Jordan, confessing their sins." Matthew and Luke say the same thing, in substance. Josephus, the great and approved Jewish historian, confirms the same statement.

The land of Judea comprehended more than half of the entire territory of Palestine, west of the river Jordan. By "the region round about" we are to understand the great and fertile valley of the Jordan, lying between the mountains of Israel on the west, and those of Hermon, Gilead, and Abarim on the east, embracing the entire territories of Samaria, Perea, and Galilee.

Now, to make the most liberal calculation in favor of our Baptist opponents, let us suppose that John baptized but *one-half* of the entire population of Palestine—the presumption then would be that he baptized, in all, upwards of *three and a half millions* of persons. Now, mark, it was the *duty* of the Jews to submit to John's baptism. Well, there must have been *time* allowed for the process—otherwise, it was not the duty of the multitudes to submit. But a natural impossibility precluded such an act of submission, if *immersion* were the mode of baptism. The time allotted to the continuance of John's ministry —his physical strength—the manner and circumstances essentially connected with a valid administration of baptism—all, we say, taken into the account, prove most conclusively that immersion was not John's mode of baptizing.

3. The foregoing observations bring us, as a matter of course, to speak of the duration of John's public ministry The evangelist Luke informs us that John opened his ministry in the fifteenth year of the reign of Tiberius Cæsar, which, according to our most approved chronology, answers to the thirtieth year of John's life. Chronologers, with but few exceptions, agree that our Saviour was born December the 25th, A. M. 4000. John the Baptist was born the 24th of June previous, and consequently was six months older than Christ. For the scriptural evidence of these two positions, see the first and third chapters of Luke.

The last account we have of John, previously to his arrest and imprisonment, states positively that he was "baptizing at Enon near Salim." This was immediately after our Lord had attended his first Passover, which, according to the manner in which the Jews reckoned their years, *i. e.*, by lunar months, was celebrated on the 14th day of March. The inevitable conclusion, therefore, is, that John was arrested during his stay at Enon; and Christ, in view of the commotion excited in Judea by that event, and of the controversy between the *Baptists* on the one hand, and the *Christians* on the other, as to who was the greater man of the two, prudently withdrew for a season into the remoter parts of Galilee.

Thus we have briefly followed John, in his public ministry, during the space of nine months, and till, by the by, he had introduced Christ to the Jews; and having thus fulfilled the object of his mission, he retired, by a singular providence, from the field of his labor in the month of April, A. D. 27. That John continued his ministry longer than nine months, cannot be proven from the Bible, by all the Baptist preachers and writers in existence; and the utmost limit to which his labors can be extended, with any shadow of evidence, is *ten months.*

With the remarks now submitted, the whole chain of facts runs thus:

1st. John must have preached several days, or even weeks, before he began to baptize, as the people were not likely to submit to his baptism before they formed some tolerably correct acquaintance with his character and the purport of his mission.

2d. John's nine months of public labor included the winter season, and though the climate in Palestine is much milder than ours, still, those who are acquainted with the history of that climate know that the inhabitants never fail to experience storms in the winter, and severe rainy seasons, at which times there is no travelling about. These facts will require a second deduction of lost time.

3d. Forty Sabbaths of lost time, which is more than one month, are to be deducted, wherein, according to the Jewish observance of those days, it was unlawful for John to baptize. This will leave, in all, about 220 days in which we may reasonably suppose John exercised the functions of his ministry.

4th. Our estimate is, that the whole number of hours in which John was employed in the act of baptizing amounted to about *one thousand three hundred,* supposing him to have devoted six hours of each day to the work of baptizing, which is a liberal allowance. If he immersed according to the modern mode, he could not have stood it longer, for 220 days in such rapid succession. John was unsustained by miracles—made no pretensions to them—and we must calculate his labors just as we would those of a common preacher in our day, allowing him a medium ratio of bodily strength. The conclusion then is, that no mortal man—nor even a *beast*—could have stood in three feet water *six* hours in the day, for 220 days, with only an occasional rest day, caused by storms, or rain, or the intervention of a Sabbath. With these remarks we proceed to the concluding argument, and hope that we may be patiently heard.

First, John baptized, in all, just three millions of human beings. Next, the time in which John was engaged in the act of baptizing, did not exceed *one thousand and three hundred hours.* This gives him a fraction over *two thousand* to the hour, *thirty* to each minute, or *one* to every two seconds! This, then, is baptizing with too great speed. No mere human that ever lived could do this. No sort of ceremony could be said in this rapid work. No man on earth could pass along a row of mortals, and pat one on the shoulders for every two seconds, much less plunge him under water and raise him up again.

The conclusion, then, of the whole matter is, that it is *wholly impracticable* for John to have immersed the multitudes he is said to have baptized. But we are asked the question, in what way could he have baptized these multitudes, in the length of time we allow him to have been engaged in baptizing? We answer, the Jews had a mode of purifying the people by dipping a branch of hyssop* into water, and *sprinkling* it upon them. It is said of Moses, in Heb. ix. 19, that he took the blood of calves and of goats, and with hyssop sprinkled all the people. It is not reasonable to suppose that John, in purifying with water, departed from the usage of Moses. For had he introduced any new and external rite, the Jews would beyond all doubt have disputed his authority. But we have no account of such dispute. Moreover, John was not sent, as he himself confessed, to abolish the Jewish rites, but to observe them, and to give a new impetus to the Mosaic religion by urging upon the Jews the necessity of repentance and baptism.

I shall here consider Christ's baptism; and although I intend brevity, I shall assign to the baptism of our Saviour special importance. Having concluded my remarks on John's baptism, something special should be said of the baptism of Christ; and the present stage of the general argument is the appropriate place for such remarks. It cannot be charged that I am wandering from the issues made by Elder Graves, because he, and all immersionists, rely upon the baptism of our Saviour as affording unquestionable authority for their *mode*, and that, too, to the exclusion of all other modes. I quote again from my work on Baptism:—

As to the *mode* of the Saviour's baptism, the Scriptures do not say whether it was by pouring, sprinkling, or immersion; but as the great probability is that John did not immerse, we may reasonably infer that Christ was not immersed. At all events, the only information afforded in the New Testament as to the mode, is what we gather from the import of the word *baptize.* This word is derived from the Greek word *baptizo*, and more remotely from *bapto*, and properly signifies *a washing;* and the learned agree that whether the sub-

* Hyssop is an herb generally known, and often mentioned in Scripture. The hyssop commonly used in purification as a sprinkler was a sort of reed or cane, like a sponge at the end, which was imbued with the blood, etc.

stance washed, cleansed, or purified, be partially or wholly immersed in the liquid, or the liquid be *applied* to the substance, it is alike baptism. Brown says, in his Encyclopedia, that to apply the liquid or element by pouring, running, rubbing, dropping, sprinkling, or effusion, is *baptism* to all intents and purposes. But as we intend to enlarge on this topic in another place, we say no more at present.

The *character* of Christ's baptism is a question of far greater importance, and is more immediately connected with the subject-matter in dispute, than that of the *mode* can be. Our Baptist brethren have assumed that the Saviour received a *Christian* baptism. We take the negative side of this question. Hence, the whole task which devolves upon us is to disprove the correctness of their assumption. Therefore, let the end, the nature, origin, object, or design of the Saviour's baptism have been what it may, one thing is certain—*it did not partake of the nature of* CHRISTIAN *baptism.* Stick a pin down here, O ye immersionists! blow the dust of prejudice out of your eyes, and look at the *scriptural* truths which we now present.

1st. John baptized his subjects "*unto repentance*," and in testimony of the fact that they had repented. Therefore, if our Lord's baptism partook of the nature of John's, inasmuch as the latter witnessed to the repentance of the candidate, the Saviour must have previously repented of *sin!* Will any one endorse this blasphemous sentiment?

2d. But the proper import of John's baptism could not apply to the Saviour in any form. The ultimate design of John's baptism was to "prepare the way of the Lord." This was the great aim of all his labors. Was our Saviour baptized with this intent? But it is idle to extend these arguments. If a man is so stupid, or so ignorant and uninformed, as to support the hypothesis we are opposing, it is doubtless trifling with time and with reason to oppose him.

3d. But John required of the candidate for baptism, faith in a Messiah *to come.* If, therefore, Christ was baptized in the faith of John's baptism, he must have believed in a Messiah *to come,* and to this faith John must have exhorted him. Need we dwell upon the absurdity of such a doctrine? Certainly not.

4th. The baptism of the Saviour, known as the *Christian baptism,* was not instituted till after the resurrection of our Saviour. See Matt. xxviii. 18, 19. See also other parallel passages, which show that the Christian baptism was never administered until the day of Pentecost. The conclusion, then, is inevitable, that if Christ received Christian baptism at the hands of John, it was three years before the actual institution of that ordinance, which is as blasphemous as it is absurd.

5th. Christian baptism, to be such, must be performed in the name of "the Father, and of the Son, and of the Holy Ghost." But is there not an inconceivable absurdity in the idea of Christ's being baptized in his *own name,* and as an evidence of his devotedness to *his own cause and person?* Yet this we must believe, if we suppose that Christ received Christian baptism at the hands of John.

THE DESIGN OF CHRIST'S BAPTISM.

Having shown that the baptism of our Saviour did not partake of the nature of John's baptism, it devolves upon us to show what was the real design of Christ's baptism, and wherein lay the necessity of his being baptized at all.

The Baptists allege that our Saviour was baptized in order to furnish his followers an *example*. At the same time, they allege that he was baptized by *immersion*. Hence, they exhort all to go forth and be plunged, thus following the example of Christ! The effect which this mode of reasoning has upon many minds is truly powerful, although it is founded in falsehood. In the whole range of the controversy between immersionists on the one hand, and Pedobaptists on the other, the former have never wielded a more successful argument (*ad captandum vulgus*) than this appeal to the example of Christ. But we demand the proof of this assumption. Is it to be found in the Bible? No. But is it deducible from the Bible by any correct rules of criticism? By no means. Where then is the proof? There is *no* proof of such doctrine, save in the *fruitful imaginations* of Baptists.

On the other hand, that our Saviour was *not* baptized with a view to furnish his followers an example, may be deduced from the sacred text by the strictest rules of criticism.

1. The example would be essentially defective in one of its most prominent features. Christ was thirty years old when he was baptized. Our Baptist friends, therefore, should put off baptism till they are of this age. But would this be walking in the commandments of God, blameless? We should think not. Then, if Christ set this example of *procrastination*, he set a bad example. But Luke says, chapter iii. verse 21, that "all the people were baptized" before Christ submitted to the ordinance. Why did he wait till all the people went before? Why did he not lead the way?

2. The example, if it be such, is unreasonable, because partial. If Christ submitted to Christian baptism for the sake of furnishing an example, he ought to have done the same thing in the case of the *Lord's Supper*. Example was as loudly called for in one case as in the other. But when he handed the cup to his disciples, he said, "*Drink* YE *all of it*," etc.

3. But does the Bible furnish us with any reason why baptism was necessary in the case of the Saviour? Yes, Christ himself gives the true reason in the following words, in reply to John's scruples—"for thus it becometh us to fulfil all righteousness." This answer, let its real import be what it may, perfectly satisfied John of the propriety of baptizing Christ; and all the reason that ever subsisted, rendering the baptism of Christ necessary, is couched in the above words of the Saviour. The only point to be established, therefore, is the real import of the phrase, "*to fulfil all righteousness.*" Well, the import of the phrase may be rendered thus, and then we have its real meaning: "For thus it becometh us to FULFIL EVERY INSTITUTION of the law of Moses, so as finally to answer its typical intention, and not

arbitrarily *to dissolve all obligations to its observance*, before it has thus received its accomplishment in me."

Then, Christ's obligation to baptism grew out of his assumed relation to the law as our *Vicar*, it being a function of his priestly character to accomplish the intent of the Mosaic ritual. But what law was there in vogue which required the Saviour to be baptized? We answer, it was the law enjoining and regulating priestly consecration, as will be seen by examining the code of Moses, recorded in Exodus xxix. and Levit. viii.; and that our Saviour's baptism was a priestly consecration, is corroborated by all the accompanying circumstances recorded in the New Testament. And when Christ exercised the office of a priest in purging the temple, and when the chief priests and elders demanded of him, on that occasion, by what authority he did these things, he appealed to John's baptism in vindication of the authority he exercised. See Matt. xxi. 12–27.

Enough has now been said to rescue the baptism of Christ from the erroneous construction of immersionists. If our remarks are founded in reason and Scripture, they cannot be set aside; if not, the advocates of immersion will overthrow them.

Certain it is that Christ, if he intended persons should be immersed, never intended *females* should submit to the ordinance in that public way, and after that notoriously vulgar fashion of the Baptist denomination, at their baptisms outside of large cities, where they have pools and preparations for changing their garments. The usual custom throughout the South and West is to bandage the forehead of a delicate and beautiful female, and tie a handkerchief round her waist, as a sort of *handle* for an awkward Baptist preacher to fasten upon; and thus she is led into the water, step by step, in the presence of a mixed multitude, who are making their vulgar remarks and criticising her steps as she *fights down her clothes*, which rise to the top of the water, and float round her delicate and exposed limbs! She is taken by the preacher, who fastens one hand in her *belt*, and the other on the back of her head; and after planting his big feet firm upon the bottom of the stream, and *squaring himself* as though he were about to knock a beef in the head, he plunges her into the water! If, in her struggle to guard against *strangling*, her forehead or face should not go under, he takes his hand full of water, and wets the parts, as though such wetting were essential to her salvation! Take, for instance, the following extract from a leading editorial in the "Baptist Banner and Pioneer," of February 24, 1842—a mammoth sheet, edited by *five Baptist preachers:*

> We regard nothing as gospel baptism but the immersion in water of a believer, in the name of the Father, Son, and Holy Ghost.
>
> How frequently do Baptist ministers, if but a hand or a part of the subject be uncovered in the water, immerse again. And whoever thought that this was *Anabaptism.* And yet, we risk nothing in saying that it is as decidedly re-baptism, as it would be to reïmmerse an individual who had been immersed by a Pedobaptist minister, [a Methodist, Presbyterian, etc.,] OR ANY OTHER UNAUTHORIZED ADMINISTRATOR!

On different occasions I have witnessed these indecent personal exhibitions, of respectable females coming out of the water with their thin garments sticking close to their skin, and exhibiting their *muscles* and *make* in so revolting a manner, that ladies present have felt constrained to surround them, so as to hide their persons from the gaze of the vulgar throng. I witnessed this disgusting sight several times in the spring of 1842, at the edge of Green's Mill-pond, in Jonesborough.

CHAPTER XI.

The Sacraments of Baptism and the Supper not duly administered by Methodists—The Methodist not a Christian or Gospel Church—Ought not so to be recognized by Baptists—Methodists baptize infants and unbelievers—Two dreams by two preachers—Seekers and infants entitled to baptism, as shown from Scripture and reason.

On page 445 of the "Wheel," Elder Graves thus rebukes Methodist preachers for administering the Lord's supper to seekers, and baptism to the same class:—

But who will say that the sacrament of baptism is duly administered, when administered according to the teachings of your Discipline, explained by Mr. Wesley, and the standard works published by your Book Concern? And what intelligent Christian man will say that the Supper is duly administered in your Church, when it is administered to *unregenerated* and *unbaptized seekers?*

I repeat what I have before said, that, according to the above article, your societies are *not visible churches of Christ, and ought not to be so recognized.*

On page 435, he concludes a bitter harangue upon baptism in these remarkable words:—

In consideration of these teachings, can Baptists, with any kind of reason, be called upon to recognize the Methodist Episcopal Society *as a Christian or Gospel Church?* Is it a congregation of believers, according to the definition of the Discipline, in which the word of God is faithfully preached, and the ordinances duly administered?

If the practice of Methodists is not always according to the Discipline, it is only because the preachers and members violate their solemn oaths and promises to observe it in "every point, great and small;" and who can tell what it would be were it not for the *counteracting influence of Baptist doctrines and practice in this country?*

What rigid sectarian proscription characterizes the course of Baptists generally, in all the South and West! I am here reminded of two *dreams* by two preachers, the one a Baptist, the other a Methodist. They had been holding a protracted meeting together, which lasted for days, and which resulted in the conversion of a number of souls to God. The two preachers now agreed to open the doors of their respective churches, and gather in the fruits of their labors. It was agreed that the Baptist brother should lead the way. He stated to the audience generally, and to the young converts in particular, that he had had a remarkable dream, in which he had died and gone to hell! His Satanic Majesty received him very politely, and proposed to escort him through all the apartments of the infernal regions before assigning to him his position. He travelled extensively through the dark dominions, and met with quite a number of Methodists, Episcopalians, Presbyterians, and Catholics, but did not see one Baptist in all the infernal regions—their compliance with the ordinance of *baptism* having carried them all safe to God's habitation!

The Methodist minister followed. He too had dreamed a remarkable but similar dream! He had died and gone to hell, as he stated to the audience; and, like his Baptist brother, the Devil had conducted him through all his dark dominions. He saw "lots and squares" of Methodists, Presbyterians, Episcopalians, and Catholics, but not a single Baptist. He inquired of the Devil, with anxious solicitude, if there were no Baptists there? His Satanic Majesty seized him by the arm, turned him suddenly around, and said, "Come out here!" The Devil raised a large trap-door and pointed to a multitude, grappling in "a lower deep," and exclaimed, "These, sir, are all Baptists holding *close communion!*" The result was, that two to one of the new converts joined the Methodists, as they did not wish to share the fate of the *close communionists!*

I have premised thus much, with a view to enlist the reader's attention while I demonstrate that *believers* are not the only proper subjects of Christian baptism—that all other denominations beside Baptists are not *Antichristian*—and last, but not least, while I give Christian examples of baptizing unconverted adults, and show that they are proper subjects of Christian baptism. I again quote from my book on Baptism:—

Who are proper subjects of Christian baptism? The proper answer to this question is one of great importance to the Christian Church; for, if the sentiments of the Baptists be correct, the visible Church of Christ on earth is reduced to a mere handful of professing Christians—a mere "corporal's guard," as is sometimes said of a certain political clique at Washington. The true point at issue, therefore, is this: Is the Baptist Church, so called, the only visible Church of Christ on earth, as alleged by Mr. Howell, [Graves, and others of their "faith and order;"] or do other professing Christians, of other denominations, belong to the visible body of Christ? If none are proper subjects of Christian baptism except BELIEVING ADULTS, then the Baptist Church is the only Church of Christ on earth, and all the rest are Churches of *Antichrist;* inasmuch as the majority of all the members of all other denominations ARE BAPTIZED IN THEIR INFANCY. This is a horrid conclusion, we allow; but desperate as it is, it is unavoidable, provided the premises of the Baptists, from which it is drawn, be correct. Let us, then, throw the Baptist argument into a syllogistic form. The Church of Christ, say they, is composed of baptized believers only, immersed by regular Baptist preachers. No mode is baptism but immersion, and none are baptized but such as are members of the Church of Christ on earth—such as have been immersed, by regular Baptist preachers, after they became believers. This is the argument. And if this conclusion be correct, it will follow that none are Churches of Christ but those whose members were immersed AFTER they became believers, upon a profession of their faith, and that, too, by Baptist preachers. But a large majority of the professing world are Methodists, Lutherans, Presbyterians, and members of the Church of England, and were baptized before they were capable of making any profession of their faith, and that, too, by sprinkling; therefore the Methodists, Lutherans, Presbyterians, and Episcopalians, are not members of the Church of Christ. This conclusion is inevitable likewise. And this is just what the Baptists contend for. For, says Mr. Howell, on page 275 of his notorious book:

We are not *Protestants*, nor Dissenters, Lutherans, Calvinists, Arminians, nor *Reformers*, but what we *have been in all ages*, *THE CHURCH OF OUR LORD JESUS CHRIST!!*

With these declarations before us, and under this view of the subject, to contend for the validity of infant baptism, as Methodists, is to contend for our existence as a Church of Christ; and not for ours only, but also for that of all other Churches except the Baptists. A principle, then, which involves such important conclusions should be supported by the most indubitable evidence—by evidence far more indubitable than the Baptists are able to bring forward. And whether the sentiments of the Baptists on this subject be thus supported or not, the reader will see before we have done with this question.

The Methodists baptize three classes of persons, to wit: *converted* believers, *unconverted* believers, and *infants.* And for doing this they have Christian examples and scriptural commands. That believers in Christ, not previously baptized, are proper subjects of Christian baptism, is not denied by any one. On this point, therefore, there can be no controversy. And by a *believer* we understand the Baptists, and all others on this subject, to mean one who is a believer in the full sense of the word; that is to say, one who is justified freely, and renewed by the grace of God. That such believers are proper subjects of baptism is not doubted. But that these are the only proper *adult* subjects of Christian baptism is explicitly denied.

In proof of this position just assumed, let us consider a few of the cases recorded in the New Testament, which go to prove, most conclusively, that baptism was received without the justification or regeneration of the subject at the time of its administration. The first case of this description is the well-known case of the Samaritans, as recorded in the 8th chapter of the Acts of the Apostles. In this chapter we have an account of a mission of Philip to Samaria, a city of whose inhabitants it is said, "And the people with one accord gave heed unto those things which Philip preached, hearing and seeing the miracles which he did." The sorcery of Simon, and its effects upon the people of that place, having been introduced by the evangelist, he thus continues the account of the Samaritans: "But when they believed Philip, preaching the things concerning the kingdom of God, and the name of Jesus Christ, they were baptized, both men and women." We have here, in a very concise manner, the religious character and history of the Samaritans, up to the time of their baptism. They had been aliens from the true God, and outcasts from Israel; as such, Philip preached to them; under his ministry they were convinced of the truth and divinity of Christianity; and upon a faith which *assented* to the truths which he advanced they were baptized. Let any one interested turn to the history, and it will be seen that not one word is said about the remission of sins, or about these Samaritans having received the gift of the Holy Ghost. The nearest they approached to a Christian character was, they were *baptized penitents*, who exercised honestly and conscientiously what theologians call a historical faith. It is not said in the inspired word that they believed *in* Christ, or *on* Christ Jesus, to the saving of their souls; but it is simply, though distinctly stated, that "They believed the things *concerning* the name of Jesus. This view of the case is fully sustained by the following statements, found in this same chapter, and at the 14th including the 16th verse:

> Now, when the apostles which were at Jerusalem heard that Samaria had received the word of God, they sent unto them Peter and John, who, when they were come down, prayed for them that they might receive the Holy Ghost, (*for as yet he had fallen on none of them;* only they were baptized in the name of the Lord Jesus.) Then laid they their hands on them, and they received the Holy Ghost.

A clearer case than the foregoing, of persons receiving Christian baptism without regeneration, or without an "experience of grace," as the Baptists term it, could not be presented. It speaks its own language. It proves that genuine penitents are as proper subjects of this ordinance as are justified believers.

But if further proof were wanting to establish this point, we mean that a person who has not the faith of a justified child of God may nevertheless be a proper subject of Christian baptism, we have it in the case of Simon Magus. Speaking of this case, the inspired historian says: "Then Simon himself *believed also;* and when he was baptized, he continued with Philip, and *wondered.*"—Acts viii. 13. Here it is expressly said Simon believed and was baptized. And yet, Peter said to him after this: "Thou hast neither part nor lot in this matter; for thy *heart* is not right in the sight of God." And again, "Thou art in the gall of bitterness, and in the bond of iniquity." Therefore, that Simon was neither a justified believer nor a true penitent is certain. What, then, was his state? Either he never was converted, or he had fallen from grace. We leave the Baptists to determine this question for themselves. To say that he never had that degree and kind of faith which would entitle him to Christian baptism, or render him a proper subject of it, would be to censure the administrator Philip, and flatly to contradict the testimony of the *inspired historian*, who says—not that Simon *professed* to believe, but that *he did believe*, and was baptized. What, then, was Simon's true state? Why, he believed in the Lord Jesus Christ as the true Messiah, and had some *undefined* desires to be saved through his grace, while he was destitute of the faith of a Christian believer. And yet, Simon was a proper subject of Christian baptism, or Philip, the *inspired* administrator, was guilty of profaning the ordinance. From the foregoing considerations, we consider that a person may be a proper subject of Christian baptism who has never obtained the forgiveness of his sins, or rather the regenerating grace of God. And by a proper subject of Christian baptism, we mean one who is not to be *rebaptized.*

INFANT CHILDREN PROPER SUBJECTS OF CHRISTIAN BAPTISM.

That the infant children of baptized parents are as proper subjects of Christian baptism as are adult believers, is maintained by Methodists, Presbyterians, Lutherans, Episcopalians, and others, but denied by Baptists. Here, therefore, these denominations and the Baptists are plainly at issue. Let us, then, hear the grounds on which "the *only* Church of our Lord Jesus Christ" rests its objections to the baptism of infants.

1st. They (the Baptists) object that there is no explicit warrant for baptizing infants in the New Testament—there is no "Thus saith the Lord," authorizing the baptism of infants; and hence they conclude that infants should not be baptized. That there is no such explicit warrant for the baptism of infants, we have the candor freely to acknowledge. But an explicit warrant is altogether unnecessary, when the right of infants to Christian baptism can be proved by other legitimate scriptural evidence. Those who complain that we have no "Thus saith the Lord" for baptizing infants, in effect dictate to the infinitely wise God in what manner he shall reveal his will to us. Our duty is humbly, thankfully, and reverently to receive his revelation as he has been pleased to communicate it to the world. The Baptists, therefore, should not say there is no explicit warrant for infant baptism, and that in consequence thereof they should not be baptized. But if they object at all, they should take the ground, that there is no SCRIPTURAL AUTHORITY for infant baptism, and therefore they should not be baptized. But they will not take this ground, because they know that those denominations who practice infant baptism can easily make the contrary appear. As it is, we have to consider the objection which is founded on the want of a "Thus saith the Lord." But it is wholly unnecessary to spend time in refuting this objection, as the Baptists themselves do not believe a "Thus saith the Lord" necessary in a perfectly parallel case—we mean that of female communion. The sacrament of the Lord's Supper and the ordinance of baptism rest on the same authority, and are of equal dignity, importance, and obligation. If, then, a "Thus saith the Lord" be necessary to determine the proper subjects of Christian baptism, the same explicit warrant is equally necessary to determine the proper subjects of the Lord's Supper. This conclusion cannot be avoided. Why, then, do the Baptists admit women to the Lord's table? Perhaps they may take the ground that *theirs* is not the *Lord's* table, but an *exclusive feast*, which amounts to a *Baptist table!* This, indeed, is the only score on which we can excuse them for administering the sacrament to females, seeing that there is no explicit warrant for such an act. Recollect, we take the bold stand, that there is not a solitary passage in the Bible which teaches either that females *should* or that they *did* communicate.

2d. But it is objected, that none are to be baptized until they believe; and that infants are incapable of believing, and therefore must not be baptized. This objection proves entirely too much, for the purpose of a Baptist, for if it prove that infants ought not to be baptized, it equally proves that none who die in infancy can be saved. Hear the text relied upon: "He that believeth and is baptized shall be saved: but he that believeth not shall be damned." The Baptists hold that faith is required of all as a prerequisite to baptism: that infants are incapable of faith; and, therefore, they ought not to be baptized. They must also maintain that faith is required of all as a prerequisite to salvation; that infants are incapable of faith; and therefore infants cannot be saved, but must be damned. For faith is made in this text as necessary to salvation as to baptism. If, therefore, infants are excluded from baptism by this text, they are by it equally excluded from heaven. This is a horrible conclusion indeed! And yet it is as legitimately drawn from the text, as that infants are not to be baptized because they cannot believe. For our own part, we believe most firmly that all who die in infancy are saved. And if they are saved in heaven, their salvation, though of grace, must be without faith. But the Baptists, for aught we know, may believe that infants are incapable of being made holy even by Divine influence, or of being saved. And in order *consistently* to reject infants, this should be their faith. Because if infants may be saved without faith, they may be baptized without faith, for any thing that is said in the foregoing text, or any other passage in the Bible, to the contrary. The conclusion of the whole matter, then, is, that the argument contained in the objection we have been considering is a perfect sophism.

3d. Having given the sum of the arguments of the Baptists against infant baptism: having shown, too, that they do not disprove it, we would, in this connection, attend to the arguments on the other side of this question, but for having anticipated them in the preceding pages. Let the reader turn to page 147, where we have considered the covenant entered into with Abraham, the subject of circumcision, etc., and it will be there seen that we have shown most conclusively that it is scriptural and right to baptize infants. And for further scriptural authority for baptizing infants, as well as the fathers favoring the baptism of infants, we refer the reader to two chapters of this work, commencing the first on page 42, and the other on page 46.

4th A few brief remarks just here, touching the relation which baptized infants sustain to those Churches within whose pales they receive baptism, and we have done with this branch of the subject. In the first part of this work we took occasion to state that "Elder Cate," of the Baptist Church, at a protracted meeting in this town, in December last, gave as one reason why his denomination would not commune with certain other denominations, that they "received infants into their Churches and made them *intellectual* members." We then rose up, and on behalf of the Methodists and Presbyterians denied the truth of what the gentleman had said, provided he alluded to either or both of these denominations. The result was, that he denied having any allusion to either, although every candid man in the congregation believed he alluded to them, and to no other people. The substance of what we then said is herewith repeated:

Baptism, administered by a proper person, and in the name of the holy Trinity, introduces a person into the catholic Church of Christ. But baptism *alone* does not constitute him a member of any particular Church. To become a member of the Methodist Church, or of the Presbyterian Church, something more is required besides being baptized. Therefore, when an infant is baptized he is introduced by baptism into the Church of Christ—he is not thereby constituted a member of any particular branch of Christ's Church; and if the baptism be performed by a Methodist or Presbyterian minister, he does not baptize him by virtue of his being a Methodist or Presbyterian minister, *but by virtue of his office as a minister of Christ.*

CHAPTER XII.

Elder Graves's position, no baptism without going into the water —Criticism on the word *baptizo*—Greek particles considered—Figurative language considered—The scriptural argument for immersion —The river Jordan a bold and dashing stream—Testimony of Stevens and Brown—Immersion utterly impracticable in such a stream!

ELDER GRAVES quotes Mr. Wesley's approval of the Catechism of the Church of England, explaining the meaning of the sacrament of Baptism, and then adds, on page 437:

> All this is sound doctrine. I most heartily accept of this definition of the sacrament of baptism, even to its *action;* for it evidently teaches that the subject must be *put into* the water. It reads: "Water, *wherein* the person is to be baptized." But if this definition be correct, *is the baptism of an infant a sacrament?*—and if not, *is it baptism at all, in any sense?*

I make the above extract my *text*, and the foundation for such criticisms on the word *baptizo*, and of Greek *particles*, as may come up in this chapter. And here, again, I fall back upon my arguments of 1842, as applicable to the present controversy, and fair and legitimate answers to all Mr. Graves has said upon the subject of baptism:

> Much that categorically belongs to this chapter will hereafter be brought forward in the course of the general argument on the mode of baptism. This will become necessary to the complete development of that subject, and we shall not anticipate our remarks and arguments in this place. As derivative words branch off from their roots, they lose much of their primitive force, and assume new shades of meaning. Hence, whenever we would attain an accurate knowledge of the meaning of derivative words, we trace their "*pedigree;*" and, as we follow them back to the parent word, we find their sense more restricted and definite. It is lawful, therefore, to presume, antece-

dently to all investigation, that, in the case under consideration, *baptizo* may lose some of the force and restrictedness of meaning that belongs to its primitive *bapto.*

We are now entering upon an important point of this controversy —a point upon which the whole must hang; and, therefore, we beg the reader's patient attention to a candid consideration of what we are about to say. Every thing depends upon correct and intelligent views of the subject now under consideration; and we need scarcely advertise the reader that, if he start with wrong notions or form wrong premises, he never can expect to arrive at a safe conclusion. Many—from mistaken notions of the proper point of inquiry here, and of the proper field of argumentation—have undertaken to show what is the primary meaning of the original word, and have gone to the classic Greek for arguments and illustrations in support of their views. From these sources they have argued the point, setting forth the New Testament meaning of the word, and its proper use in a religious sense. But they might as well have applied to Homer and Aristotle to sustain and uphold the doctrines of the great apostle to the Gentiles.

The real issue, and the only question here to be settled, is: *What is the meaning of the term* BAPTIZO, *in the New Testament, when used in a religious, or ritual sense?* The proper answer to this anxious interrogatory must for ever put this controversy at rest with candid and intelligent minds. Scripture *usage* must be the criterion for judging of Scripture *terms.*

Before we proceed further, then, we must be permitted to apprise the reader of the difference between *classic Greek* on the one hand, and *Hebraistic Greek* on the other. Classic Greek is the writings of those Greek authors who were educated in the philosophy and doctrines of heathenism; and Hebraistic Greek is to be found in those books written by Jews who had been educated in the doctrines of the Bible: though they spoke in the Greek language, yet they *thought* as Jews or Christians. Homer and Aristotle would naturally express only the *ideas* of heathens, in Greek *words;* but the apostles, or St. John and St. Paul, when called upon to write in that language, would as naturally express in Greek the ideas peculiar to Jews converted to Christianity. Hebraistic Greek is, therefore, nothing more nor less than Hebrew *ideas* expressed in Greek *words.* And where converted Hebrews have written the history and doctrines of Christ in the Greek language, it is evident that their words have not, at all times, been used in strict accordance with the classic Greek, as defined by us in the preceding remarks. Not only so, but many Greek words have been entirely changed in their meaning by being transformed from a native Greek to a Hebrew, and then to a Christian. Indeed, the doctrines of Christianity could never have been expressed in Greek, as they have been, *without altering the meaning of many words.* The reason of this is obvious. The Greeks never had any conception of many of the doctrines of Christianity, and, consequently, they had no words in their language primarily adapted to express them, pliant as was their language. These statements will not be denied by any man, unless his ignorance and party spirit outweigh all appreciation of truth and justice, as is unfortunately the case with too many men in the Baptist Church, called *preachers.*

Furthermore, we wish to premise that whatever the meaning of *baptizo* may be, when used in a ritual sense in the New Testament, in any one place, it must be uniform in its meaning throughout, in all similar connections. If it describe an external act, or the manner of performing an external rite, in one place, then also must it have the same restricted sense in all other places. But if it have a *generic* sense, (comprehending a genus,) if it signify the *effect* of some outward mode of using water, as, for instance, *purify* or *cleanse,* then also must it be uniform in this sense, in all similar places. If it mean to *sprinkle,* it cannot mean to *immerse,* and *vice versâ.* And if it mean either sprinkle or immerse, pour or plunge, it cannot mean *purify,* and *vice versâ.*

Baptism, to proceed, is a word whose meaning, or rather usage in the sacred writings, has given rise to a vast amount of disputation. The word baptism is derived from the Greek words *baptisma* and *baptizo,* and more remotely from *bapto,* and properly signifies A WASHING, whether the substance washed be *immersed* in the liquid, or the liquid be *applied* to the substance by running, pouring, rubbing, dropping, or sprinkling. So there were "divers washings" or baptisms enjoined under the former dispensation, (Heb. ix. 10,) some of which were performed by immersion, others by bathing, but more by affusion. The apostle having there mentioned these "divers *baptisms,*" goes on, in the following verses of the same chapter, to speak expressly of "divers *sprinklings,*" which shows satisfactorily that they were included.

This, then, is the primary meaning of the terms *baptisma* and *baptizo,* as used in the wide range of classic and Hebrew Greek; nor will any man, not grossly ignorant and uninformed, dispute the correctness of our views. But we are to show, not what are the "divers" meanings of these terms, in the wide range alluded to, nor yet what is their general use in Scripture, but *what is their meaning when used in a ritual sense in the New Testament;* and we take the ground that they mean, in all such connections, to *purify* or *cleanse,* without any allusion whatever to the *mode* of cleansing.

But suppose we understand the Greek word *baptizo* as the Baptists do, in the sense of IMMERSE, and take the ground that the Saviour used it thus, and that, therefore, the command to BAPTIZE is a command to IMMERSE. This is the point contended for by the regular Baptists. But is this satisfactory? Is it definite? Is it at all intelligible? But suppose the Saviour had commanded the disciples simply to IMMERSE, that is, to put the converts *under* water: would the command have had any definite meaning whatever? As immersion is performed for various purposes, why should they immerse the converts? The word immerse would never give a clue to the solution of this question. History might determine it, but philology never could.

But suppose we understand the word BAPTIZO in the sense of PURIFY, and that our Saviour said to the disciples: "Go teach all nations, PURIFYING them in the name of the Father, and of the Son, and of the Holy Ghost." This would make the sense complete, and BAPTIZO would then denote the grand INTENTION, or ceremonial use of water. This is, indeed, so plain a case, that we cannot think it will be misunderstood by any, nor need we dwell longer thereon. Thus, then, we rest the philological argument from the import of the word BAPTIZO. Our aim has been to simplify the subject, so as to bring it within the comprehension of all classes of readers. And if the reader has attended to what we have said, he, we apprehend, will agree with us that BAPTIZO, when used in connection with the subject of Christian baptism, in the New Testament, may be translated by PURIFY, *consecrate*, or even *wash;* that it is a *generic* term, in all such instances, signifying the *effect* of the ceremonial use of water, without any allusion to or stress put upon the *mode.*

GREEK PARTICLES CONSIDERED.

In the preceding chapter the reader has found nothing to justify the vain-confidence with which Baptists have asserted that *baptizo* necessarily signifies to *immerse;* but from the evidence arising from the word itself, it has been clearly shown, we think, that its true import is against this Baptist hypothesis. In this chapter we propose briefly to notice the Greek *prepositions* employed in connection with the history of baptism, in the New Testament. They are—*in, at, by, from,* etc., etc. The frequent interchange of these particles, the various senses in which they are used, together with the rareness of their occurrence in connection with water baptism, all and singular concur to render their testimony dubious to the cause of exclusive immersionists; so that we should deem it altogether unworthy of any formal notice, had it not assumed an importance in the estimation of some who, from ignorance or want of investigation, seem not to have appreciated its real merits. It is not, however, our purpose to treat of the prepositions at large; and, in order to the greater perspicuity, we shall treat them separately.

1st. *In.*—The first sense we shall notice as belonging to this preposition, where it stands connected with baptism, renders it synonymous with our English preposition AT. Thus—as our common English version of the Bible has it—the people were baptized by John "*in* Jordan." It is well known that the Baptists claim this passage in their favor, alleging that if John stood *in* the waters of Jordan when he baptized, it could only have been for the purpose of IMMERSION. But in this they assume the very point to be proved, and assume it, too, *against* proof. If John stood *in* the water—and we will not say that he did not—still, it is wholly gratuitous to assert that, therefore, he *immersed.* As well might we maintain that because it is said a man is *in* America, or *in* Tennessee, the preposition certainly imports that he is *under the soil of America,* or *under the soil of Tennessee.* In translating *in* AT, as above, we do not intend to deny that John ever stood *in* Jordan, when he baptized. We allow that he may sometimes have stood *in* the water, sometimes *out* of the water, and sometimes *at* the water's brink, when he performed the ceremony. Our only object is to show—which is the fact—that the force of the preposition has nothing to do with the *mode* of baptism. This will appear still more evident from the following facts: Mark says John baptized "*in the desert;*" Luke says he came preaching repentance, and baptizing in all the "*country* ROUND ABOUT Jordan;" while John himself declared that he preached and baptized "BEYOND Jordan *in* Bethabara," and also "*in* Enon." What, then, becomes of the force of the preposition *in?* What connection has it with the doctrine of immersion? Now the whole story is, when told, that the evangelists merely intended to say that John stood AT, or *in the vicinity of* Jordan, Bethabara, Enon, etc., when he baptized. Again: "On whom the tower AT (instead of *in*) Siloam fell." And Matthew says: "Thou shalt love the Lord *with* all thy heart"—not *in* all thy heart! Once more: "I indeed baptize WITH water"—not *in* water. In the book of Acts it is said: "But ye shall be baptized BY the Holy Ghost," and again, "WITH the Holy Ghost." And Luke says: "The Holy Ghost SAT UPON the apostles;" although the Baptists would have us believe that the apostles were *immersed in* the Holy Ghost!

2d. *Into, out of, from.*—We have placed these prepositions together, because it will not be convenient to treat of them separately. It is said in Mark i. 9: "Jesus was baptized by John *into* the Jordan," as it is properly rendered, though the same thing is not said anywhere else in the New Testament. Now this is a plain case of the interchange of Greek particles, where *into* is put for *in* or *at.* See Matt. iii. 6, and Mark i. 5, where the preposition *in* is used, not with reference to the *mode*, but to the *means* of baptism. The second and last place where *into* is used in connection with baptism, in a way to affect the question under examination, is found in Acts viii. 38: "And they went down both *into* the water, both Philip and the eunuch," etc. But wherein lies the stress of this passage favoring immersion? Certainly not in the circumstance of their going "*into* the water," for that is affirmed of "*both*" of them. Will the Baptists contend that Philip was baptized likewise? If he was, *who* baptized him? Did he do it *himself*, or did the eunuch baptize him, after the fashion that WILLIAMS did HOLLIMAN "and the other ten?" In Acts xxvi. 13, it is said, speaking of Saul and his company, "And when we were all fallen *to* the earth," not *into* the earth. In John xi. 38, it is said of the tomb of Lazarus, "Jesus therefore cometh *to* the tomb," not *into* the tomb. Again: "Then cometh Simon Peter, following him, and went *into* the sepulchre." As to the preposition *into*, it oftentimes stands in contrast with *from*, instead of *out of.* Instance the following passages: "*from* city *to* city"—"*from* Jerusalem *to* Jericho"—"the way that goeth down *from* Jerusalem *to* Gaza," etc.

We have already observed that both Matthew and Mark use *from* instead of *out of*, when they describe the act of our Saviour in leaving the water after baptism. They simply say he came *from* the water, and not *out of* the water.

In concluding our remarks under this head, we have a passing remark or so to make touching the *body of water* in which the eunuch was baptized. The account says, "They came *to* SOME *water*." But what is *some* water? How much is *some?* The pronoun (*some, any*) sometimes has a diminutive sense—it sometimes means *a little;* and who will say this is not its meaning here? The eunuch exclaimed with evident astonishment when he discovered the water, *Behold water!* He does not say, behold the *quantity*, but was surprised to find *any* water in *such* a place. Indeed, he knew the country, and knew it was in that vicinity—in the Valley of Gerar, where, as every man of information knows, the city of Gaza stood—where Abraham and Isaac were obliged to dig wells to procure water for their flocks. It was here, too, that "the herdmen of Gerar did strive with Isaac's herdmen, saying, *The water is ours.*" Would different parties have contended fiercely for water, if it had been abundant as the Baptists say it was in the valley? Would Abraham and Isaac have incurred the expense and delay of digging wells, if there had been rivers or creeks in the vicinity large enough to immerse a man in, after the manner of the Baptists? Certainly not. Whence, then, has arisen all this fancied abundance of water sufficient for an immersion, where herdmen would quarrel and fight for a "*well*" out of which to water their flocks? Reason and presumption are against it, else might it have been said:

> But, children, you should never let
> Such angry passions rise;
> Your clumsy fists were never made
> To gouge each other's eyes.

FIGURATIVE LANGUAGE CONSIDERED.

The branch of the general argument which we now propose to notice very briefly, is one of much more importance than may be supposed. Men of intelligence and candor will not doubt the correctness of this position. There is no controversy as to whether baptism be *emblematical;* nor is there any dispute, to our knowledge, in regard to the fact that outward baptism is an emblem of inward purity. And all agree, except perhaps the Baptists and Catholics, that baptism with water derives its entire efficacy from its emblematical character, while none others deny that it also signifies *purity of heart.*

If we scan the figurative language of the Bible, we shall find that two distinct ideas are comprehended under the general ceremonial use of water; namely, REGENERATION and PURIFICATION of heart. The one is founded on the *resuscitating*, and the other on the *purifying* qualities of water. These facts, then, clearly show the necessity of *divers forms of administration of the consecrating element*, in order to create the foundation and *similitude* on which the very notion of an *emblem* is founded. On this point, DR. DICK, in the second volume, and at the 377th page of his Theology, beautifully and justly remarks: "It is by no means probable that God would speak of his own operations in *one way*, and symbolically represent them in a *different way:* that he should promise to *sprinkle* or *pour out* his Spirit *upon* us, and, to confirm this promise, would command us to be *plunged* into water!"

It now only remains for us to inquire into the ancient Jewish import of the ceremonial use of water. The whole history of this use of water among the Jews speaks but one language. We shall content ourselves, however, with a few passages, and leave the reader to extend the line of citations *ad libitum*, and so on *ad infinitum.*

In the Psalms, we hear David pray, "*Wash* me thoroughly *from mine iniquity*, and *cleanse* me from my sin." Again: "*Purge* me with hyssop, and I shall be CLEAN: *wash* me, and I shall be *whiter than snow.*"

The Prophet Isaiah says, "*Wash* you and make you CLEAN: put away the *evil* of your doing." Again: "O Jerusalem! *wash* thy heart *from* WICKEDNESS." And in the forty-fourth chapter of Isaiah, it is observed, "I will POUR WATER upon him that is thirsty, and floods upon the dry ground: I will POUR MY SPIRIT upon thy seed, and my blessing upon thine offspring."

The Prophet Ezekiel says, "Then will I SPRINKLE CLEAN WATER upon you, and ye shall be CLEAN: *from* all your filthiness and *from* all your idols will I CLEANSE you." What a severe, what a merited rebuke is here given to those Baptist preachers who have been plunging men and women in Green's muddy and stinking mill-pond, and in the mud and filth of the Cherokee creek, south of this!

In the tenth chapter of Hosea, and at the 12th verse, the command is recorded, "Seek the Lord till he come and RAIN *righteousness* upon you." And in the fourteenth chapter of the same book it is said, "I will be as the DEW unto Israel." In the seventy-second Psalm it is said, in reference to Messiah, "He shall COME DOWN like RAIN upon the mown grass."

In these three citations the inspired writers most beautifully represent the *refreshing* influences of the Spirit by a metaphor taken from the falling of DEW and RAIN. What lively—what beautiful figures! How expressive! But not a word about *immersing* in all this. No *purifying*—no *cleansing*—no *washing*—is here represented by a command to PLUNGE!!

The conclusion, then, to which we are conducted by express declarations of holy writ, and by ancient usage, and which have never been either contradicted or impaired, is that the practice of IMMERSING persons in baptism is an innovation upon the established and ancient meaning of the emblematical use of water. This innovation we cannot allow, first, because there is no necessary demand for it; and, next, because it alters in many important and vital respects the sense and aspect of the doctrines and allusions of the New Testament.

We cannot close this chapter more appropriately than to give a paragraph touching these points from Hibbard's Christian Baptism, a work inferior to none we have seen on this subject. This paragraph, moreover, will enable the reader the more readily to appreciate the entire bearing of the foregoing remarks. Hibbard very justly remarks:—

> If, therefore, according to the general analogy of Scripture, water be used ceremonially as an emblem of the purifying and regenerating operations of the Holy Spirit; and if God has uniformly spoken of the latter as being *poured out* upon men—as *falling upon*—as *sitting upon* them, etc.; and has also signified it symbolically, by the *falling of dew*—by the *descent of rain*—by the *pouring out of water*—by the *sprinkling of water*—by Christ's *breathing upon his disciples*—by the "*laying on of hands*;" and if to this general emblematical sense of ceremonial ablutions accord the particular teachings of the New Testament in regard to Christian baptism, it follows that, by the sanction of all Jewish usage—by the analogy of water and spiritual baptism—and by the common law of interpretation of all symbolical rites—the water of baptism should be applied by SPRINKLING or POURING.

THE RIVER JORDAN.

Jordan is the largest river in Palestine, and affords more water than all the streams of the Holy Land united together. This celebrated stream is formed by the junction of two rivulets, the *Jor* and the *Dan*, from which it takes its name. It rises in Mount Libanus, and runs into the *Dead Sea*.

Editor Howell recently quoted Stevens's Travels in Egypt, Arabia Petræa, and the Holy Land, to prove that this river afforded sufficient water for John to have immersed Christ in. We now quote an item from the same author, dated March 31, 1836, to prove a man *could not be immersed* in Jordan:—

> The bank of the river Jordan here (where Christ was baptized) is about ten or twelve feet high—a clear level table of land, covered with rich grass, and large bushes on the edge overhanging the river. Judging by the eye, the river is here about thirty paces broad; *the current is very rapid, and the pilgrim in bathing is obliged to hold on by the bushes to avoid being carried away.* Immediately below this the river narrows to ten paces. It is (thence) a small, broken, and muddy stream, running between banks of barren sand, without bloom or verdure.

Now, is it not strange that Mr. Howell should introduce the testimony of Mr. Stevens to prove that Jordan was so bold a stream that a man could not wade into it without being carried away by the current, when the same testimony would show that no one could be immersed in it for the very same reason? Was Christ immersed in such a stream as this? Or did John and Christ "*hold on by the bushes to avoid being carried away?*" It would seem so, for the river, just at the point where Christ was baptized, was "*very rapid.*" Wonder how many females could be induced to encounter "bold Jordan" with a Baptist preacher who acknowledges himself that he *can't swim!* What would one of these large, fleshy, overgrown women do, with her several garments on, in such a rapid current? Or, forsooth, what would a female *in a peculiar fix* do in such a scrape?

To show that Mr. Stevens is not singular in his description of the

Jordan, we give the following very brief extract from Brown's Encyclopedia, page 700:—

> The *current* [of the Jordan] *is so violent* that a Greek servant, belonging to the author, who attempted to cross it, though strong, active, and an excellent swimmer, found the undertaking *impracticable.*

The same author says, page 701:—

> The *rapidity and depth* of the Jordan are admitted by every traveller, although the volume of water seems to be much diminished from its ancient greatness.

The fact, moreover, of there being no *fords* or *ferries* on the Jordan goes to establish its character as a bold and dangerous stream. The regular passages over the Jordan were only four, as we are taught in Scripture.

1st. Jacob's bridge, near to the Lake Genesareth, said to be the place where Jacob met his brother Esau, and where he had the night's wrestle with an angel.

2d. The second crossing-place was a bridge at a place called Chammath, at the issue of the Jordan from the Lake of Genesareth.

3d. There was a ferry at Bethabara, mention of which is made in 2d Samuel. Here there was an eddy, but the water was deep.

4th. Last of all, there was a bridge at Bethshan, or Scythopolis, a city belonging to the half-tribe of Manasseh, on the west bank of Jordan. This is the city on the wall of which the Philistines hung the body of Saul, after the celebrated battle of Mount Gilboa.

CHAPTER XIII.

No serving of God without immersion, according to Elder Graves—None but immersed believers can constitute a Church—Eight scriptural examples of Christian baptism—Inhabitants of the Polar regions of the earth excluded from the service of God, if immersion be the true and only mode of baptism—Indecent personal exhibition, growing out of immersion—Summary of the whole.

On page 547, under the head of "Declaration of Rights," our author says:

> We hold it to be the personal and bounden duty of every accountable person,
>
> To acknowledge and serve God—believe in and obey Jesus Christ—to be *immersed* upon a profession of that faith—to unite with a Christian Church—to participate in the Lord's Supper—and to labor for the glory of God and the extension of the Redeemer's kingdom; etc.

On the same page, under the head "Proofs," intended to sustain his position as above given, he quotes the following passage, which I suppose he takes from the *New Baptist Version* of the Scriptures, as it is not to be found in our present authorized English version of the Bible:

> Go ye, therefore, disciple all nations, *immersing* them in the name of the Father, and of the Son, and of the Holy Ghost; teaching them to observe all things whatsoever I have commanded you.

And on page 552, where his "Wheel" is about to call a halt, he gives the constitution of a true Church. The first section of the first article is in these words:

> SECTION 1.—A Church of Christ is a company of BELIEVERS IMMERSED upon a profession of an evangelical faith, voluntarily asso-

ciated, on terms of perfect equality, in a covenant or agreement, implied or expressed, to receive the New Testament as their only rule of faith and practice, and to be governed by its teachings in all things.

Making these three extracts the foundation of my remarks, I shall conclude my argument upon *baptism* in this chapter. We quote again from our little book :—

EXAMPLES OF CHRISTIAN BAPTISM.

At this stage of the argument, it is proper to inquire into the practice of the early Christians, with a view to determine the specific bearing of their example on the question in dispute. We therefore proceed, and without further preliminary, to examine the Christian baptisms recorded in the New Testament, and especially those cases alleged to have been cases of *immersion.*

1. The first case we design to notice, is the baptism of three thousand persons on the day of Pentecost, as set forth in the 2d chapter of Acts: "Then they that gladly received his word were baptized, and the *same day* were added unto them about three thousand souls." These were all added to the Church on the day of Pentecost; but the *mode* by which they were baptized is not pointed out. The Baptists say it was by immersion. But any one acquainted with the circumstances of this occasion, will readily see that the weight of evidence is against the idea of immersion. Peter began to preach about the third hour of the day, *i. e.*, about nine o'clock A. M. Judging from the nature of the occasion, and from the drift of his discourse, as reported by Luke, he could not have delivered his sermon in less than an hour. Luke says—"With *many other words* Peter testified and exhorted," etc. Sermon being ended, the candidates for baptism must be selected from the vast multitude, and questioned as to their "experience of grace." If they were immersed, they must have been provided with a change of raiment; but how could they have been prepared to change clothes? They came together, at first, a promiscuous multitude, without any expectation of Christian baptism, or of their conversion. These and many other things considered, we have no idea that the apostles proceeded to baptize their converts before one o'clock. The Jewish day closed at six P. M., and Luke says they were baptized and added to the church the "same day." This granted, they had but five hours left in which to baptize three thousand persons. Divide these among twelve apostles, even supposing them to have all assisted, and each man had an average of 250; which would be, for each man, 50 persons per hour, or 5 persons in every 6 minutes. This, we need not say, would have been impossible. The Baptists allege that the seventy disciples aided on the occasion. This allegation has no foundation either in the text or chapter in which this event is recorded. Besides, there is no proof that the seventy were commissioned to baptize. Luke is so explicit as to say—"But Peter standing up with the *eleven,*" etc. Why did not Luke say—"But Peter standing up with the *seventy,*" etc.?

But on this occasion, the apostles *had no place for the immersion of such a multitude.* The brook Kedron, which ran along the east side of the city, was at its maximum but a turbid stream—for ever dry in the hot season, and it was now about June; so that, if it were not dry, its waters must have been failing fast. Besides, soon after this stream issued from its source, it received from a common-sewer all the blood and ordure of the daily sacrifices, and the common filth, both of the temple and the northern section of the city. If one of the apostles had taken a wife or daughter of ours, and *plunged* her into this filthy brook, he would not have immersed another female soon again.

As to public pools, the Scriptures give an account of but *two,* Bethsaida and Siloam. The latter was one mile from where the great meeting was on the day of Pentecost. Do the Scriptures give any account of the marching of these three thousand persons, and as many spectators, to this pool? But if they had gone there, could three thousand persons have been immersed in one pool, between the hours of *one* and *six?* Are there no difficulties attending this Baptist hypothesis? Is it not evident that *pouring* or *sprinkling* was the mode on the memorable occasion we have been considering? Let the candid reader answer.

2. The second example of baptism mentioned in the New Testament is that of the eunuch, by Philip. Here, says the Baptist partisan, they both *went down into the water,* and they both *came up out of the water,* and this certainly makes out a case of immersion. There is nothing in the text from which immersion can be inferred, but the circumstance of their *going down into the water,* etc. If, then, this circumstance prove the immersion of either, it will prove the immersion of both, for it existed alike with respect to both. Let us throw the argument into a syllogistical form, and see what it proves. Going down into the water necessarily implies immersion. Philip and the eunuch both went down into the water. Therefore, of necessity, they were both immersed. But many persons go down into the water, and come up out of it, without being immersed. Of this we are absolutely certain, both from our own experience and daily observation. But as this question is examined on former pages of this work, we will add nothing more in this place.

3. The third example of baptism recorded in the New Testament, is that of the Apostle Paul at Damascus. And we unhesitatingly affirm that there is nothing in this text which, either directly or indirectly, justifies the conclusion that Paul was *immersed.* Hear what the evangelist says, Acts ix. 17, 18: "And Ananias went his way and entered into the house, and putting his hands upon him, said, Brother Saul, the Lord, even Jesus, who appeared unto thee in the way as thou camest, hath sent me that thou mightest receive thy sight, and be filled with the Holy Ghost; and immediately there fell from his eyes, as it had been scales; and he received sight forthwith, and arose, and was BAPTIZED." Was Paul immersed? It is not so written in this text. It is not so much as *hinted* at in this text. It is not in the book of God. It is a mere Baptist conjecture which no man is bound to believe, because no man can prove it true. Nay,

more—there is every reason a man of sense should require for believing the very reverse. Paul had been three days and nights as blind as a bat, greatly enfeebled by fasting and anguish of spirit; and from the fact of his rising up to be baptized when Ananias came to him, it appears that he was either *sitting* or *lying down*—certainly in a bad condition to be led off and plunged into some pool or pond, for there was no river or creek suitable in the neighborhood. The text does not warrant the conclusion that Paul left the house or room in which Ananias found him; and inasmuch as he received meat and was strengthened, immediately after his baptism, the presumption is that he did not.

4. The fourth example of baptism afforded us in the New Testament, is that of Cornelius and his friends at Cesarea. See Acts x. 48: "Then answered Peter, Can any man forbid water, that these should not be baptized who have received the Holy Ghost, as well as we? And he commanded them to be baptized in the name of the Lord Jesus."

Does any part of this text say that Cornelius and his friends were immersed in water? A person who had never heard tell of the practice of plunging, might read this narrative a hundred times over, and he would never think of a baptism by immersion: nay, there is not a word or an allusion, in the text, from which such an idea could originate; but there are several indications of baptism by *pouring* and *sprinkling*.

Look at the mode of Peter's question, "*who shall forbid water*," etc. As if he had said, in the preceding verse, Christ has *poured* upon them the promised baptismal purifying of the Holy Ghost. Who shall forbid us to *pour* on them the baptismal water which represents it? These considerations prove to our mind that *pouring*, and not *immersion*, was the mode of baptism on this occasion.

5. The fifth example of baptism that we meet with in the New Testament, is that of Lydia and her household. See Acts xvi. 13–15:

> And on the Sabbath, we went out of the city, by a river side, where prayer was wont to be made; and we sat down, and spake unto the women which resorted thither. And a certain woman named Lydia, a seller of purple, of the city of Thyatira, which worshipped God, heard us: whose heart the Lord opened, that she attended unto the things which were spoken of Paul. And when she was baptized, and her household, she besought us, saying, If ye have judged me to be faithful to the Lord, come into my house, and abide there. And she constrained us.

Now we ask the Baptists, who demand explicit proof for the mode and subjects of baptism, to show us in what part of this text they find "Thus saith the Lord," Lydia and her household were immersed or plunged in a river? There is nothing resembling it in all the text. There is nothing resembling it. The scriptural narrative of this case of baptism is plain, unvarnished, and complete. And what does the whole narrative amount to? Why to this: Lydia went to the place of prayer—heard Paul preach—the Lord opened her heart—she believed the gospel—was baptized, and invited the apostles to abide at her house. Does this prove that Lydia was immersed? Not one word is said as to the *mode* of her baptism. It is said she was baptized, but no mention is made of the *how*.

6. The sixth example of Christian baptism recorded in the New Testament, is that of the Philippian jailer. See Acts xvi. 33: "And he took them the same hour of the night, and washed their stripes; and was baptized, he and all his, straightway." Now tell us, ye advocates of immersion, did the jailer and his family put off at the hour of midnight to a river, creek, or pond, or other collection of water, to be plunged? Did the Spirit of God, under whose influence the jailer acted, direct him to leave an important and responsible charge, both in violation of the laws of God and his country, and upon the strict observance of which his life—to say nothing of the happiness of his family—depended, and follow one of his prisoners through the streets and back alleys, and over garden fences, at midnight, in search of a river, or pond, or pool of water, in which he and his family could be plunged? An ignorant and prejudiced Baptist may believe this, but we never can. We cannot believe it, moreover, because it has no foundation in Scripture or fact.

But, says a blind, infatuated Baptist, there was a *bath* in the prison, in which the jailer and his household were immersed. Where is this written? Not in the Bible. But what was a bath doing there? Were any so sharp-sighted as to know beforehand that the administrators of Christian baptism would be committed to prison, and that the keepers of the prison would "become obedient to the faith," and desire baptism? Imbecility itself, without the aid of Baptist bigotry, cannot exceed the weakness of such a conclusion.

7. The seventh case of Christian baptism to which we shall allude in this connection, recorded in the New Testament, is that of the twelve disciples at Ephesus. (See Acts xix. 1–7.)

And it came to pass, that while Apollos was at Corinth, Paul having passed through the upper coasts, came to Corinth; and finding certain disciples, he said unto them, Have ye received the Holy Ghost since ye believed? And they said unto him, We have not so much as heard whether there be any Holy Ghost And he said unto them, Unto what then were ye baptized? And they said, Unto John's baptism. Then said Paul, John verily baptized with the baptism of repentance, saying unto the people that they should believe on him who should come after him, that is, on Christ Jesus. When they heard this, they were baptized in the name of the Lord Jesus. And when Paul had laid his hands upon them, the Holy Ghost came on them; and they spake with tongues, and prophesied. And all the men were about twelve.

This text only says that the twelve disciples were baptized, without once referring to the *mode*. Of course it proves nothing for or against the practice of immersing persons. Having, however, spoken of this case of baptism in the preceding part of this work, we shall merely add that the idea of these disciples having been immersed has no foundation in Scripture or fact.

8. The eighth and last example of baptism mentioned in the New Testament which we shall bring to view, is the baptism of Crispus and Gaius, and the household of Stephanas, by St. Paul. On these cases we cannot enlarge, because the apostle Paul does not tell how, nor where, nor when, he baptized either of these persons, or this

household. Therefore, nothing can be inferred therefrom concerning the *mode* of baptism.

We have now examined all the cases of Christian baptism recorded in the New Testament, which took place after the new or Christian dispensation, and upon which the Baptists rely for authority to *immerse;* and we arrive at this conclusion, that it cannot be proven from the New Testament that the apostles ever immersed a single person. Nay, we unhesitatingly affirm that no one ever was immersed in the days of the apostles. And we defy every Baptist on earth to produce explicit proof from the Scriptures of any persons ever having been immersed in the primitive Church. On the contrary, the nature and design of Christian baptism prove that *affusion* or *sprinkling*, rather than *immersion*, was the mode.

In 1842, I had a controversy with the Baptist Banner, published at Louisville, Kentucky; and I urged the utter impracticability of immersion in those terrible regions of frost and snow traversed by the sixtieth parallel of northern latitude. My article entire, on that occasion, compiled from the views of Hibbard and Humboldt, and Woodbridge's Universal Geography, was as follows:

We cannot allow, by any means, that baptism by immersion is essential to salvation, because nature, in some portions of the world, has interposed an insuperable barrier for nine out of every twelve months in the year—a barrier which, to the inhabitants of those countries, would render immersion *instant death*. Not less than eight millions of human beings now inhabit the polar and frozen regions of the earth. Many of these are to be found in the *sixtieth* parallel of latitude northward, where the temperature is such for two-thirds of the year, that wells freeze to their bottoms, and the inhabitants can only get water to use by melting snow or ice. In the region of the Esquimaux the lakes and streams, however deep, are frozen to the bottom for nine months in the year. In Greenland and Lapland even baldface and mercury freeze during the winter. The inhabitants of these regions, during the winter, remain crowded together in small huts. The inhabitants of Siberia, especially, stop the openings in their houses with ice and snow, and use ice instead of glass. Every part of the body must be covered in going out, or it is instantly frozen. The cold often causes trees and rocks to split, and make loud reports!

In these sections, we ask, in all candor, how could immersion be performed? Not by melting snow or ice. Not by baths, for they would freeze up. And yet in these cold regions dwell millions of human beings, as good by nature as we are; and if this mode of baptism be essential to salvation, they must be lost. It is not saying much for either the wisdom or goodness of God, to contend that he has established an ordinance of perpetual obligation which, though adapted to the convenience of the inhabitants of the burning sands of the south, excludes from his Church all whose misfortune it is to reside amidst the perpetual and eternal snows of Lapland, Greenland, or that more frozen region, Siberia! Even with us there are six months of the year during which immersion is performed with great inconvenience, producing sensations we should think by no means pleasant to the "outward man;" unless, indeed, we attach a merit to such sensations, according to a Catholic's idea of penance, or a Brahmin's notion of *self-mortification.*

This objection to immersion, arising from climate, has always kept Baptist missionaries within warm latitudes. While other Protestant sects of Europe have penetrated northward into Norway and Lapland, ay, and Greenland, the Baptist missionaries have confined their labors to Germany, the southern parts of Poland, and some of the states of Austria. They have missionaries in India, Africa, and among the aborigines of America; but no Baptist missionary ever yet attempted to organize a society in the frozen regions of Lapland, Siberia, Labrador, or Central Russia, and for this very good reason too, that nature has rendered the ordinance of baptism by immersion wholly impracticable!

A single quotation from Woodbridge's Geography, page 145, seventh edition, will sustain me in the views here expressed:

During the winter the inhabitants of the coldest parts remain crowded together in small huts. The whole inside of a hut or ship is usually lined with ice from the vapor of breath, which must be cut away every morning. The inhabitants of Siberia stop the openings of their houses with ice, and use it instead of glass. If the cold air suddenly enter the house, the vapors fall in a shower of snow. Every part of the body must be covered in going out, or it is instantly frozen. The air, when breathed, seems to pierce and even rend the lungs. The cup often freezes to the lips if it be touched in drinking. The provisions must be cut with hatchets and saws. Trees and the beams of houses are split by the frost, and rocks are rent with a noise like that of firearms.

To this article the Rev. editor of the Banner replied, charging me with ignorance of history and geography. To which I, in part, replied as follows:

It has been ascertained by Humboldt and others, who have carefully traced those lines of equal temperature usually called the *isothermal lines*, that not less than eight millions of human beings inhabit the polar regions. To these souls the gospel must be promulgated, and its ordinances administered. Churches must be organized in the very centre of these most frozen regions. But the Baptists cannot organize those churches, nor administer those ordinances, especially that of baptism, because, nine months in the year, their *mode* of baptism would be more galling than the bloody rite of circumcision.

But we are boastingly asked if we "know that the Greek Church prevails in Central Russia, and that they are all *trine*-immersionists?" We do know that the Greek Church claims the *territory* of the whole Russian empire in Europe, a great part of Siberia in Asia, the entire country in Palestine, Syria, Mesopotamia, Egypt, Arabia, and, in short, the whole of the old world; and, in this respect, is truly the *universal Church*. But we happen to know, likewise, that the head of the Greek Church, the patriarch of Constantinople, resides in that famous capital, where a synod convenes monthly, for the transaction of ecclesiastical business, the twelve bishops attending. And while we know all this, we happen to know more: we know that this Church has never organized churches in one-tenth part of the extent of territory they claim the control of; and we know, too, that she baptizes *children*, and admits them to the table of the Lord. Unlike the Baptists in every respect. This editor can find an account, on the eightieth page of his own History, (Benedict's, vol. i.,) of a Greek priest cutting a hole in the ice, and immersing a child, when unintentionally he let it slip through into the water and drown! The holy administrator exclaimed: "*Give me another, for the Lord hath taken that to himself!!*" The parents on the bank declined, however, and said they were not willing the Lord should receive any more in that way. Better *sprinkle*, we should think. Query: Have the Baptist missionaries kept out of "Central Russia" for fear of having to encounter these Greek "*trine*" immersers of children? Verily, "when Greek meets Greek, then comes the tug of war."

From the ignorance manifested by this reverend editor, it is more than likely he labors under the impression that "Central Russia" is in the "Canadas, Nova Scotia, New Brunswick, and other British possessions in North America!" On this point it may be well enough to enlighten the gentleman. Russia proper is a very large empire, partly in Asia and partly in Europe: bounded on the north by the Frozen ocean; on the south by Great Tartary, the Caspian sea, and Persia; on the east by the sea of Japan; and on the west by Sweden, Poland, and the Black sea. The greatest part of this empire lies in the temperate zone, within which limits the Greek Church operates, baptizing *children* by "*trine*" immersion, and administering to them the sacrament of the Lord's Supper. "Central Russia" is in and beyond the sixty-sixth degree of latitude, lies in the frigid zone, where there are neither Greeks nor Baptists, for reasons heretofore named. Does the editor consider himself instructed?

RUSSIAN BAPTISM.

It is always performed by immersion. In the rich houses, two tables are laid out in the drawing-room by the priest: one is covered with holy images, and on the other is placed an enormous silver

ELDER B. CHANGING CLOTHES BEFORE THE LADIES, AFTER IMMERSING!—See chap. xiii.

basin filled with water, surrounded by small wax tapers. The chief priest begins by consecrating the font, and plunging a silver cross repeatedly in the water: he then takes the child, and, after reciting certain prayers, undresses it completely. The process of immersion takes place twice, and so rigorously that the head must disappear under the water: the infant is then restored to its nurse, and the sacrament is finally administered. In former times, when a child had the misfortune to be born in winter, it was plunged without pity under the ice, or into water of the same temperature. In the present day that rigor has been relaxed by permission of the Church, and warm water is substituted for the other; but the common people still adhere scrupulously to the ancient practice, in all seasons. On these occasions numbers of children are baptized at the same time on the ice, and the cold often proves fatal to them. It sometimes happens, also, that a child slips through the hands of a priest, and is lost; in which case he only exclaims: "God has been pleased to take this infant to himself: hand me another;" and the poor people submit to their loss without a murmur, as the dispensation of Heaven.

AN INDECENT PERSONAL EXHIBITION.

During the cold spring of 1842, on two different occasions, at Cherokee Church, in Washington County, Tennessee, the Baptist pastor, Elder B., after immersing several persons, came out of the water and changed his clothes in the presence of the multitude, as indicated by this engraving, and all in the presence of males and females! He was a very tall man, knockkneed and rawboned—any thing but handsome when dressed!

At one time he stripped himself to his *shirt*, on the plain, around a fire, and in the presence of a crowd of females, some of whom actually ran! At another time he changed his clothes in the pulpit, before the congregation, preparatory to administering the BAPTIST, not the *Lord's* Supper.

Now, for this contempt of the decencies of life, the reverend gentleman ought to have been indicted *for an indecent exhibition of his person.* It is a shame and a disgrace to any Church, and to the entire Church, and calculated to bring religion into contempt. And for this, as well as other reasons, we denounce such practices. Let the people of every order frown down such vulgarities. And let all females who have not a *taste* for such *sights*, stay away from such places until better order be observed.

SUMMARY OF THE WHOLE.

We have now said what we desired to say in this work, and what we deemed necessary to be said; and from what has been said we may learn:

1. That baptism is a sacrament of the gospel, which was instituted by our Saviour for very important purposes; that he designed it to be perpetuated in his Church, in every clime, to the end of time; that it

is the duty of all Christian people to attend to it, and no less the duty of all authorized ministers to administer it in all proper cases, who, by the way, can alone lawfully administer this sacrament, but who have no authority to *rebaptize.*

2. That penitent adults, adult believers, and the infant children of all baptized parents,* together with the servants of such persons, provided they are charged with their education or training, are proper subjects of Christian baptism, and, as such, should not be kept from the ordinance.

3. That no one mode of baptism is laid down in the Scriptures, to the exclusion of all others; that it may be validly administered either by *sprinkling*, or *pouring*, or by *immersion;* but that, nevertheless, the Scriptures do afford more evidence in favor of sprinkling and pouring than of immersion.

4. That too many persons substitute an attention to this outward ordinance that ought to be paid to inward piety and an upright life; that, instead of using baptism as a means of grace, they abuse it to their own destruction; that, instead of laboring to become holy here, and of being fitted for the inheritance of saints in light, they seek after a mere *shadow*, in the vain hope that it will lead them to the uninterrupted enjoyment of that eternal and enduring SUBSTANCE which baptism is designed to represent.

---

* We of course hold the doctrine that all infant children, whether of believing parents or not, are entitled to baptism on account of *their own* relation to Christ and to his kingdom, and not of that of their parents—"for of such is the kingdom of God."

CHAPTER XIV.

Elder Graves perpetrates twenty-five falsehoods in one chapter of twelve pages, being over two lies to a page—Espouses the cause of local preachers, at the expense of the travelling ministry—Plays off the demagogue, and misrepresents the laws of the Methodist Church—Proves himself unworthy of the confidence of honest men of all denominations!

J. R. GRAVES, of Nashville, and "Editor of the Tennessee Baptist," claims to be one of the clerical successors of the apostles; and by virtue of his lineal descent from *John the Baptist*, claims, in connection with the ministers of his own "faith and order," the exclusive right of administering the ordinances of the Church, exclusive qualifications to instruct mankind in the important doctrines of salvation, and, as a matter of course, to reform the manners and customs of the several *spurious* sects of the country. I propose to show that this man Graves and his associates are not the only authorized expounders of God's word—the only authorized administrators of the ordinances of the Church—and that they have by no means been set for the general reformation of men and manners by the Head of the Church! I propose to show, in other words, that if the arrogant claims set up by these bigoted sectarians are even well founded, neither the *temper*, nor *morality*, nor *example* set by Graves, qualifies him for the position he has assumed!

I propose to show that Graves has perpetrated TWENTY-FIVE FALSEHOODS in one chapter of his book, a short chapter at that, composed of only *twelve pages*, making more than *two lies to a page.* Not so bad for one of the successors of the apostles, in a direct lineal descent from John the Baptist! The chapter I allude to is Chapter 20th, commencing on page 225; and I declare, upon the honor of one who expects to give an account in the future to the Judge of all men, that this is but a fair specimen of the other *thirty-nine* chapters of his book!

An able article from the pen of Rev. WESLEY SMITH appears in the Texas Christian Advocate of September, 1855, taking the same view of this subject; but as it is written more in detail than answers my purpose, I will present an abridged view of the subject. Graves is really so ignorant of the economy of Methodism, that he takes the absurd ground that all local preachers in our Church were once itinerant preachers; whereas, a great majority of them never were members of our Annual Conference, and never even desired to be. And when ministers of our Church locate, they do it *voluntarily.* When local preachers join a Conference, they are received or rejected by a majority vote of the Conference, just as young men are when they first enter the travelling ministry, according to their merits or demerits, talents or want of talents. I was ten years an itinerant preacher, and in that time a member of the General Conference. I have been twenty years a local preacher—I know what are the rights and privileges of local preachers—and I am pleased with the government of my Church *as it is.* The dedication, then, of this *lying* chapter to local preachers, in its conclusion, is a species of *demagogueism* that all high-minded and well-informed local preachers will treat with scorn and contempt! But I will turn my attention to the celebrated chapter alluded to.

FALSEHOOD NO. 1.

A travelling preacher is evidently considered the most useful to your society, and indeed *the only legitimate preacher.*

This is a *palpable falsehood*, inasmuch as a local preacher receives the same kind of license that an itinerant does: takes upon him the same ordination vows: holds the same order of credentials: administers the sacraments: solemnizes the rites of matrimony; and attends to the burial of the dead. The only difference between them is, that the one is the *pastor* of the church, while the other preaches when and where, in his own judgment, there seems to be a demand for his services.

FALSEHOOD NO. 2.

Consequently, the strongest possible influences are brought to bear upon the preachers to keep them in the saddle.

To my own knowledge, the above statement is false. No influences are ever brought to bear upon itinerant preachers to keep them in the regular work, when their pecuniary necessities and the increasing demands of their families require them to locate. Every man in the work can locate at his Annual Conference, if he is in good standing, and take with him a *certificate* of his location and good character. Both a man's connection with and retirement from the work are *voluntary*. It is a matter of regret, at all Conferences, that some useful men are *forced* to retire, from a want of that support necessary for their families.

FALSEHOOD NO. 3.

And every obstacle thrown in the way to deter them from locating or *becoming pastors*.

When our preachers locate, instead of *becoming* pastors, they really *cease to be pastors*. Here, then, are three *bare falsehoods* found in one short sentence!

FALSEHOOD NO. 4.

The office of pastor, the most common office of the Christian minister, in the days of the apostles, is wholly ignored by you, and that of evangelist substituted in its place.

This is false, inasmuch as we have *a regular* pastorate, though the Discipline requires the pastor to be changed every two years. The Baptist, and other *congregational* churches, have a great deal of trouble at times in ridding themselves of men who do more harm than good. The Baptist Church in Nashville refused, last October, to *endorse* J. R. Graves's Christian character, after a severe struggle on his part. He had lived among them *too long*, and they *knew him too well!*

FALSEHOOD NO. 5.

They (the people) are not even allowed the right to petition for his (the preacher's) return.

This is a more deliberate falsehood than either of the foregoing, inasmuch as our people regularly petition for preachers, and are as regularly granted their requests. We local preachers are regularly consulted by the Bishops and Presiding Elders, as to who will best serve the interests of the Church on our circuits and stations. In our Quarterly, Annual, and General Conferences, the *right* of our people to petition is conceded, and their petitions are always treated with the utmost respect.

FALSEHOOD NO. 6.

Speaking of a meagre fund provided by our Church for the support of worn-out preachers, and the widows and orphans of deceased preachers, Graves says:

Who doubts that multitudes of Methodist preachers *become such* through the influence of this strong consolation held out to them by the elders?

That Methodist preachers enter the itinerancy for the sake of an annual dividend of fifty or sixty dollars per annum, *after they are broken down*, or a dividend of fifteen to twenty for each of several children, *after the death of the father*, carries the lie upon its very face. Every candid and sensible man knows that many join our ranks *with means*—travel and preach until they exhaust their means, and then locate because their support is inadequate.

FALSEHOOD NO. 7.

And who doubts that multitudes continue their connection with the Methodists through the influence of this fund for superannuated preachers?

No man having any acquaintance with Methodism supposes any such a thing. Graves, and such understrikers as the "North Carolina Publishing Society of the Baptist Church," may suppose such a thing. Honest, candid, and well-informed men *know it is a lie!*

FALSEHOOD NO. 8.

But he (the preacher who locates) is degraded at once in the eyes of the whole travelling connection, in the eyes of his Bishop, of the world; for they (the travelling preachers) take care that it shall be so.

This discovery never was made by any local or travelling preacher! Dr. Bond, editor of the New York Christian Advocate, O. B. Ross, late of Kentucky, Judge Longstreet, of Mississippi, United States Senator Colquitt, of Georgia, and ex-Representatives in Congress, SENTER and TAYLOR, of East Tennessee, were local preachers. These men were never degraded in the eyes of their brethren, or of the world. And these are only a few of the dead and living evidences of the falsehood of Graves's statement.

FALSEHOOD NO. 9.

He (the preacher who locates) is degraded from the *rank* he held with them (the travelling preachers.)

This is notoriously false; for if he were a deacon or elder, he is still the same, retaining his credentials, and carrying with him an additional *certificate* of his *honorable* withdrawal from the Annual Conference!

FALSEHOOD NO. 10.

His name is carried down and put upon a *class paper*, and some smooth-chinned and brainless boy of a class-leader now has jurisdiction over the aged veteran, in conjunction with some equally endowed circuit-rider. What a fall! How humiliating to a man possessed of self-respect!

Every word of the foregoing is false, in the connection in which it stands. The Quarterly Conference, and not the class-leader, has jurisdiction over all the local preachers in the circuit or station. This Conference is composed of all the preachers, exhorters, leaders, and stewards in the circuit or station. The local preacher, moreover, has the right of appeal to the Annual Conference. (*See Discipline.*)

FALSEHOOD NO. 11.

He (the local preacher) is subjected to the most rigid and oppressive *espionage* on the part of those whose love of rule is gratified in subjecting their former sovereign to their wills, if they have no old scores to settle with him.

This entire statement, in every particular, is false. I have been a local preacher for twenty years—I never heard of this "oppressive espionage"—I never felt it—I have enjoyed the largest liberty—so do all local preachers—it has no existence in the Methodist Church!

FALSEHOOD NO. 12.

They (the class-leader and preacher in charge) cannot exclude him (the local preacher) without a hearing, but they can arraign him as often as they please before the quarterly court, the majority of it being *class-leaders* and *preachers in charge*, and he being *nothing* but a local minister; and can be represented as *troublesome*, disposed to exercise too much authority and influence, and greatly in the way; the class-leader and circuit-riders can easily come to the conclusion that, *upon the whole*, he had better be divested of his ministerial office.

This statement is false by *suppression*, false by *denial*, and false by *misrepresentation*. No local deacon or elder ever was deprived of his ministerial functions by the arbitrary conduct of class-leaders and preachers in charge. He can only be suspended from his ministerial office by a committee of local preachers. His court of trial is the Quarterly Conference—if dissatisfied with its decision, he can appeal to the Annual Conference, whose decision is final. See our Discipline, under the head "Local Preachers," and see how it puts this villainous slanderer to the blush!

FALSEHOOD NO. 13.

By simply removing to a distant neighborhood, he (the local preacher) does it at the forfeiture of his ministerial office, for the law empowers the presiding elder or preacher in charge to give or *withhold a certificate* of his official standing as they please.

This is an inexcusable and a most *malicious* falsehood. Every local preacher's character is examined once a year in his Quarterly Meeting Conference, and if nothing appear against him, the minutes must show that fact. And whenever he desires to remove from one circuit to another, or from one State to another, the presiding elder or preacher in charge is *bound to grant him a certificate of removal*, setting forth that he is in good standing. This is the *law* of our Church, and I know it to be the *usage*, from Maine to California, as well as in Great Britain and Ireland!

FALSEHOOD NO. 14.

Local preachers are generally a persecuted class.

This is false, unless Graves intends to say they are *persecuted* by Baptist preachers, bigoted sectarians under their influence, and by wicked men and devils!

FALSEHOOD NO. 15.

A local preacher thus expostulates with Mr. McFerrin, the editor of the Methodist Advocate in this city, (Nashville,) who, living at home on a *fat salary*, can even write disrespectfully of local preachers.

It is false that Dr. McFerrin ever wrote or spoke "disrespectfully of local preachers." On the contrary, he has spoken and written of them in terms of high regard. He may have denounced some *one or more cases*, but this has no more to do with local preachers, as a class of men, than my denunciations of Graves's falsehoods has to do with pious and gentlemanly Baptist preachers, to whom I make no allusions!

FALSEHOOD NO. 16.

If the preacher locates with a very extensive and powerful influence, he becomes obnoxious at once to the preacher in charge.

The very *reverse* of this is the truth! The practical workings of Methodism show, that the more popular the local preacher, and the greater the influence he exerts, the more apt the preacher in charge is to be on terms of intimacy with him; and for two reasons—first, because of his supposed merits, and next, because of the service he can render the travelling preacher in building up his church, and in procuring his support.

FALSEHOOD NO. 17.

Suppose he (the local preacher) is a far superior preacher, and the people far more desirous of hearing him, and his opinion far more influential in the town or community: the circuit-rider is not long discovering it, nor long in putting on foot a course of treatment to remedy the *evil*.

Graves measures other men's corn by his own half bushel. These unworthy motives governed him in his war upon Professor Duncan, of New Orleans,' and those Baptist preachers of Louisville, as well as his opposition to Hillsman's Baptist paper in Knoxville. Methodist preachers, as a body of men, both local and travelling, are on terms of as much kindness and confidence as any equal number of men on earth.

FALSEHOOD NO. 18.

It is bruited about that he *wont* or *don't* observe the *rules*—very good, but not pious—not much of a Methodist in his feelings, for he don't attend class.

This is false, for no such stuff is "bruited about," only among Baptist opposers of Methodism. And the insinuation that local preachers don't attend to *rule* is maliciously false.

FALSEHOOD NO. 19.

It is *distasteful* telling his *experience* over fifty-two times a year.

The falsehood of this short sentence consists in the insinuation that local preachers are opposed to class-meetings, as *distasteful* meetings. Local preachers are expected to circulate as widely as they can, and preach, and are not therefore required to attend class-meetings every week.

FALSEHOOD NO. 20.

The preacher may reprehend him on a *bare report* that the local preacher has used improper words, and the preacher is the judge what words are improper in a local preacher; or is reported to be guilty of improper tempers, and the preacher is the judge; or improper actions, and his reverence, the preacher in charge, is the judge!

Now, the difference between Graves and our Discipline on this point, is just the difference between TRUTH and FALSEHOOD; and falsehood has the advantage, as set forth by Graves. Here is what the Discipline says:

QUESTION 1.—What shall be done when a local elder, deacon, or preacher is reported to be guilty of improper tempers, words, or actions?

ANSWER.—The person so offending shall be reprehended by the preacher having charge. Should a second transgression take place, one, two, or three faithful friends are to be taken as witnesses. If he be not then cured, he shall be tried at the next Quarterly Conference, and if found guilty and impenitent, he shall be expelled from the Church.

FALSEHOOD NO. 21.

Where is there a local preacher who ever left the circuit with a commanding character and controlling influence, who was ever able to keep it five years?

The LIE here perpetrated consists in the charging, by way of interrogatory, that no Methodist preacher ever located with character and influence, who did not forfeit both in five years! The slander needs only to be stated.

FALSEHOOD NO. 22.

More: lives there a local preacher who enjoys to-day one-tenth the influence and reputation he did when a member of the preacher's church?

Yes, hundreds are to be found. I know many local preachers who wield more influence than the presiding elder and all the circuit preachers of their district!

FALSEHOOD NO. 23.

He is a degraded man.

Poor fellow!! I should be sorry for him if the charge came from a source entitled to credit.

FALSEHOOD NO. 24.

He is snubbed about and domineered over by beardless class-leaders and circuit-riders until he loses his self-respect.

This statement carries the LIE upon its face; and if it did not, its utter want of foundation in truth has been demonstrated in my preceding remarks, and quotations from the Discipline.

FALSEHOOD NO. 25.

What chapters of the lives and wrongs of local preachers might be written! The iron has pierced through the soul of hundreds; and they who have been the faithful servants of their society through the vigor of youth and strength of manhood, are going down to their graves dishonored and oppressed by its unfeeling, unkindness, and tyranny

Now, I have only to say to Graves, his "North Carolina Publishing Society," and other understrikers, that there is not a single local preacher in the Methodist Church, South, out of the thousands in good standing, who will not unhesitatingly pronounce the foregoing false in every particular. After *thirty* years of close and intimate fellowship with local preachers, in different States, I pronounce the foregoing quotation from Graves's book an unmitigated slander. The whole book is a FALSEHOOD, and the man himself is a LIE!

CHAPTER XV.

Three specimens of deliberate lying—A vulgar, false, and slanderous caricature of a Methodist revival—The challenge by the North Carolina Publishing Society of the Baptist Church—Replies of Doctors Lee and Deems—Graves publicly caned for slander—The Baptist "Western Recorder" against Graves, alluding to his Church troubles in Nashville—His abuse at Bowling-Green—Damages obtained against Graves in Tennessee, for libel, to the extent of $7,500—Mortgages all his property away, under peculiar circumstances!

WHENEVER Graves has told a truth in his strictures upon and exposure of Methodism, he has told it in such a way, and so worded his expressions, as to make a *false impression;* which is not only equivalent to, but is the very worst species of lying. And as this chapter will be occupied with the challenge of the "North Carolina Baptist Publishing Society" to DOCTORS SMITH, LEE, and DEEMS, to meet Graves in the city of Raleigh, and discuss the issues made in the "Iron Wheel" of the latter, I will give three specimens of Graves's mode of lying, when he even *seems* to be telling the truth, that this Baptist committee may have no room for escape. I could give many others equally palpable, but these three will suffice as *specimens:*

1st. The bishops have every press in all Methodism under their control, as much as Pio Nino or any absolute monarch in Europe. *They appoint the editors, and change them at pleasure.*—P. 192.

Now look at the Discipline:

"All of whom (the editors) shall be elected by the General Conference," etc. (Dis., ed. 1846, p. 191.)

2d. He must obtain the privilege from his society or class-meeting to exhort. This is of easy accomplishment. And, mark it, this is the only instance in the life of a Methodist preacher when his name comes before the laity.—P. 208.

Now look at the Discipline:

"Provided, that no person shall be licensed to *preach* without the recommendation of *the society of which he is a member*, or of a leaders' meeting." (Dis., p. 34.) A leaders' meeting is composed of the laity.

3d. The objection I have to the Methodist confessional above the Romish, is this: In the former I am required to confess all my sins of deed or thought as particularly and rigidly as Rome requires, *to a preacher*, etc.—P. 386.

Now look at the Discipline:

"The design of our (band) meetings is to obey that command of God: 'Confess your faults *one to another*, and pray *one for another*, that ye may be healed.'—James v. 16." (Dis., ed. 1846, p. 81.)

Here are three plain and palpable falsehoods, not to say wilful and malicious, that no man can deny, and no man could perpetrate in ignorance, with the Methodist Discipline in his possession; and Graves had it, for he pretends to give it as his authority! Now, will the "Baptist Publishing Society of North Carolina" admit that they are "involved in a great sin" in circulating this false, foul, and slanderous work, and "take speedy steps to free themselves from the guilt," as they propose in their challenge? We shall see.

If the "North Carolina Publishing Society" will take the trouble to turn to pages 531–2–3 of Graves's book, they will find a specimen of low, vulgar, and slanderous ribaldry, at which Tom Paine or the most wicked of infidel persecutors of religion would blush! It is a caricature of a Methodist revival which a friend to Christianity should blush to countenance, much less to perpetrate! He represents one preacher as calling upon the Lord "to make these sisters *shouting* happy right now;" another, with a voice trumpet-toned over all, cries, "Fire! fire! send down *fi-re!*" a third calls out "Power! po-wer! come in po-wer!" Then follows "forty or fifty crying, screaming, and praying, in a *sanctified row.*" And, to cap the climax: "See there, how those ministers are beating them upon their backs, as though religion was a wedge to be driven in between the shoulder-blades!"

After his caricature of a Methodist revival, he ought to have introduced the Baptist preacher into the same vicinity, some two weeks after the close of this meeting, preaching to the young converts, crying, *Water! water!! water!!!* shaking hands and singing:

"Go read the third of Matthew—
Go read that chapter through:
It is a guide to Christians,
And tells them what to do!"

He ought to have represented this stupid, ignorant, and uneducated man, awkward and uncouth, attempting to advocate the cause of Christianity, but doing it so badly as to bring it into disrepute. After winning over some by this *water gospel,* he tells them that they are now on the rock, Christ; that all their future sins are to be imputed to Christ, while *his* righteousness is to be imputed to them. Thus, they may *lie, cheat, steal,* and get *drunk,* and do any other wickedness, without falling from grace! Once in the Baptist Church, and under the water, they are beyond the reach even of temptation!

But to the challenging committee of the North Carolina Publishing Society. I copy the challenge from the "Biblical Recorder" of August 9th, 1855, published at Raleigh:

A CHALLENGE.

"The Great Iron Wheel" and "Orchard's History of the Baptists," recently published by Elder J. R. Graves, *having been adopted for circulation* by the Baptist Publication Society of North Carolina, and it having come to the knowledge of said Society that the Iron Wheel has been pronounced by certain Methodist ministers, through the columns of the Richmond Christian Advocate, *a false, foul, and slanderous book*—the members of said Society, feeling that they are charged with circulating FALSEHOODS AND FOUL SLANDERS against the Methodist Episcopal Church, have made an arrangement with Elder Graves to defend his book and the North Carolina Baptist Publication Society against the charge specified, and appointed the undersigned a committee to submit the following proposition first to Rev. Leroy M. Lee, D.D., editor of the Richmond Christian Advocate, and, in case of his declination, to others hereafter to be named.

We propose that Elder Graves will meet Dr. Lee in the city of Raleigh, at any time that may be agreed upon by the parties concerned, when and where all or any of the positions discussed in "The Great Iron Wheel" will be defended and substantiated in their consecutive order, or in any number of propositions so framed as to embrace the substance of the same.

On behalf of the Society, we express our earnest desire that such a discussion shall take place as early as practicable. For, if we are lending our aid in the circulation of a book which is both *false and slanderous*, we are certainly involved in great sin, and wish to be convinced of it, that we may take speedy steps to free ourselves from guilt; and if such is *not* the character of "The Great Iron Wheel," we have a right to demand that we be no longer held up to public scorn as the endorsers and circulators of falsehood and slander.

We hope Dr. Lee will favor us with an early reply, in order that all necessary arrangements for a discussion may be made, if he accepts the proposition, or that its provisions may be extended should he see proper to decline.

JAMES M'DANIEL,
A. M'DOWELL,
G. W. JOHNSTON, } *Committee.*

June 18, 1855.

In reply to this challenge, Leroy M. Lee, editor of the *Richmond Christian Advocate*, responded:

We copy the above from the Biblical Recorder of Raleigh, N.C. It contains a challenge, not to mortal combat, "resisting unto blood," but to a public discussion of the truth or falsity of "all or any of the positions discussed in the 'The Great Iron Wheel'" book. Before responding to this challenge, we have a few words to say to the committee whose names figure at the foot of it. We know nothing of them personally. They have volunteered to address us publicly, and cannot object to a reply in the same way.

1. These gentlemen act "on behalf" of the "Baptist Publication Society of North Carolina." They belong to that Society; and, in challenging us, they are acting under its direction and by its authority.

2. We learn from their missive that The Great Iron Wheel, written and published by Elder J. R. Graves, has "been adopted for circulation by the Baptist Publication Society of North Carolina:" that the book has "been pronounced by certain Methodist ministers a false, foul, and slanderous book;" and that "the members of said Society" are a little restive under, what they will excuse us for thinking, the justly merited charge of "circulating falsehoods and foul slanders against the Methodist Episcopal Church."

3. That, in order to justify themselves, quiet their consciences, and increase the circulation of the book, they "have made an arrangement with Elder Graves to defend his book and the North Carolina

Baptist Publication Society against the charge specified;" and hence the desire to have and the challenge to a public discussion, addressed first to *us*, and, if we decline it, to be tendered "to others hereafter to be named." In this matter every one must follow his own tastes. We speak for ourself: the "others" can do the same.

We beg the attention of the gentlemen of the committee, and through them of the Baptist Publication Society they represent in the matter, to the following, as *our* reply to their challenge:

1. We respectfully submit that a Society, representing a large and influential body of Christians, engaged in publishing and circulating books for the ostensible purposes of increasing knowledge and doing good, ought, as a first duty to themselves, and the cause of truth and true religion, in adopting a book for circulation, to be well assured of its character, and, at least, of the probable fruits of its circulation. This is a dictate of Christian prudence and propriety which your Society seems, singularly enough, entirely to have overlooked. The anxiety to have the book defended by its author betrays a sense of indecent haste in its adoption. If you examined the book, and adopted it because you were satisfied of its truthfulness, and believed that its circulation would be a good work, and do good in North Carolina, you ought to be satisfied with your determination, and the reasons on which it rests. If you did not examine it, or if you are now doubtful of its character and utility, you are involved in the censure of having acted unwisely for the Society, or wickedly against the good character and Christian usefulness of your brethren in Christ. In either case, it is a questionable course to meet such "a case of conscience" by arranging with the author to *defend* it. His interest in the sales, no less than in the infamy to which a righteous popular opinion will sooner or later consign his false and mischievous production, renders him too partial an advocate; and, at least, subjects to the suspicion that, in conducting a discussion on his own truthfulness, he would proceed on the old adage, that "a falsehood well stuck to, is better than a truth badly told."

There is nothing in the character of the book, in our judgment, to relieve its author of the suspicion that this adage was the governing motive and guiding principle in its composition.

2. Besides, without deciding positively, we incline to the opinion that the ostensible reason put forth for this challenge is not the real or the true one. The haste of the Society in adopting the book, the zeal for its circulation, and a desire to augment the sale, both for the pecuniary profit of the author and the Society, and with the hope that any injury it may do to Methodism will inure to the benefit of the Church whose "Publication Society" so industriously circulates it, mingle, it is at least probable, with the motives superinducing the desire for a public debate on its character and merits. Whatever might be the result of such a discussion, even if an intelligent jury of moderators decided the work to be false and slanderous, the publicity of the discussion would enhance its sale, and what seems to us to be the prime cause of seeking it would be secured. We can sym-

pathize with you as Christian gentlemen when you say: "If we are lending our aid in the circulation of a book which is both false and slanderous, we are certainly involved in great sin, and wish to be convinced of it, that we may take speedy steps to free ourselves from guilt;" but we doubt the propriety of the mode by which you seek "to be convinced of it." We could suggest "a more excellent way;" but we are neither "lords of your faith," nor "keepers of your conscience." "One is your Master, even Christ." By His judgment you are to stand or fall. Whether you sought His glory, and to please Him, by adopting this vicious diatribe against Methodism, you can determine for yourselves. We doubt whether it entered into your thoughts: it was abusive of Methodism, that was enough for you: it will pay, that was enough for the Society and the author. As an opinion of ours—only an opinion—you "*are* certainly involved in great sin," and should "free yourselves from the guilt" with all speed.

3. If "Elder J. R. Graves," or either one or all of you, gentlemen, were to publish and circulate the most atrocious falsehoods and calumnies against our *personal* character and reputation, it would never enter into our thoughts to meet you in a public discussion on the truth of your statements. A proposition on your part for such a discussion would be justly regarded, by all right-minded men, as the superaddition of a deliberate insult to a gross outrage and injury. Now, "Elder J. R. Graves," and yourselves, gentlemen, and "The Baptist Publication Society of North Carolina," as his "aiders and abettors," have assailed our character and reputation *as a Methodist*, by publishing and circulating a series of false and slanderous statements, deliberately made by the one party, and voluntarily circulated by the other. That you and your Society feel the indelicacies and difficulties of your position, as abettors in a false and slanderous attack on Methodism, its ministers and members, is not surprising; and is, indeed, gratifying, as a proof that your religious sensibilities are superior to your official sagacity, and not yet hardened by the desire of gain from the workings of your ponderous Iron Wheel. But to interpose for your relief, in the way you suggest, is asking too much of our self-respect and good sense. We wish you an honorable escape from your embarrassing position. But, in the way you propose, we would not lend the strength of our little finger to aid your efforts.

4. As the occasion serves, we desire your attention to a few remarks on the subject of popular discussions of the kind to which you challenge us. We have no affinities for such modes of settling questions involving religious truth; and confess to a very considerable repugnance to "such doings." How we should get along in one, we know not, as we have never "tried our hand." Our maiden sword, if we have a sword, is yet unfleshed. It is likely to remain so. We can perceive no propriety in these public discussions; and believe very little for truth or godliness is ever accomplished by them. As feats of intellectual gladiatorship, they attract a gaping crowd of those

who admire the pugnacious combatants, or who care nothing for them or the subject they are to fight about, and who are only a little less interested than they would be in "seeing the elephant" and "stirring up the monkeys" in a menagerie. More are attracted by the fuss or the fun of the thing, than by regard for the principles discussed, or the real religious interests involved. Besides, they settle nothing; perhaps never induce any one to change an opinion; and almost invariably engender strifes and debates. We look on them as about equally disastrous to religion and discreditable to the parties. If others choose to make such spectacles of themselves, they must follow their own bent. Our tastes lead us in another direction. But if any "set of circumstances" could seduce us into such an arena, we can conceive of no possible circumstances that can induce us to accept a challenge to meet the Great Iron Wheel man! We care to say very little of its author. We only know him in his book: that we regard as a tissue of deliberate falsehood and malicious calumny, written with a cold, callous, calculating selfishness of purpose to make money by defaming a community of Christian people. Discuss that book with its author! Pardon us, gentlemen, if we suggest that your zeal for "The Baptist Publication Society of North Carolina" has blinded you to the instincts which always govern upright and honorable minds.

The "Publishing Society" replied to Dr. Lee, and charged him with *backing out* from the proposed discussion. Dr. Lee replied:

There was no *backing* in the case: we turned right round and walked away—just as we would if we were to find a skunk confronting us in walking through a forest. This is the plain truth, and we shall offer no apology to the committee for stating it; besides, we leave them to determine, between themselves and their champion, as to the subject of the figure and its appropriateness. A celebrated editress of Washington City, returning from one of her trips to the South, passed through Charlotte county, Va. The stage was filled with passengers; and while stopping at a roadside trough to water the horses, John Randolph, of Roanoke, rode up, with the same kindly object for his own steed. The female in the stage recognizing him, addressed him with, "How do you do, Mr. Randolph? I am very glad, indeed, to meet with you." "I do not know you, madam," was the shrill and chilling reply of the cynic. "Not know *me!* Why, I'm Mrs. ———, of Washington!" Looking earnestly at her for one brief moment, gathering his reins shortly up, he cried, "*phumph!*" and, lashing his horse, galloped away, elongating and elevating his voice above the clatter of his abrupt departure. *We* walked right off from the challenge with sensations of disgust quite as intense, if not as strongly expressed. We do not care, now, to say more concerning the challenge, or the strictures of the committee on our reply to it.

REV. DR. DEEMS, of the North Carolina Conference, comes next in order. Here is his reply:

GREENSBORO', N. C., July 21, 1855.

Rev. Messrs. M'Daniel, M'Dowell, and Johnston:

GENTLEMEN:—

The Biblical Recorder of July 12 has just been placed in my hands, and I have read with astonishment the degrading proposition you make me. I profoundly regret any act of my life which may have led you to believe that you could induce me to become YOUR scavenger.

Yours, etc.,
CHAS. F. DEEMS.

REV. DR. SMITH, President of Randolph Macon College, seems to have treated the challenge with silent contempt, as he did not reply to the challenging committee. He left them alone in their glory, or *shame*, to "pick the dunghill's spoil for bread," or *fame*, whichever they are seeking to turn up, by delving in the *feculent* pages of Graves's infamous book. These three ministers rank among the most distinguished of the Methodist Episcopal Church, South: literary gentlemen, able in debate. But they all three seem to have acted upon the principle—by the way, a very correct one—that persons who undertake *dirty work from the love of it,* ought not to ask decent men to help them!

One of the members of this committee, Mr. M'Dowell, I understand, at the time of his displaying this eager zeal to defame the Methodist Church, its members and ministers, had a flaming school in Raleigh. The other Churches who patronized it withdrew, and my information is, he was compelled to wind it up! So much for his officiousness in adopting and circulating a foul, false, and slanderous production. Such conduct ought to have placed him beyond the pale of Methodist patronage or courtesy. But if the gentleman choose to act as a hod-carrier for Elder Graves, let him carry on—it is only a matter of *taste!*

The truth is, however, that not one of the distinguished gentlemen named in this challenge could, with propriety, have gone into a discussion with the licentious editor of the "Tennessee Baptist"—a scurvy editor, and a blotch upon the Christian community in which he lives. He has tried, time and again, to obtain an endorsement of himself and his paper by his own denomination in Middle Tennessee, where he resides and is best known. He attempted it in Murfreesboro', and failed! He attempted it in Winchester, at a General Association, and failed. Not only so, but he was there told, to his face, on the floor of the Association, by Dr. William P. Jones, a practising physician of Nashville, and a highly respectable member of the Baptist Church, that he *was not a man of truth*, and that he, (the Doctor,) who had been a close observer of his conduct, had never seen him *acting out a Christian spirit*, or promoting the cause of God by his course!

The subject of endorsing his Christian character had been under consideration some time last fall, at Nashville; and in October, while I was in the city, the final action was had, and that Church, with which he worships, and where he has resided for years, *refused to endorse him*, and this action is now a matter of record in that city! What a commentary upon his twelve years of toil, of warfare, preaching, prayer, and praise! Certainly the private life and domestic relations of this man Graves are a sealed book to the "North Carolina Publishing Society;" otherwise, they are no better than he is, and have justly subjected themselves to the censure of the poet Cowper:

> The man that dares traduce, because he can
> With safety to himself, is not a man.

From week to week, and for years, his dirty paper has teemed with defamation and lying slanders, of the quick and

AN EX-CONGRESSMAN CANING GRAVES FOR SLANDER!—See chap. xv.

dead, male and female. It was in the month of September, 1853, just before the meeting of the Legislature, that an ex-member of Congress and an able lawyer followed him round the Square, until he found him at a drug-store occupied by a member of the Baptist Church, and there and then did chastise and publicly *cane* the aforesaid J. R. Graves—a scene which the reader will herewith find represented by an appropriate engraving! This was for slandering a female of reputable standing, through the editorial columns of his vile paper, to the detriment of good morals, and in violation of the decencies of private life! This *caning of the scavenger* met with the approbation of an outraged and insulted community; and when the Grand Jury convened, they refused to find a bill against the honorable gentleman who *thrashed* him—saying, thereby, that he served him right! And this day, every good citizen of Nashville, without reference to any artificial distinction of party, condemns the course of Graves in this matter, and believes that it was right to make him sensible of the obloquy he incurred, by "apostolic blows and knocks," well laid on upon that memorable occasion! This is the man who boasts of his arduous labors in the cause of God, and of his toils and sufferings for the gospel's sake! His professed consciousness of a well-spent life is in fact a *living lie!* Look at his deeds!

In the "Western Recorder" for October 3, 1855, a leading Baptist journal, I find this statement in reference to Graves's Church troubles in Nashville, which will not be without interest to those who are aware of his troubles there, and his former controversies at Bowling-Green in Kentucky:—

As to Brother Graves and his *Church troubles,* all we know of them is the mere statement of others, that *there were charges against him in his Church at Nashville.* We have never published any thing about him or these charges, nor have we, that we recollect, ever *even* mentioned his name in a private letter to any one at Nashville during our lives; nor do we know nor have we ever inquired what became of the *prosecution against him*. Had we been as vigilant in collating and publishing all the Baptist incidents of *Nashville* and *Bowling-Green* as the "Tennessee Baptist" has those of *Louisville*, we no doubt might have recited quite as many interesting little episodes!

This *Bowling-Green allusion* is a hard *hit* by the "Recorder!" Graves visited Bowling-Green a few years ago, and held a meeting in the Baptist church, and his abuse of other sects was so low, and his conduct so degrading, that a Baptist lady remarked that if any one would hold him, she would *cowhide him!* REV. J. S. SCOBEE, of the Methodist Church, took him up and exposed his conduct, through a public journal, most effectually. Among other things, he set forth some of the many blasphemous sayings of Graves; such as—"Of all the damnable heresies in the black catalogue which has befouled the fame of Christianity, infant baptism is the most damnable. If other heresies have damned their thousands, this has damned its tens of thousands."

Again, he said at the baptizing: "That the mark of the beast, as mentioned in Revelation, which brought the curse of God on some, was the baptism of the Pedobaptists, received by pouring."

But to return to the "Western Recorder's" charge of difficulties in Nashville! The "Tennessee Baptist," of which Graves is editor, thus replies on the 20th of October:—

But this committee denies that they are in *league* with a disaffected brother or brethren in this latitude, through whom they gather incidents to publish. We very respectfully and seriously ask them from whom they learned that we were under charges in our Church?! Did the committee visit the Southern Convention, or did they learn it from some who did go? Will these gentlemen inform us? We *demand* the names: we have a right to them. Can we get them?

The reference to a "*prosecution against him*" was an indictment for libel in Henderson county, Tennessee, tried in the Circuit Court at Lexington, where damages were obtained against him to the amount of $7500. It was for a charge of stealing made against a respectable Methodist preacher, and the clerk of the Circuit Court for that county.

In his paper for October 20, 1855, Mr. Graves tells his Baptist brethren of the corps editorial, Messrs. Caldwell, Taylor, Brannin, and Buck—some of whom had published his being indicted in this case, and others had spoken of it in no very complimentary terms to Graves—that explanations of the affair had repeatedly been given in his paper; and that *he* was not the writer of the slanderous article! True, he has repeatedly told this story in his paper, but he has failed to tell that he tried to justify the villainous publication, by defending the suit in court, thereby *aggravating* the case! And when convicted in the Circuit Court, he appealed to the Supreme Court of the State, held in Jackson in the spring of 1855, and there had the $7500 of damages fastened upon him! What followed next? We shall see.

In May, 1855, just after the Supreme Court had decided against him, he goes to the Register's office of Davidson county, and *mortgages* all his effects away; whether to avoid this $7500 damages and large costs, the reader can judge for himself. I have examined the record, and find his conveyances registered in Book xxii., and on pages 58, 59, and 62. His first mortgage is to his mother, *Louisa Graves*, the joint work of himself and partner, *Marks*. The next conveyance is Graves & Marks to A. B. Shankland, page 59. Then follow two cases, J. R. Graves to W. P. Marks, pages 59 and 62. That the reader may at once see the design of this "hot haste" in getting rid of all his effects, I will be somewhat explicit in stating them.

First case, May, 1855. Sells valuable land in the vicinity of Nashville, to his aged mother, Louisa Graves!

Second. Mortgages to B. Furguson a power-press, with all the fixtures connected therewith: one steam-engine, used in the office of the "Tennessee Baptist:" also, all the type, cases, stands, etc., and all the accounts due to said office. This mortgage includes the following publications likewise: "The Great Iron Wheel," "Orchard's History of Foreign Baptists," and "Stewart on Baptism;" also, a *one-horse barouche* and harness! This conveyance is dated May 26, 1855, which was just after the Supreme Court had decided against him at Jackson!

Third. The third case is dated May 28, 1855, and is a mortgage, by Graves & Marks to Shankland, of the same articles mentioned in the *second* case, excepting only the publications named. He seemed to have thought that *one* conveyance would do to bind a set of vile publications not in demand among those to whom fines and costs were due; but a power-press, a steam-engine, and a barouche and harness, it was deemed necessary to "*rebaptize*" in the office of the register, as they could be used profitably by all parties and sects!

Fourth. This case is one of singular interest, being a mortgage from J. R. Graves, to W. P. Marks, of his private library, amounting to 500 volumes, and the one-horse barouche and harness *once more*. This is dated May 28, 1855, the same day and date of its conveyance—I mean the *barouche*, to Shankland, and *two* days after its conveyance to B. Furguson!

Fifth. This is a case of bargain and sale, and is so recorded. J. R. Graves sells to W. P. Marks his *half* of three lots in Edgefield, for which said Marks executes his note to Graves for *one thousand dollars*, THREE YEARS AFTER DATE, and *retains no lien*. This is the more remarkable, as Edgefield, just across the Wire Suspension Bridge, is a new town growing up on the Kentucky Railroad, where real estate is increasing every day in value, and must still increase! Why sell such property upon *such terms,* and at so *low a rate?* Why, that unfeeling clerk of the Henderson County Court might make an execution upon the property. Ah, yes, circumstances alter cases!

Sixth. I will close my account of his *financial* operations with a still more palpable case of *design,* the proof of which is to be had in the Register's office. It is the case of a *note of hand,* payable to W. P. Marks, "for the use and benefit of Louisa Graves," his mother, bearing date March 23, 1854. Circumstances prove that he had *redeemed* the note, although provided for in the mortgage. He had out a bundle of papers in the Register's office, and accidentally let this note fall under the edge of the table, without intending to exhibit it! The Register afterwards found it—kept it two or three months before he met with Graves, when he handed it to him! Does any one suppose for a moment that he owed his helpless old mother any thing, who was living with him, and for whom he was providing, as was his duty? How came *he* to hold the note, and not Marks? The case is too palpable for further comments!

Now, is not this man Graves a pretty disciple to set himself up for the general reformation of men and manners! *He* write whole chapters of abuse against Mr. Wesley, for having been indicted at Savannah by an ill-natured family, when Wesley demanded a trial at "six successive courts!" Wesley gave to the Church and the poor all he made, and died a poor man. Not so with Graves: he does not give away, but *hides behind the records of the Register's office* all he possesses. Like the lurking, midnight resurrectionist, he haunts the charnel-house, and drags forth the mutilated memory of departed worth, to mock and slander! Mean wretch! not only is his sordid soul hardened against the humanizing sentiment of speaking no evil of the *pious dead*, but, hyena-like, he defiles the sanctuary he has profaned, by his huge financial exploits! Verily his licentious career, his malicious and false publications, are doomed to receive the retribution he has so stoutly defied!

CHAPTER XVI.

Graves's reckless slander of Rev. F. A. Owen—Falsehood in reference to a debate with Chapman—Cornered in both cases and made to square out—"Christian Magazine" *vs.* Graves—The Baptist "Western Recorder" *vs.* Graves—A Correspondent of the "South-western Baptist" *vs.* Graves—"New Orleans Weekly Baptist Chronicle" *vs.* Graves—Professor Duncan, pastor of the New Orleans Baptist Church, *vs.* Graves—"Knoxville Baptist Watchman" *vs.* Graves—Scriptural advice to Graves and his understrikers!

THE conduct of Graves for years past has been characterized by a degree of recklessness, slander, and falsehood, which shows, clear as demonstration, that he does not care whether he speaks the truth or its opposite. What an example he is of ministerial propriety! What a stab his conduct is to our holy religion!

To illustrate the character of the man more completely, I will show what he has been guilty of on different occasions. REV. FRANCIS A. OWEN, at present one of the Book Agents for the Methodist Episcopal Church, South, residing in the vicinity of Nashville, was, in 1852, the editor of the MEMPHIS AND ARKANSAS CHRISTIAN ADVOCATE. Mr. Owen is a native of Virginia, and I have known him intimately for a quarter of a century; and a more honorable, high-minded Christian gentleman I never knew. His character never had a stain upon it, nor were his piety and integrity ever called in question among those who knew him. While he conducted the "Advocate" at Memphis, he passed unnoticed the frequently repeated attacks of the vile editor of the "Tennessee Baptist," both personal and otherwise. His friends understood well the cause of his silence: he did not regard Graves as a gentleman, and would not *stoop* to a controversy with him. Graves, knowing the reason of his declining any war with him, and that he viewed him as a reprobate to the editorial profession, determined in his malice to assail Owen; and, accordingly, in the "Tennessee Baptist" of April 24th of that year, assailed him in this false, slanderous, and cowardly language:—

> We say to Mr. Owen, and every other editor or enemy, we are willing for our character to be investigated any day; and we challenge him or any other man to stain it with one foul blot—to darken it with a shade.
>
> We never drew the will of dying men or women, in which we were made guardian, the money to remain in our hands for *ten or twenty years without interest!*
>
> *We have heard of an Owen that did!*

Now, the application of this foul and slanderous insinuation to Rev. F. A. Owen, of the "Memphis Advocate," and now of the Methodist Publishing House at Nashville, involved a wilful slander; and when he came to meet it, *Graves backed square out of it.* It was false in every particular, from beginning to end, and no word or syllable of it ever was true, Owen having written no *will*—having been no such guardian—having had no such moneys in his hands, at any period of his life. He drove the lying editor of the "Tennessee Baptist" to the wall; and, to avoid a prosecution, he abandoned the slanderous charge, and, as I have already said, *backed square out of his daring lie!*

AND STILL ANOTHER CASE! In 1852, after Graves had discussed the subject of baptism with REV. JAMES L. CHAPMAN, of the Methodist Church, at Lexington, in Henderson county, Tennessee, Graves published in his paper, in substance, that Mr. Chapman, in that debate, admitted that our Saviour was baptized by immersion in Jordan, by John the

Baptist. This *falsehood* led to the publication of the following certificates in the "Memphis Christian Advocate:"—

We, the undersigned, do hereby certify that we were in attendance, some of us all, and some part, of the time during the debate between Rev. J. L. Chapman and J. R. Graves, at Lexington, in the summer of 1851, and that we *distinctly understood* Mr. C. as emphatically denying the immersion of Jesus Christ; nor did he use any expression, by a fair and just construction, that could be made to favor the idea of his immersion; for this was one of the points against which he directed his arguments.

Mr. Graves, closing the debate, did taunt Mr. C. with the admission, to which Mr. C. made no reply, not because of the truth of Mr. G.'s remarks, but because the truth was so manifest to the audience that it needed none.

J. B. Wadley,
James Story,
G. H. Buck,
J. G. Warren,
Rev. R. S. Reeves,
Clinton Brigance,
R. B. Jones,
John Brooks,
H. McClamrock,
D. O. N. Wadley,
F. M. Story,
Thomas Fesmire,
Ransom Cunningham,
A. T. Johnson,
Alfred Middleton,
Jarrett Taylor,
John T. Cavness.

I was present all the time, and heard every word of the above debate. Mr. C. said, for the sake of "argument," he would admit that Christ waded into the water up to his waist, "yea, he might have gone in up to his arm-pits;" but even then he was baptized "with," etc., emphasizing the word. Mr. C. made no admission of "immersion" in the case. J. W. G. Jones.

Lexington, May, 1852.

I was not present at the close of the debate between Mr. Chapman and Mr. Graves; but during the time I attended, I did not hear any remark of Mr. Chapman's calculated to leave an impression upon any of the audience that Christ was baptized by immersion.

Wm. A. Warren.

Lexington, May 26, 1852.

And yet another document! The following article is from the "Christian Magazine," of 1852—a religious periodical published and edited by a Campbellite preacher at Nashville. It shows in what light the editor of the Tennessee Baptist is viewed at home—not by Pedobaptists, but by an advocate of *immersion*, and one who is utterly opposed to *infant baptism.* Hear what this editor says of the low per sonal abuse and unchristian spirit of Graves:

THE TENNESSEE BAPTIST.—We publish the article below with regret, and would not consent to it but that good brethren, upon the ground that persons unacquainted with Mr. Graves, and the reckless character of his assertions and editorials, may be misled by our silence. We have for years been constrained, reluctantly, to look upon the "Tennessee Baptist" as a reproach to the editorial profession, and never felt ourselves warranted in noticing any thing that might appear in its columns. Nothing that can appear in it, as it is now conducted, could excite our resentment. There is not a sheet in the land, either political or religious, that we do not regard as being under the control of higher, more decorous and honorable principles than those which seem to dictate many of its editorials and communications. To the article to which Brother Howard replies below, did we feel called upon to notice it at all, we could only say of it that it is indecent and slanderous; but yielding to the judgment of others, we admit it and the reply. The Tennessee Baptist has been reckless enough to state that our marriages were illegal; that the property of our meeting-house was fraudulently obtained, and has made sundry similar unfounded declarations. With a paper that could unblushingly publish such statements, we can have no controversy.

For Mr. G. and his brethren we do not entertain an unkind feeling. For his course as an editor of a religious journal we can have no fellowship; and common decency forbids that we should notice the often-corrected and now stolid slanders he chooses to publish against the community we have the honor to be associated with. To his frequent and violent provocations, we consider it more noble to oppose forbearance than contest—preferring rather to endure all the injury he can inflict, than to contend with a wrong-doer so apparently destitute of common candor and decency. He is at perfect liberty, as we stated years since, to say any thing of us he may please; and our only hope for him is that he may yet see the error of his way, seek the change of *his* heart, from what it has appeared for many months, to the love and approbation of truth, decency, and we would say charity, but we fear it is too great a virtue to command his efforts for many years to come. J. B. F.

ONE MORE OF THE SAME SORT! The Louisville "Western Recorder," a Baptist journal now before me, dated September 26, 1855, published and edited by a committee of Baptist clergymen, to wit—"Associate Editors: S. W. LYND, A. W LA RUE, A. D. SEARS, WM. M. PRATT, L. FLETCHER"—thus takes off Graves, for his unmanly assault upon one of the former editors of that paper:

"COOL AND INDICATIVE."—Under this caption the Tennessee Baptist, in speaking of Brother Ford's name being withdrawn from the list of editors in the Recorder, says: "Did Prof. Farnam's letter take effect upon Brother Ford? We think the decapitation and the silence indicative." We have intentionally passed in silence the many *false insinuations* made in the Tennessee Baptist against us, a committee conducting the Recorder; but are unwilling that a brother should be assailed through us. There was no decapitation in the case. Brother Ford having purchased and become the sole proprietor of the Repository, voluntarily withdrew his name from the list of editors to the Recorder, with perfect good-will on both sides; and will, we hope, convince his Baptist readers that he is not "decapitated," and cannot be, even by the little *garroting* machine at Nashville. The editor's caption to such editorials should read, Cool and Vindictive. Then all will understand him.

Graves published, in his paper, that the "Recorder" had been influenced by *Campbellite money* in its course! To this charge of bribery and corruption, the "Recorder" of October 3, 1855, replies:

How these things come we cannot tell, but we fear brothers Pendleton and Graves permit our enemies to poison their minds against us unwarrantably; for every reader of the Tennessee Baptist has seen how familiar its editors and correspondents profess to be with the affairs of the Louisville Baptists at large, and the Recorder and its Committee in particular. Do such things look like sustaining the friendly relations of the papers? Do they not rather look as though they were on terms of intimate confidence with secret spies and false friends of the Recorder? Will not such a course necessarily excite suspicion that there is a secret plan of espionage carried on by the Tennessee Baptist for the sole purpose of injuring the Recorder? How else do they obtain those distorted and perverted accounts of our acts and doings? We appeal to brothers Pendleton and Graves: will they not be convinced, yea, do they not know these things are hurtful to the Church, and must ultimately injure them in common with us and the cause? Will they not learn that those who are sufficiently depraved and vicious to retail to them the private affairs of their brethren for publication, would not scruple to misstate, misrepresent, and slander? We again repeat, we must believe brethren Pendleton and Graves are imposed upon by designing tattlers. In this way alone can we account for the strange infatuation which seems to have taken possession of them—that there were those connected with the Recorder who were in a conspiracy with brethren in Nashville to kill off J. R. Graves, and, as they have it in Bowling-Green, if necessary brother P. must fall too, and he even intimates how hard he will die. At first we treated this matter seriously, and assured brother P. and his friends that we had no such wish, the whole matter was a fabrication; but the idea of being a martyr in the cause of J. R. Graves seems to possess him as an infatuation; his every act and thought seems colored with the fancy, until the ridiculous so far exceeds the serious that really in spite of ourselves we can but be amused.

AND YET ANOTHER WITNESS! The "SOUTH-WESTERN BAPTIST" of June 7th, 1855, published at Tuskegee, Alabama, and edited by ELDER SAMUEL HENDERSON, contains a communication of four columns, in which we find the following remarkable language:

I think it due the public to state that I find a large part of the article from the "Western Watchman,' in the Great Iron Wheel, a work written by a Baptist—the Rev. Mr. Graves; a portion of the piece is without quotation marks. See pages 291, 292, 295, 296, 299, 300. A few precious extracts will show the spirit of the author. Mr. Graves charitably classes "ruling elders of the Presbyterian Church, and Methodist Conferences, with Pio Nino, and styles them big and little Popes." Page 45 Iron Wheel. "We see bishops and ruling elders lording it over God's children." Page 50. "Any Pedobaptist Society is a huge clerical despotism itself." Page 50. On pages 254, etc., he calls "all Protestant sects harlots and abominations of the earth," and the communing together of Methodists and Presbyterians "a blasphemous farce, prostituting the holy emblems to the propagation of a falsehood." On page 265 he says, "Protestant ministers have usurped Christ's place, and exercise his authority over his Church." You may imagine my surprise, then, on discovering that the piece, ascribed in the "Watchman" to some profound philosopher unconnected with any Church, was surely an effusion of the tender mercies of the lovely Mr. Graves, whose charity is so strikingly displayed in the foregoing extracts. What meant this concealment of the author? For charity of this description, however, I never gave you credit, and therefore did not look for you to endorse the beautiful sayings of such a writer.

WORSE AND WORSE! I have before me the "NEW ORLEANS WEEKLY BAPTIST CHRONICLE" for November, 1854, edited by WM. C. DUNCAN, in which Professor Duncan is defended against the slanderous assaults of Graves. Professor Duncan is one of the most intelligent and able of Southern Baptist ministers. He is a professor in the University of Louisiana, and pastor of the Baptist church in New Orleans.

The article in the "*Chronicle*" occupies EIGHTEEN columns, and is headed, "*Defence against False Charges and Misrepresentations of Rev. J. R. Graves.*" I quote only the two following paragraphs, and they will serve as fair *specimens* of the whole:

There is much dependent upon the decision which the denomination may render respecting these libels of the Tennessee Baptist on Professor D.'s History of John the Baptist. Mr. Graves, while he affects wonderful zeal for the Baptist denomination, aims a stab at one of its cardinal principles, *freedom of opinion*, and a right to differ from *any* or *all* in the denomination on points of doctrine not essential to Christianity. Mr. D. does not agree with many Baptists touching the baptism and ministry of the Forerunner. Is he on that account to be injured in his character for orthodoxy, to be frowned down in his publication enterprises, and to be opposed in all his undertakings for the advancement of the Baptist cause? And, above all, is this to be done by a man who, possessing power, abuses it most shamefully; a man noted alike for his vanity, his ignorance, and his hot-headed folly; and who has not one worthy qualification for acting the part of leader and adviser of the denomination? These are, just now, momentous questions, which are to be decided by the Baptists of the South-west.

In what we have written, we deliberately arraign J. R. Graves, Baptist editor, of Tennessee, before the denomination, on the charge of *repeated falsehood and misrepresentation.* Our proofs have been adduced. Judge between us, ye that are interested. Acquit him of falsehood if you can, acquit him of misrepresentation if you can. One thing, however, do. Say now, whether a man so careless of truth, so hasty, so fell in his hostility, so incapable of discussing any subject with candor and fairness, so unjust to his opponents, is fit to lead (nay, to govern, for *govern* is what he is clearly trying to do) the denomination in the South-west. Decide now, Baptists that are free, whether the despotism of this man is to stand or fall. His committed partisans, no doubt, will uphold him, be he false or be he true. But will the intelligent, the thinking, the freedom-loving among our Baptists, defend and sustain him in his high-handed course of injustice and iniquity? We have done, we trust, with this unpleasant subject for ever.

L. ALEX. DUNCAN & Co.
WILLIAM C. DUNCAN.

New Orleans, Nov. 1, 1854.

AND STILL THEY COME! I have before me a pamphlet of fourteen pages, from this same Baptist office in New Orleans, in reply to the "false charges and misrepresentations" of

Graves against Professor Duncan; and on the fourteen pages are enumerated FIFTY-THREE FALSEHOODS by Graves! I will trouble the reader with but two short extracts:

Mr. Graves has endeavored in three ways to injure the standing of the Chronicle: in all three modes by *misrepresentation*. 1. By studiously creating a false impression as to the sentiments advocated by the Chronicle. 2. By not truly stating the views held by Professor D., or advocated by Von Rohden, in the work "John the Baptist." 3. By misrepresenting Mr. D.'s acts and opinions in other particulars.

4. Mr. G. asserts, with only the above Notice, then before him, as his authority, that the Index "has unqualifiedly pronounced all its [the book's] doctrines sound, and of course sound Baptist doctrines." One wonders that his hand did not wither as he penned these untruthful words. Ought such a man to be credited on any point?

The long and the short of the matter is, that Graves seeks to put down, and otherwise override all other Baptist papers. He attempted to prevent the starting of the "Baptist Watchman" in Knoxville; and John L. Moses, I think it was, an intelligent and respectable member of that Church in Knoxville, took him off through the columns of the "Watchman!" I am unable to lay my hands upon the paper, or I would quote from it at length.

This is an *outline*, gentle reader, of the character of Elder J. R. Graves. Strange to say, some of the prominent ministers and members of that Church in Tennessee, Georgia, Alabama, and the Carolinas, are circulating and defending his book, with all its false and slanderous affirmations! This is giving his falsehoods currency to a very great extent, and will in the end bring a crash upon the Baptist Church in the South and West, as it will involve her ministers and members, in the estimation of the public, in the guilt of bearing "false witness against their neighbor." This will necessarily close against them the door of usefulness with thousands to whom they might otherwise be profitable. It has already injured the "North Carolina Baptist Publishing Society." The Methodists have outlived, and lived down, greater opposition than this; and will certainly come out of this unhurt. But the Baptist Church is to suffer by it—*mark what I say!*

In concluding this chapter, allow me to call the attention of Mr. Graves and his endorsers, especially at Raleigh, to one or two passages of Scripture, and earnestly entreat both him and them to reflect seriously upon their solemn import, before it is too late! The first is found in Revelation xxi. 8:

> And all liars shall have their part in the lake which burneth with fire and brimstone.

The second passage is found in 1 Tim. iv. 1, 2, and reads as follows:

> Now the Spirit speaketh expressly, that in the latter times some shall depart from the faith, giving heed to seducing spirits, and doctrines of devils; speaking lies in hypocrisy; having their conscience seared with a hot iron.

CHAPTER XVII.

Methodism "Republicanism Backwards"—Graves's pictorial representations of the oppressions of Methodism—Methodism "death to all the institutions for which Washington fought and freemen died" —Washington taught the contrary in his letter to Bishops Asbury and Coke—The Baptist Churches pure democracies—Robert Hall thought otherwise—Hall's opinion of Wesley—Wesley's Address to the American Methodists—Strength of religious parties in this country—Churches dividing upon the slavery question—Elder Graves a Northern man, and strongly suspected of Abolitionism!

ELDER GRAVES is peculiarly unfortunate in his *pictorial* representation of the Methodist Wheels, on page 161 of his book, which he classically styles "Republicanism Backwards!" He has the Bishops on the outside, holding the handles and keeping the machinery in motion. It would have been much more appropriate to have had the "Wheels" propelled by a steam-engine, (such as he *mortgaged* to a Baptist friend, to avoid paying for his slanders in Henderson County!) while the Bishops act as chief engineers. For as tyrannical, oppressive, and arbitrary as the powers of the bishops, presiding elders, circuit-riders, and stationed preachers may be in the eyes of their traducers, they are dependent upon the *voluntary* contributions of the people for their support. Amongst the Methodist laity are Senators and Representatives in Congress, Governors of States, Judges of the Supreme Court of the United States, the Supreme, Chancery, and Circuit Courts of States, presidents and professors of colleges, doctors and lawyers, merchants and capitalists of every grade, and as learned, intelligent, and patriotic citizens as can be found in any other Church on the American Continent, and *more of them!* How, then, can any one suppose that such men would quietly crouch under a huge platform, beneath the oppressive weight of a pyramid of itinerant preachers, such as is represented on page 306 of his book, where he represents Methodism as a religion of "Preachers on the People's Backs?" To say the least of it, the idea is superlatively ridiculous!

But Graves tells the world in his book, that

> The Methodist system is death to all the institutions for which Washington fought and freemen died.

It seems that GEORGE WASHINGTON thought differently. He says, in a letter addressed to the Bishops of the Methodist Church, about the time of the close of the Revolutionary War:—

> I must assure you in particular, that I take in the kindest part the promise you make of presenting your prayers at a throne of grace for me, and that I likewise implore the Divine benediction on yourselves and your religious community.

Now, would *George Washington* have given "aid and comfort" to a *despotic* organization—to a set of anti-republicans, whose religious "system is death to all the institutions for which *he, Washington,* fought and freemen died?" Surely not! But Washington did give "aid and comfort" to the Methodist Church, and *prayed the Divine benediction upon its bishops, ministers and members!* The Methodist Church is now what she was when Washington patronized her, and prayed the "Divine benediction" upon her clergy and membership; and he who charges that she is *"despotic and anti-republican,"* is guilty of knowingly slandering the "Father of his Country"—the immortal Washington! Verily, the prayer of that matchless patriot, offered to God for his blessings to rest upon the Methodist bishops, and the Methodist community, is a lasting shield to their patriotism, which the poisoned darts of Graves's malignity, backed as they are by the "North Carolina Publishing Society," can never penetrate! The proof that will establish the anti-republicanism of Methodist episcopacy, will also convict the great and good Washington of being a traitor to the cause of republicanism!

On page 311 of his book, Graves makes this assertion:

> The Baptist Churches are pure democracies—are the only form of purely democratic government in the world.

ROBERT HALL, the great apostle of the Baptist Church, thought otherwise, and really vindicated the Baptists against the *foul* charge of being republicans! Hall thus repels the charge of republicanism from all Dissenters, Baptists, and others:—

> Dissenters are reproached with the appellation of republicans, but the truth of this charge has neither appeared from facts, nor been supported by any reasonable evidence.—Works, vol. ii., p. 82.

As proof of Elder Hall's position in regard to his Church, he could refer to the licentious madness of the German Baptists, or Anabaptists, as they were termed, who utterly detested the principles of republicanism, and considered it unjust to charge them with the sin of *democracy!*

Graves tells us that John Wesley was a loyal subject of an English king; therefore our Methodist episcopacy, to which he tells us Wesley was hostile, is anti-republican! Five out of six Methodist preachers who were Englishmen returned to their native country when the war of the Revolution broke out; and, therefore, the SIXTY American preachers who, in 1784, organized the Methodist Episcopal Church, some years afterwards, were anti-republicans, and their Church is hostile to our free institutions—to all "the institutions for which

Washington fought and freemen died." Admirable logic, Mr. Graves!

At the close of the war, Mr. Wesley addressed the American Methodists, and in part in the following noble strains:

> As our American brethren are totally disentangled, both from the State and from the English hierarchy, we dare not entangle them again, either with the one or the other; they are now at full liberty, simply to follow the Scriptures and the primitive Church. And we judge it best that they should *stand fast in that liberty wherewith God has so strangely set them free.*

Thus nobly spoke John Wesley. Could he be hostile to our institutions, when he believed *God* had set these colonies free? See Bangs's History of the Methodist Church.

Even the great and good Baptist, Robert Hall, believed and taught that John Wesley was one of the greatest, purest, and most useful men, since the days of the apostles—in relation to whom Mr. Hall said,—

> Whitefield and Wesley will be hailed by posterity as the second Reformers of England.

As the Baptist Church has been under way in the United States at least one hundred years longer than the Methodist, one would suppose that it is much the most numerous denomination. But no: the Methodists outnumber them two to one! But the "Methodist system is death to all the institutions for which Washington fought and freemen died," and it is presumed that all native-born Americans and true patriots would scorn to unite with such a despotic organization! But no: there are two to one of the best patriots and most talented statesmen in the country connected with the Methodist Church, preferring it to that of the Baptist communion. There is no accounting for men's *tastes* in these days of railroads, steamboats, and progress!

In this connection, I will introduce a chapter from the work I published in 1842, as peculiarly applicable here:

STRENGTH OF PARTIES.

On page 290 of Mr. Howell's work, the eighteenth and last chapter commences, and is headed—"Firm adherence to original principles —our ultimate triumph!"

This chapter contains a labored argument against free communion —calls close communion "original principles"—boasts that Baptists, by adhering to this selfishness, will finally take the world! The concluding remarks of the chapter are, "Light is spreading—darkness is receding.—Our triumph is not distant!"

In order to show how far Mr. Howell has missed the mark in his confident boastings, we need only to submit a few historical facts relative to dates, accompanied with an aggregate of each religious denomination. According to CHARLES BUCK, it appears that the Baptist denomination was first formed into a sect of stability in 1526 —316 years ago. This was first formed in Europe. Well, according to BENEDICT, their own historian, the first Baptist church in America was organized in Providence, Rhode Island, in 1639—203 years ago.

The rise of the Methodist Society in Europe, under JOHN WESLEY, was in 1739—only 103 years ago. And in 1749 Mr. Wesley drew up the "General Rules" contained in our Discipline, which have continued to be the general rules of the societies, both in Europe and America, to this day. The first Methodist preacher who ever held forth in America was PHILIP EMBURY, who commenced preaching in the city of New York in the year 1766—only 76 years ago! And in 1768, the first Methodist house of worship was erected in John street, in the city of New York—only 74 years ago. For the correctness of these statements, we refer to Bangs's History of the Methodist Episcopal Church, Vol. i. p. 46.

Now, the number of Baptists in the United States is 492,496, while the Methodists number 850,000—nearly two for one! Thus it will be seen that, although the Baptists commenced operations in the United States 127 years before the Methodists did, the latter have nearly *doubled* them. Whose "ultimate triumph" would seem to be near at hand, according to this rule of figuring? Before whom does it seem that "darkness is receding?" In whose hands is the sword of truth used, so as to "take hold on the hearts of men?" Or, rather, whose *tardy* movements, for the last two hundred years, in the language of Milton, have seemed to "*beam darkness visible?*" Let Mr. Howell answer.

But it may be said that we take sinners into the Church, and that in this way we have swelled our numbers. Indeed, this is said. Not only so, but many other invidious remarks are made, by way of comparison, evidently intended to *lower* the standard of personal and religious character in our Church. We have only to say, that the members of the Methodist Church will bear an honorable comparison with those of the Baptist Church, *in any and every respect;* and that there are as few thieves, liars, drunkards, Sabbath-breakers, swearers, and loafers, among the Methodists, as there are among the Baptists.

For the sake of establishing the truth of our calculations, and for the further information of the general reader, we copy the following aggregate of each religious denomination, from Brown's Reference Book of 1841, page 29:

PRINCIPAL RELIGIOUS DENOMINATIONS IN THE UNITED STATES.

Denomination	Number	Denomination	Number
Baptists	492,496	Christians	150,000
Methodists*	850,000	German Reformed	30,000
Protestant Methodists	50,000	Unitarians	180,000
Presbyterians	358,083	Mennonites	30,000
Congregationalists	160,000	Friends	100,000
Catholics, population	1,300,000	Jews	15,000
Episcopalians, do	600,000	Moravians	5,800
Universalists, do	600,000	Mormonists	65,000
Lutherans	63,000	Shakers	6,000
Dutch Reformed	22,550	New Jerusalem	11,000

Making, together, 4,859,030 professors of religion, and allowing three or four among the family or friends of each, and the number so ascertained will include very nearly the entire population of the United States as professors, friends, or believers in the eternal truths of Divine revelation.

Graves *ridicules* the Methodist Church for the separation which took place in 1844, and attributes the cause to the government of the Church, and the ambition of a corrupt and designing ministry! That was a glorious act on the part of the Methodist Church, and a proud day in her history. It was the *Abolitionists* of the North who rent in twain the Methodist Church, in 1844. I will let MR. CALHOUN state the case, as he did in his *dying speech* in the United States Senate, on the 4th of March, 1850. He was posted on the slavery question, in all its bearings. Speaking of the effect of the Abolition agitation upon the religious cords which assisted in holding the Union together, he said:

The first of these cords which snapped under its explosive force (Abolitionism) was that of the powerful Methodist Episcopal Church. The numerous and strong ties which held it together are all broke, and its unity gone.

---

* The above calculation was made from the Methodist Minutes of 1841, since which time the increase of our societies has been unprecedented. We now number 900,000, and upwards! What the increase of other Churches has been, we have no means of ascertaining. [We number now—1856—over a million and a quarter.]

The next cord that snapped was that of the Baptist, one of the largest and most respectable of the denominations. That of the Presbyterian is not entirely snapped, but some of its strands have given way.

It is in evidence, then, that the Methodist and Baptist Churches have divided upon the slavery question. The DUTCH REFORMED CHURCH has since followed suit; and during the sitting of the synod of this Church or denomination, in New York, in October last, there was a warm discussion on the subject of fellowship with slaveholders, and an *anti-slavery position was taken!* The question of admitting the Classis of North Carolina into the Synod was decided in the negative, in a resolution offered by the Rev. Dr. Bethune, of Brooklyn, by a vote of 55 to 34—showing the Abolitionists to have a majority of *twenty-one* in the Synod! The cause of exclusion was slavery, which is now agitating and dividing the country, as it has done the Churches. The same agitation is embracing the Presbyterian and Episcopal Churches, and I believe they, too, will be rent in twain by it, as they ought to be, unless the Northern fanatics cease their aggressions.

I have not intended to say, nor did MR. CALHOUN, that any *organic bond ever united the Baptist Church.* The loose and confused nature of their Church government is such, that every Baptist congregation is a separate and independent organization. They never had a General Assembly, a General Conference, or a General Convention. Nothing over, under, around, or through, ever formed them into one body! *Outside* of the Church, certain voluntary societies were formed several years ago, consisting of individuals of the Baptist persuasion, whose objects were the publication of books, and the sending of missionaries into foreign fields of labor. To these societies, churches of that "faith and order" sent their money, or withheld it—purchased books from them, or got them elsewhere, just as they pleased. Even in this there was no organic bond of union, and no obligation acknowledged! In process of time, certain Northern Abolition Baptists raised an outcry against sending slaveholders abroad as missionaries, upon the funds of said society! The North and the South agreed to separate amicably, and partition out the missionary ground. This took place in 1845; and this is what Mr. Calhoun meant by *the division of the Baptist Church*, because it was occasioned by means of the Abolition agitation! Since that period, a *Southern Baptist Publication Society* has been organized, which has widened the breach between the North and South!

And now, people of the South, why is it that *Elder Graves* can publish a book of 570 pages, north of Mason and Dixon's Line, WHERE HE WAS BORN, and discuss so many different subjects, some of them growing directly out of the slavery agitation, and never say one word AGAINST ABOLITIONISM, or one word in favor of SOUTHERN SLAVERY? After leaving New England, it is said that he took up his abode in the "Western Reserve," in Ohio, and in Indiana, the great theatre of Free-Soilism! It has, moreover, been said of him, that he was *an Abolitionist* before he came here to reside! One thing is certain—he *keeps very dark* upon this grave question, and ought to be made to come out explicitly, if he concludes to take up his permanent abode in the South!

We are on the eve of unconjecturable events, and every Southern man ought to show his hand. Look at the conduct of Congress! A struggle of unequalled fury is swiftly approaching us; and if the ties of our cherished Union come out of it unrent, they are made of sterner stuff than the history of the past would seem to warrant! The bonds of the Union have resisted political agitation, but can they withstand religious fury? Abolitionism has travelled from political dominion to religious conviction, and has infected the whole mind and heart of the North. Under its palsying touch, some of the strongest cords that held the Union together have snapped: others are now assailed, and I fear will give way! Elder Graves is suspected of unsoundness upon this question; and if these suspicions be well-grounded, as I have reason to fear they are, he is a dangerous man to be operating in the South!

GRAVES HAS ONE FACE FOR AND ONE AGAINST KNOW-NOTHINGISM.—See Chap. xviii.

CHAPTER XVIII.

Graves for and against Know-Nothingism—A two-faced and insincere man—The "State Line Baptist Association" endorsing Graves's paper and book—Criticisms upon that endorsement, and the characters of the members of the Association—Their endorsement of Orchard's History of Foreign Baptists—New Version Baptists—Their fraudulent demagogueism, and ulterior objects!

BEING identified with one of the great political parties of the country, and being the editor of a *political journal*, it has been my constant aim, in the preparation of this work, to avoid any collision with an opposing political party, or the introduction of any matter into this work that would arouse the prejudices of political parties. My design has been, and still is, in this work, to preserve the mind free from all improper bias, and to discuss the great issues involved in the slanders of Elder Graves against the Church of which I have had the honor to be a member and a minister, for these thirty years past.

But to show up the inconsistencies of *Elder Graves*, and his *two-faced* course even in politics, which is but faintly shadowed forth by the engraving attached to this chapter, I will present him as THE KNOW-NOTHING CHAMPION of 1854, and again as the REV. ANTI-KNOW-NOTHING of 1855! This exposé—not intended to have any bearing in politics, either *pro* or *con*—will aid in illustrating the character of the man, as the dirty *ear-wig* of Baptist exclusiveness—the geographical location of whose moral and political principles is *nowhere*, and the tenants of whose heaven are the haggard phantoms of an overheated imagination—a mockery of a man not entitled to the confidence of *Southern* men, coming, as he has done, from an *Abolition* State, and being suspected of orthodoxy upon the great and exciting topic of slavery! For by the same rule and in the same manner that he would be a Know-Nothing in 1854, and an *Anti* in 1855, he might still harbor all the *Free-Soil* prejudices of his native State and raising. Ay, his code of morals, and his mode of reasoning, enable him to assume the position of an "illustrious predecessor," of whom the poet says:

> He 'd prove a buzzard is no fowl,
> And that a lord may be an owl:
> A calf an alderman, a goose a justice,
> And rooks committee-men and trustees.

In 1854, when Know-Nothingism was sweeping every thing before it—at least as was supposed—Elder Graves came out with the following editorial, in the "Tennessee Baptist" of August 26:

KNOW-NOTHINGS.

If we can read the "signs of the times," the Know-Nothings are organizing in great strength in this city, and the order will spread with great rapidity throughout the State, and without doubt will carry the next elections triumphantly over all parties.

Nothing is more evident than that our political parties have become sadly, deplorably corrupt. Our politicians, like so many wolves, wrangle and fight for the spoils of party. Congress has become a most shameful and disgraceful scene of drunkenness, riot, and caucussing for the Presidency, and the minor offices of the government. The foreign element is increasing in fearful ratio. Nearly one million per annum of foreign Catholics, German infidels—who, though opposed in all else, are agreed in the subversion of our free institutions—are pouring in upon us, and the tide is increasing. These foreigners have already commenced their warfare upon the use of the Bible in our public schools—against our free school system—against our Sabbath—against our laws. They boldly threaten to overthrow our Constitution, through the profligacy of our politicians; and we see our candidates for political preferment pandering more and more to the Catholic and foreign influence. We see from the last census that the majority of the civil and municipal offices of this government are to-day in the hands of Catholics and foreigners: an overwhelming majority of our army and navy are foreign Catholics. They hear the editors of Catholic papers, who are endorsed by their Archbishops, threatening in these words:

If the Catholics ever gain—which they surely will do, though at a distant day—an immense numerical majority, religious freedom in this country is at an end. So say our enemies. So we believe.

"The Rambler," an organ of Popery in England, says:

Religious liberty, in the sense of a liberty possessed by every man to choose his own religion, *is one of the most wicked delusions ever foisted upon this age by the father of all deceit.* The very name of liberty, except in the sense of a permission to dc certain definite acts, ought to be banished from the domain of religion. It is neither more nor less than a falsehood. No man has a right to choose his religion.

Thousands and hundreds of thousands of American citizens and Christians, who love their country better than party, and who nobly prefer to struggle and sacrifice even blood if it shall need it, to perpetuate this glorious legacy of our hero-fathers and martyrs of the Revolution, rather than to wrangle and prostitute their principles for the spoils of party, are banding themselves together, determined to Know Nothing but the safety and best good of their country, and of their whole country. The following are said to be the leading principles of the Know-Nothings:

1. Repeal of the Naturalization Laws.
2. None but NATIVE AMERICANS for office.
3. A pure American Common School System.
4. Opposition, first and last, to the formation of military companies composed of foreigners.
5. War to the hilt on Romanism.
6. The advocacy of a sound, healthy, and safe Nationality.
7. Hostility to all Papal influences, in whatever form and under whatever name.
8. American institutions and American sentiments.
9. More stringent and effective Emigration Laws.
10. The amplest protection of Protestant interests.
11. The doctrines of the revered WASHINGTON, and his compatriots.
12. The sending back of all foreign paupers and convicts landed on our shores.
13. The formation of societies to protect American interests.
14. Eternal enmity to all who attempt to carry out the principles of a foreign Church or State.
15. Our country, our whole country, and nothing but our country.
16. And finally, American laws, American legislation, and death to all foreign influences, whether in high places or low!

If we could be allowed to add one or two more, we would Know Nothing in politics save these principles. We have for years clearly seen, and so preached and so written, that within a few years there would be but two great parties in this Republic—the American Protestant party, and the Foreign Catholic and infidel party; and every true patriot and Christian will be compelled to take sides, or be branded as a traitor. Then it will be the duty of the *minister*, as well as the *member*, to become a politician; and the politics of that day will needs be preached from the pulpit and prayed around the family altars, and enter into and affect all the interests and relations of life. When the crisis comes, we expect to be found in the field; and upon the stump, if we shall possess an influence that is needed. We hail the omens of this day: this society, or party, or whatever it is, is the budding of great hopes. It bids fair to revolutionize and obliterate the existing political parties; and if it does nothing more, it will have done a good and saving work.

We commend the above principles, and a few more, to the serious and favorable attention of Christians and patriots.

Now, in October, 1855, when the current of public opinion *seemed*, at least, to have set in against these principles—principles which the *reverend elder* so much cherished, and in defence of which he was ready to TAKE THE STUMP—he came out and *denied any approval* of said principles, or sympathy for them; and published such an article as drew from JUDGE LONGSTREET, a Methodist preacher of Mississippi, the following card, which I copy from the Memphis Appeal for October, 1855:

THE REV. J. R. GRAVES, OF TENNESSEE.

Through the kindness of a Baptist friend and brother, I have just been favored with a perusal of the following from the pen of the Rev. J. R. Graves:

"JUDGE LONGSTREET.—We understand that this gentleman is charging us with being a Know-Nothing, and the Great Iron Wheel is a Know-Nothing work. We pronounce both statements false. The work was written years before Know-Nothingism was born, and we have never been a Know-Nothing."

In answer to the foregoing, I have to say that there is not one word, syllable, or letter of truth in the information which Mr. Graves has received. I do not think that I ever uttered his name five times in my life, and I am confident that I never uttered it since the rise of Know-Nothingism in this country. Nor did it ever pass my lips in any unkind, uncharitable, or unbrotherly connection whatever. I never saw the "Great Iron Wheel," and, of course, never read a line of it in my life. No Methodist has ever been upon better terms with his Baptist brethren than I have *always* been; and never was I upon better terms with them than I am just at this time. I respectfully inquire of Mr. Graves, whether he has gained any thing by forcing this correspondence before the public? Would it not have been as well for him, and, perchance, far better for me, that it should have been conducted privately? But, as I have said, for the kindness of a member of his Church, I should never have seen his publication; and then, after waiting a reasonable time for a reply, he might have proclaimed me to the public as neither a "Christian," a "gentleman," nor an "honest man." He will, of course, give my reply a place in his paper. I will thank him for the number in which he inserts it.

A. B. LONGSTREET.

The honest truth is, Graves had never heard that Longstreet had charged him with being a "Know-Nothing." He *fabricated* the charge for the sole purpose of having a chance to deny that he was one. He had been talking, writing, and even *preaching*, in favor of the new political party. He supposed that they would carry every State by storm; and if his expectations had been realized, he would have continued their advocate. But at the time of writing the editorial from which Longstreet copies, the elections had generally gone against the Know-Nothings. Besides, at the time of Graves's denial, there were strong prejudices getting up against many *Methodist preachers* in Tennessee, who were either justly or unjustly charged with favoring the principles and aims of the new party! So far as Graves *honestly* entertained any political principles, they were doubtless in accordance with those of the Know-Nothings, as published by him; but his determination was to be on the strong side, and hence he was hesitating, doubting, hoping, and expecting—while his motto was, and still is—

Some said, Graves, go it; others said, not so.
Some said, it might do good; others said, no.
At last I thought, since you are so divided,
I'll mount Sam not; and so the case decided.

It is this disposition to "become all things to all men," for the sake of gain, or rather the *sale of his book at the North*, where he was brought up, that he has waded through 570 pages, without defining his position upon the slavery question! Nay, when the question came up as connected with the division of the Methodist Church South, from that of the Church North, which was alone on account of slavery, he seems not to know it, and accounts for the separation on the ground of the *defects* in our system!

I now have before me a pamphlet copy of the "Minutes of the Ninth Annual Meeting of the State Line Baptist Association, held with the Antioch Baptist Church, Bradley County, Tennessee, October 20th, 1855, and days following." I copy from this remarkable publication the following "Report," signed by "B. Williams, *Chairman*:"

Report on Publications.—We recommend the Bible, the book of all books, the source of all knowledge, the pilgrim's way-bill from earth to heaven. Also, the Library, the Encyclopedia of Religious Knowledge, and *Orchard's History of Foreign Baptists;* and as periodicals, the Home and Foreign Journal, the TENNESSEE BAPTIST, in particular, inasmuch as it is a fearless and bold advocate of the PRINCIPLES OF OUR HOLY RELIGION; also, the IRON WHEEL!!!

Now, this "State Line Association" I know to be a *one-horse association*, composed of a body of ministers who, to say the least of it, if called of God to preach and expound his word, are not equal to the task, for the want of sense, education, and other acquirements! Let any one of them attempt the discussion of an important passage of Scripture—one which has been, and still is, the subject of theological disputations—and the mind of an intelligent man passes successively through the stages of regret, pity, disgust, and finally contempt, for one who, instead of proving himself "a Greek indeed," sinks at once into a deformed, wrangling bigot, whose claims upon public respect, even for his office's sake, vanish at the first touch of analysis! Some of them are distinguished about the "State Line," among *their people;*

but they have risen to distinction, however, upon the principle that a *dwarf* will tower when surrounded by *pigmies!*

Without intending to call in question the *piety* of these men, we are warranted in saying that in their discussions, nine times out of ten, nothing can be found worthy of the name of an argument. Logic, eloquence, wit, sarcasm, grammar, illustration, argument, taste, unction—all and singular, are utterly wanting. Their sermons (if it be lawful to dub their incoherent ravings thus) are at best but the undigested outbreaks of those who have more partisan zeal than scriptural knowledge, conveyed in language which the revision of a competent reporter can scarcely make grammatical, and adorned with vulgar comparisons, exceptionable interjections, stale quotations, hackneyed phrases, and "halt and blind" metaphors! And yet, these men alone have a right to execute the ministerial office—they alone have received a Divine commission; and the exclusive right of granting this commission is vested in them, as successors of the apostles! BISHOP SOULE, of the Methodist Church, or DR. ELY, of the Presbyterian denomination, may each baptize a person, and baptize by *immersion*, too; but neither of these distinguished divines being in the regular line of succession from the first immersionist down—a requisite without which a *valid Christian ministry* cannot exist—should these persons conclude to attach themselves to the Baptist Church, they must be *rebaptized* by a Baptist preacher, because, forsooth, he alone has the authority to baptize, and he alone possesses the power of ordaining and commissioning ministers to feed the flock of Christ!

This ignorant Association, it will be seen, has styled Graves's book of 570 pages a "*periodical,*" and classed it with the "Home and Foreign Journal," and "Tennessee Baptist." One might think they had never seen the work, and labored under the mistaken idea of its being a weekly or monthly magazine! Or, forsooth, they may have heard that the *Olympiads* among the Greeks, and the *Jubilees* of the Jews, were *periodical!* But this could not be, for the whole Association could not tell that *Olympiad* took its name from Olympus, a mountain of Macedonia; or that the period of four years, reckoned from one celebration of the Olympic games to another, constitutes an important epoch in history and chronology! The first Olympiad commenced 776 years before the birth of Christ, and 23 years before the foundation of Rome. But that Association would not admit these facts, lest they might invalidate *John's baptism!*

"Orchard's History of Foreign Baptists" is a very absurd and contradictory, not to say ridiculous work, published by Graves for the two-fold purpose of making money out of the sales, and of bolstering up his favorite theory of *immersion,* and of a *regular succession from John the Baptist* on the part of Baptist preachers! It was well enough for the "State Line Baptist Association" to endorse that work, although it is questionable whether any one of the body had ever critically examined it.

In their endorsement of the "Tennessee Baptist," I suppose they intended to approve its abuse and slander generally, and with it to go for and against Know-Nothingism. This is well enough!

In reference to the "Iron Wheel," I presume they act *understandingly,* as it is now in very general circulation among their people. A reference to what I have brought to light, in the preceding pages of this work, will show *what* this Association have approved!

In their recommendation of the "Bible as the book of all books, the source of all knowledge, the pilgrim's way-bill from earth to heaven," much depends upon *what edition* or *version* of the Bible they are for! If they go for the present authorized version of the Holy Scriptures, known as King James's translation of the Bible, I am with them, and agree with them that it is all they have represented it to be, and even more! But if they go for the *new Baptist version* of the Bible, intended to teach that *immersion* is exclusively baptism, thus *perverting* the word of God, I receive no such "pilgrim's way-bill from earth to heaven;" for when I leave for that "immortal clime," I desire to go the "overland route," and not by *water!*

I have with me the united opinion of Protestant Europe and America that there exists no necessity for a new translation of the Bible. Those who believe otherwise are a set of men whose hopeless lapse into bigotry would prevent their belief of the truth "though one rose from the dead" and testified thereto! Discreet, learned, and thinking men, in the South and West, are tired of listening to the prating of a little, ignorant, plebeian dynasty, in this State, and another in that, about "*the new version, the pure word of God*"—a set of ignorant pretenders, who have scarcely mastered *the spelling-book!*

Just in this connection, I deem it proper to call the attention of the reader to a hypocritical fraud which is being used by *Revision Baptists,* both in the pulpit and through the press, to gull and deceive the masses upon this subject. They are pleading, in justification of a new version, that "the American Bible Society had found TWENTY-FOUR THOUSAND ERRORS IN OUR PRESENT ENGLISH BIBLE." In the spirit of demagogueism, these "*new version*" Baptist preachers appeal to the people, asking them, "Who would plead for a Bible that has twenty-four thousand mistakes in it?" These vile sectarians, these *specious deceivers,* never tell the masses the nature of those errors—that they are *unimportant, consisting of errors in orthography, punctuation, italic words,* etc., etc., *such as in no way affect the sense of the reading!* I close my remarks upon this point by quoting a few paragraphs from the pen of one who is well posted in all that relates to the subject under consideration :—

The only thing that can be pleaded from the action of the American Bible Society is that our present English Bible has these errors, which have multiplied in process of time to this enormous extent, and which they have already corrected, as their report shows, and the edition thus corrected is now for sale in various parts of the country. The American Bible Society reported the necessity of correcting the mistakes, not the necessity of a *new version.*

The American Bible Society, after a rigid scrutiny of our English Bible, pronounce it "inimitable:" the Baptists denounce it as "*impure!*"

How ridiculous to meet in Memphis in April, 1852, and plead that the American Bible Society has found twenty-four thousand errors, and, therefore, we must have a new version, when every member of this convention might have brought the Bible, corrected by the Society, with him to Memphis for sale. The American Bible Society desired our English Bible *corrected:* the Baptists desire a new *translation*, which will translate *bapto*, *baptizo*, and their cognates, by terms which signify to immerse.

How, then, can any man plead the action of the American Bible Society as favoring the project of a new version? while it is clear the former condemns the action of the latter, and absolutely reports that there exists no necessity for such version.

We may call the attention of the reader to another subject intimately connected with the above. It is this: That our brethren who believe in ultra-immersion will not agree to be governed by the original copy published by the King, and denominated in the parlance of the historian the *standard Bible.* Nor is it likely they will agree to make the Bible translated by Archbishop Cranmer the *basis* of any subsequent version.

The whole class of ultra-immersionists most manifestly design to condemn and bring into disrepute the present received version, and by this manœuvre pave the way for the reception of such a version as will teach clearly and irrevocably their particular views on the *mode of baptism.*

CHAPTER XIX.

The consideration of certain miscellaneous items bearing upon the merits of this controversy—The "Biblical Recorder" charges that Methodism is a human invention—Defends Graves against Methodist slanders—Methodists shrink from investigation—Speech of Rev Dr. Slambangus in Raleigh—Powell's Valley Association—The renegade Jewett, of Ohio—North Carolina Baptists *vs.* Missionary, Bible, Tract, Sunday-school, and Temperance Societies—Methodists falsely accused of rebaptizing—Absurd position of Close Communion Baptists—Guilty of treason against God!

TIME and space—those potent and universal influences—compelled me to conclude some of the preceding chapters of this work more rapidly than I should otherwise desire, and consequently to omit a notice of divers *small* points and issues raised by Elder Graves and his ghostly conscience-keepers, especially of the "North Carolina Publishing Society" of the Baptist Church! It is my purpose now, however, to dwell somewhat at length upon the beneficial results accruing to the religious world from the learned criticisms of the *organ* of that society at Raleigh—which is proving, by the clearest demonstrations, that upon Baptist journalists, of the *Graves school,* devolves the duty of propagating refined and general intelligence, critical and correct ideas of literature and art, and a true taste for exalted and enlightened Christian charity!

To be serious, there is no other power in the United States which has within its immediate reach the means of doing so much public good as the PRESS. Compared with it, the school-house, the bar, the pulpit, sink into insignificance. I confine this sweeping declaration to the United States. The productions of the periodical press of this country are the morning and evening companions of the American citizen; and, like the eyes of Argus, its admonitions, for good or for evil, are seen and felt everywhere in the land. Unfortunately for the character of the *religious* portion of the press, there are to be found such sheets as the "Tennessee Baptist," now published at Nashville—a most delectable, sweet-perfumed nosegay for such of our Baptist brethren to smell at as conduct the "Biblical Recorder," a Baptist journal published in Raleigh, a truly spiritual mustard-pot, every issue of which will make the soul of a Baptist *sneeze* with devotion to the cause of *immersion!* That print arrogates to itself, like the "Canon of the Covenant," published at Nashville, the right to pronounce judgment upon all matters of public or private import—religious, social, or political; and this right seems confirmed by general Baptist acquiescence!

Some unknown friend has sent me a number of the "Biblical Recorder" of recent date, in which I find a correspondent, *endorsed* by the editor, referring to Graves's publication, in which the Methodists as a denomination, and Methodism as a system, are caricatured, traduced, vilified, and blackguarded after a style derogatory to the heads of Billingsgate fishwomen, and to the spirit which governed the *Spanish Inquisition!* This correspondent, a welcome contributor to the "Recorder's" chaste columns, gives these crumbs of comfort for the *chickens* of the Baptist covenant:

If Methodism is a work of God, will it not bear the closest scrutiny and the strictest examination? What will the opponents of Methodism think, when they behold its advocates shrinking from the light, and endeavoring to overwhelm with calumny and slander a man who has dared to investigate the subject, and to express the decided convictions of his judgment? Human workmanship will not bear close scrutiny.

There is a falsehood involved in this declaration against which I enter my protest. The Methodists fear the "closest scrutiny and the strictest examination!" When did Methodists shun the "closest scrutiny and the strictest examination" into their entire system, whether of doctrines or polity? They never did—*they never will!* This is a vile misrepresentation of the whole of the eventful career of Methodism, both in Europe and America. Methodism has been assailed on both sides of the Atlantic by men of much more force of character and brilliancy of intellect than the *reverend blackguard* of the "Tennessee Baptist" could bring to bear against it, and it not only stood firm, but *faced* the foe, and battled successfully for its principles. Wesley, Fletcher, Clarke, and Watson, investigated all the peculiarities of Methodism against a host of learned and profound enemies beyond the Atlantic, overturning their flimsy arguments, driving them to call for quarters, and actually conquering a peace! In America, Doctors Bangs, Fisk, Bond, Emory, and others, investigated the charges against Methodism, and scrutinized the slanders of her enemies, until some of them were ashamed to avow themselves the authors of what they had written, and others retired upon their dignity, leaving their own cherished Rabbinical legends and Brahminical vagaries to vanish before the light of truth! Go back to the assaults of 1825, '30, and '32, upon Methodist doctrines and polity, and it will be seen that the holy fathers and friars of the infernal Inquisition were not more vindictive and implacable than were those enemies against whom Drs. Bangs and Emory contended. Their horribly intolerant, bigoted, and persecuting spirit, came in thunders and anathemas from their desks; in cants, whispers, and innuendoes, among the throng: it came larded with much *holy grimace*, and many sanctimonious sighs for the credulous and pious; with much logical jargon and "*biblical*" criticism for smatterers, such as admire the style of the "Recorder;" with spleen and gall enough, when the company had sufficient pride and malice to bear it; and with fire-brands for all the young foxes they could catch!

Methodists shrink from investigation—shun close scrutiny—dodge strict examination! The history of Methodism in every State in this Union gives the lie direct to the insinuation. Methodists invite discussion, and challenge investigation into all they have ever said or done, or the founder and fathers of their Church before them. And by the time the "Biblical Recorder" and its blustering correspondent wade through the pages of this work, they will conclude that some of the Methodists are looking into matters wholly without the precincts of their own territory! But the cry is raised in advance that this is a case in which Methodists are "shrinking from the light, and are endeavoring to overwhelm with calumny and slander." The "Recorder" had no doubt learned, or if it had not its correspondent had, that a reply to the "man who has dared to investigate the subject" of Methodist polity would be forthcoming in due time, and that this war-horse of "Iron Wheel" notoriety would be made to look *less* like a successor of the apostles than they could desire! Cry slander, if you choose—it will not protect your man Graves: the atrocity of *his* slanders shall stand forth without a rival and beyond comparison. A pretty set to speak of a resort to slander! Who is more prone to denunciation and slander than the author of the "Iron Wheel?" When he has exhausted his topics of argument, and that he can soon do, without a miracle, he resorts to a low species of sarcasm and ridicule, and to downright and outright lying, and here his talents are wonderful: Hercules comes in "head and shoulders." The conductors of the "Biblical Recorder" and the editor of the "Tennessee Baptist" have contrived a reciprocity of interest and obligation, and they advance upon each other with the proper overture, "*Titilla me et titillabo te;*" and then they meet without the fear of a repulse. But the man of the "Recorder" and his *sapient* correspondent would do well to pause and reflect, and see that they are not led astray by Graves, and swayed by prejudice and malice, at the expense of truth—a tool for others to work with, till they find themselves in a condition to use such tools as they themselves once were—sectarians, bigots, false accusers of the brethren; any thing which the pliant qualities of Proteus can be wrought into, and every thing which their sectarian jealousy and unsanctified ambition may dictate. I fear their blustering assaults upon Methodism arise from too high an opinion of their own importance, and of the overshadowing greatness of their Church. Men may become very extravagant on these points. It is recorded of two Roman emperors—I believe Diocletian and Galerius—that they once, in conversation, expressed themselves in the following manner:

DIOCL. When I am dead and in my urn,
May earth and fire together burn,
And all the world to cinders turn!

GAL. Nay, while I live I would desire
To set the universe on fire!

To give force and grandeur to the language of passion, rage, and falsehood, in connection with Methodism, seems to be the chief aim of Graves, whose striking characteristics are restless pride without gratification; ostentation without motive or reward; professions without sincerity; ceremony without comfort; laughter without joy; smiles with concealed rancor; approbation alloyed with *envy;* and vociferous praises dying away into the whispers of calumny!

The reader will bear in mind that this "Recorder" is the *home organ* of the grave "Publishing Society" whose learned and conscientious members challenged Drs. Smith, Deems, and Lee, to meet their idol Graves, in the city of Raleigh, "in mortal combat," upon the issues made in his book. Let us fancy to ourselves that the battle is to come off, and, fur ther, that we see some oracle of ecclesiastical jurisprudence, who had been regularly immersed, rising slowly from his seat. Ah! 'tis he: it is the Rev. Dr. Slambangus, correspondent of the "Recorder," whose endorsement of Graves's slanders has well-nigh got him out of temporal employ! While he lays back his foretop, and raises and waves his hand, to put the *humeri extensores* in tune for harmonious action; while the ophthalmic muscles, with awful convergence, point the visual ray level, beneath a superciliary nexus of majesty and thought, as when the sun from the eastern horizon shows half its orb beneath a line of darkness, an attention spreads that would almost render *thoughts* audible, and give an echo to *silence* itself. He speaks, the chair being filled by an admirer of Graves, who has "gone down *into* and come up *out of* the water!"

MR. MODERATOR:—

When I consider the dignity of the chair you fill, the dignity of the occasion upon which we have convened, which dignity is all derived from the dignity of HIM who fills the chair, and of HIM who wrote the book which has caused this discussion, who is promoted by the dignitaries of the Church to be the chief dignitary of all the dignitaries of this ECCLESIASTICAL COURT, I feel MYSELF dignified while I dignify YOU, Sir, who are dignified by those whom all men dignify! Sir, I rise to move you, that there shall, at the close of this debate, be established a seminary of Ecclesiastical or Canon Law, in which there shall be three professorships, all to be filled by *Baptist preachers:* the first, to form into a body of reports the decisions of all judicatories, drawn from their records and judgment-rolls, every Baptist congregation being a judicatory; the second, from these reports, and from our *standards,* "Orchard's History of Foreign Baptists," and "The Great Iron Wheel," to form regular *digests*, pandects, or *codices legum ecclesiasticorum;* the third, to arrange and complete a lexicon of legal terms and phrases, adapted to the "New Version," to be entitled, *Lexicon Verborum Theologiorum Ecclesiasticorumque;* and furthermore, that the theological course of every candidate for the ministry in our said Baptist Church shall be the study of the "Iron Wheel," *without prayers*, and of "Orchard's History of Foreign Baptists," with a mixture of *corn whisky*, which I presume every one will see to be of vital importance to the ministerial character! Sir, this would be a shot aimed at the Devil's head-quarters of Methodism! It would be baking our biscuits in the big Dutch oven of Charity, carefully conserved with the spirit of the *Reverend Rooster* of the "Tennessee Baptist," leavened with the leaven of *Free-soilism* from the "Western Reserve," and perfumed with the honeysuckles of the slander suit in Henderson county!

But Methodism is "human workmanship, and will not bear close scrutiny." Indeed! Were we living in the days of the inspired apostles, we might pause to argue this question of a "Divine right" to preach the word and to administer the ordinances of the Church. Or did this charge come from an inspired prophet or apostle, we should pause to look into its merits; but coming from a Church having no *regular and uniform* system of government, every separate congregation doing just as it may choose, and undoing to-day what a neighboring congregation may have done on yesterday; a Church professing one faith in one county or State, and another and a different faith in an adjoining county or State; a Church making war upon Bible, Tract, Sabbath-school, Temperance, and Missionary Societies here, and advocating each and all of those yonder, as the intelligence of the community may seem to call for it; a Church commissioning and sending forth a set of young and old, ignorant, uneducated, and uncouth men to preach God's word, who have not sense enough to tell whether the United States are in North or South America—all held together by the cohesive power and attraction of *water*—to talk about "human workmanship" in other branches of the Church is preposterous! But if it be true that the Methodist system is even a well-regulated *human invention*, it has greatly the advantage of the Baptist organization, for that is *a botched affair* in every respect.

Methodism is "human workmanship, and will not bear close scrutiny," writes the "Recorder," and so writes Elder Graves before that print, and in divers places! The design of this figure is to convey the false idea to the mind that the doctrines and discipline of the Methodist Church have no foundation in Scripture, and are only the works of man. Judge Blackstone somewhere remarks, that a man ignorant of *human* laws, who falls into transgression, may, through the imperfection of *human* administration, be holden to the legal penalty, but, nevertheless, cannot be, in the eyes of society, or even of the law itself, impeached of moral or political turpitude, unless the transgression be of a nature which the universal laws of society forbid; which qualification supposes that *he might have known better!* In this case, I cannot enter the plea of ignorance for the "Recorder" and Graves: they both knew better. They have wilfully and intentionally *lied*, and have thereby committed an offence which the *universal laws of society forbid*, to say nothing of the express law of God. The shameless and strenuous vindication of error and selfishness, so prominent in all the writing, conversation, preaching of Graves, and, I am sorry to add, in the conduct of his understrikers dispersed throughout the South and West—for they are all of a piece—the virulence with which they attack all idea of disinterestedness, even in the great concerns of *religion*, justify the conclusion that the pursuit of self-interest is their supreme object.

All that is charged in this Baptist journal is repeated, and even more and worse, in Graves's slanderous book, which goes out to the world with the endorsement of the "North Carolina Publishing Society" of the Baptist Church. What is charged? Why, that the Methodists, far and wide, are a generation of sectarian dupes, or of pious knaves. Their whole system of doctrines and polity is the wicked contrivance of men—it is the result of "human workmanship." If *human*, of course it is not *Divine:* if of *man*, it cannot be of *God*, and ought not to be sanctioned in Protestant Christendom. The Methodist common masses are all ignorant dolts; their leaders are all wicked deceivers; their doctrines are all unscriptural; the whole Church is a mass of corruption and moral putrefaction! This is substantially the charge, and it is endorsed by the "North Carolina Publishing Society" of the Baptist Church!

As the Baptist denomination is *superhuman*, and its acts are all by *Divine authority*, let us look into some of them, and see how they will compare with the "human workmanship" of Methodism. The "Powell's Valley Association," in East Tennessee, consisting of *nineteen* churches, reported its proceedings in the "Louisville Banner," for the year 1842, the *organ* then of the denomination in the South-west, as it still is to a very great extent, though the name of the paper is changed. From this report and this paper I make the following extract, which, though coming from a Church claiming to be in a regular line of succession from John the Baptist, and even *Christ himself*, I must say, argues a *dark-minded* Christianity:

Powell's Valley Association.—This is a *new test* association, and carries the matter somewhat further than most of their brethren. They do not recognize as valid the baptism of any one who has received that ordinance from a *Baptist* minister who is friendly to missions, *or from a Baptist minister who is friendly to any minister who is friendly to missions!* All such persons, if they join them, must be rebaptized. We have *some* "out and out" brethren in Tennessee. The Powell's Valley excommunicated at their last session three other *associations and all who correspond with them.*

Here were THREE ASSOCIATIONS EXCOMMUNICATED—the bull of the true Church hurled at them, because they were friendly to the cause of *Christian missions!* Will it be said these were *Hard-shells?* They were *immersionists,* holding to the *loose form of Church government* adhered to by the hundred and one factions into which immersionists are divided, some contending for one peculiarity, and some another; but all agreeing harmoniously that there is no salvation out of their fold!

A certain *Mr. Jewett,* a renegade from the Presbyterian ministry, one whose order of talents did not secure to him a comfortable support in that Church, went over to the Graves and Howell wing of the Baptist denomination a few years ago; and at Marietta, Ohio, published a book in favor of his new associates, and against all others not of that "faith and order." On page 110 of this work, Mr. Jewett thus boasts of the absence of all system, order, and government in the Baptist Church—unimportant items, which had given him some uneasiness while a Presbyterian:

Without creed or catechism, without General Assemblies, or other high judicatories of the Church, without Archbishops or Bishops, Baptists have walked together harmoniously, uniting with each other in efforts to extend Christ's kingdom, till they embrace in their churches a larger body of believers than any other denomination in the United States.

"A larger body of believers!" Believers in what? Why, in *baptism by immersion,* as the only scriptural mode, and the only possible road to heaven! Well, I grant it; and God forbid that "any other denomination in the United States" should ever equal them in numbers of this faith!

A few years ago, the Baptists of North Carolina published a pamphlet, officially setting forth their views of missions,

Bible, tract, Sunday-school, and temperance societies, as of "human workmanship," and not entitled to the esteem and confidence of true believers in Christ! This infidel production was republished, with approbation, at Jonesborough, by ELDER BAYLESS, the bell-wether of the Graves wing of that Church in Upper East Tennessee, and extensively circulated. From this singular production, commencing on page 11th, I give such extracts as follow:

The fourth religion I shall notice as having been established in the world, is the *missionary establishment;* and will examine that for the marks of craft. It is abundantly harped upon that Jesus Christ and his apostles were all missionaries: that is agreed to, as to words or office, but here lies the great matter in dispute: were they craft men? did they make gain by godliness? did they make a craft of their religion, like modern missionaries? I hope to show presently, from the New Testament, they did not. The first moneyed missionary society that ever was established in the world, as I can find on the pages of history, was established in the year 1622, by Pope Gregory XV.,—for the New Testament knows nothing of money-established religion,—and then called the Congregation for Propagation of the Faith. It had, like our modern missions, an incredible number of donors, rich, and emulous to excel in the greatest gifts, as well as being greatly enriched by Urban VIII. And, by this Congregation's money, a vast number of missionaries were sent to the remotest parts of the world, among the most barbarous nations, and in India, China, and Japan.

The sect of Christians called Moravians founded the second mission, about one hundred years ago. The third missionary establishment was formed about twenty or thirty years ago, in London, called the Evangelical Society. The fourth, called the Baptist Missionary Society, in England. And, lastly, the Baptist Missionary Society in America, with others of like occupation. All of which are founded on beggars and money, like that of Pope Gregory's. These are all important establishments of the craft kind,—for their like cannot be found in the New Testament—the basis of which are money, honor, and titles.

But, as I am limited to a mere sketch, I shall begin with the Baptist Missionary Society founded in England. In the year 1784, at an Association held at Nottingham, England, it was agreed to set apart an hour of prayer the first Monday evening of every month, for a revival of religion, and the extension of Christ's kingdom in the world: so far plausible. Now, who were at the head, plan, or seem to have had the chief management of this society? Why, John Ryland, Reynold Hogg, William Carey, John Sutcliff, and Andrew Fuller. Were they priests? Surely; for do you not know that the priests were, are, and must be at the head of all the schemes of the day? And Mr. Carey was one of the committee, and helped form the plan that has got him along, according to the best accounts I can get, to $6,000 a-year—a good business indeed for a preacher: neither the prophets, John the Baptist, nor Christ, nor his apostles, ever shared such a loaf as this. Mr. Robertson and wife were allowed $840 per year, and Mr. Chater and wife and two children were allowed $960 a-year for missionary services. Now, my hearers, say whether you think either of these men would have left the British shore, if it had so turned out there had been no money. I think not.

Much is said about the Temperance Society, but, if I am rightly informed, those who join are not to drink one drop: if so, it has a wrong name, for it ought to be called the Abstaining Society. Does such a society agree with Scripture? "Drink no longer water," says Paul to Timothy, "but use a little wine;" and of deacons he says: "Not given to much wine;" and the Saviour drank wine. And because some men make a storehouse of their belly, I must eat none; and because some men have burned up their kettles, I must not hang mine on the fire; and because some men have been killed by medicine, I must not use it prudently. What sophistry of priests!

And as it regards tract societies and Sunday-school unions, they are about the worst of the whole gang; for they are also the inventions of the priests, and contain craft for printers, and they should cry out, as well as the priests: "Our craft is in danger; for you know by this, our printing tracts, we have our wealth;" and the writers should cry out, since premiums are offered for the best tract on such a subject; and the traders in tracts also may cry out; but the worst of all the effects, is the sectarian principles infused in the minds of youths; for it is but reasonable to suppose that the writers will squint an eye to their party, and give that turn to them that will mostly establish and enhance their sect.

These *infidel* doctrines, set forth by the North Carolina Baptists, and afterwards republished by the same Church in Tennessee, show most conclusively the opposition of that sect to all *human* and *Divine* workmanship! And I would like to know how many members of the present "Publishing Society" of the North Carolina Baptists were connected with this manifesto, and took their stand upon it at the time, as a platform of principles!

The disposition among Baptist preachers and writers to misrepresent Methodism is too general, and has been ever since we have known them, now upwards of thirty dreadful years! I have before me a volume of "The True Light and

Baptist Monthly Visitor," published in Jonesborough, by MASON R. LYON, a Baptist preacher, in 1836, and edited by "Elder Rees Bayless, with associated brethren." No. 10 of this paper contains many misrepresentations, both of Methodists and Presbyterians, upon the subjects of *communion* and *baptism*. I will give the following as a *sample*, found on page 154:

> THE METHODISTS WILL BAPTIZE BY IMMERSION THOSE WHO HAVE BEEN ONCE SPRINKLED, AND BY THAT MEANS TACITLY AND VIRTUALLY DENY THE AUTHENTICITY AND VALIDITY OF SPRINKLING!

Now, this is not part of an *editorial*, for which one man would be responsible, but it is part of a letter on Close Communion, from an *association*, published by authority, and by a vote of the members endorsing it, and sending it out to the world. It is an association of Baptist ministers saying to the world that the Methodists will and do *rebaptize those whom they know to have been once baptized!* There is not one word of truth in the whole statement. It is a downright slander. It is neither the faith nor the practice of the Methodists. But, on the contrary, they hold it to be *a profanation of sacred things*, and so teach, on all occasions, to rebaptize any one, old or young, man or child, *who has once been baptized*, whether the ordinance have been administered by immersion, pouring, or sprinkling. The Methodists hold baptism, as practiced by all orthodox denominations who acknowledge the essential divinity of Christ, to be valid. Therefore, they will not rebaptize any one, though he come from another branch of the great Christian family well recommended, and ardently desiring baptism and Church membership among them.

But this same association, in this same letter, on page 155 of the "True Light and Visitor," thus shows its hand further, upon the great questions of *baptism* and *close communion:*

There is a small denomination of Baptists in this country who call themselves Christians. Though they have given themselves a very good name, yet the united Baptists cannot fellowship with them, and consequently cannot invite them to the Lord's table. They agree with us respecting the ordinance of baptism, but they *will invite Pedobaptists to commune with them;* and it remains with them to show their authority for communing with those persons whom they believe to be UNBAPTIZED!

What comment is necessary upon the foregoing? I deem it proper to repeat what I have said, in substance, in the general argument upon baptism, and the hypothesis of Close Communion Baptists, who seek to nullify the Abrahamic covenant, and, what is worse, to dispense with the sacred office of the gospel ministry!

1. The Close Baptists lay such a stress upon baptism by immersion, as to make it the sole condition of admittance to the Lord's table—a table which, they say, can only be spread by ministers who have been immersed, no others being invested with ministerial functions, or even members of the Church of Christ. And yet, of late, they will tolerate such of their members as commune with the Methodists! For proof, in this county and Greene, we refer to late occurrences at Cherokee, at Urbana, and at Milburnton!

2. The Close Baptists hold and teach that there is no Church militant but THEIRS, and that there is no ministry but such as is constituted by churches of *their "faith and order;"* but they will call on a Methodist or Presbyterian minister, at their revivals, to address the throne of grace, or to preach in their pulpits—thus making such a one their *mouth* or *organ,* either to ask God's blessings to be poured upon them, or to declare his will concerning them, which is vastly more sacred and important than to prepare and offer the bread and wine!

3. The Close Baptists believe and teach that *immersion* is the only door into the Church; but they will not receive into their communion candidates who have been regularly and properly immersed, except they *repudiate* their baptism, and the ministerial functions of all other ministers: therefore, the repudiation of the ministerial functions of all other clergymen is the door into the regular Baptist Church.

4. The Close Baptists are influenced by a spirit which is opposed to the kingdom of Christ—a spirit which would set up *another kingdom* in opposition, and nullify the covenant of God, and at the same time wear the name of Christian! God has never had but one spiritual

kingdom in the world. This kingdom was set up in the family of Abraham. It was with God's people in the wilderness, and was planted with them in the land of promise. In this kingdom Christ was born. Over this kingdom Christ reigns. The Close Baptists have set up a kingdom in opposition to Christ: therefore the Close Baptists are guilty of HIGH TREASON AGAINST GOD!!

CHAPTER XX.

Elder Graves and slavery—Separation of the Methodist Church on account of slavery — Slaveholders admitted into the apostolic Churches—Primitive Christians held slaves—Proof from the Scriptures that slavery existed in the earliest days of the Christian Church—Views of Drs. Neander and Clarke—According to the Scriptures, slavery will exist to the end of time—Concluding remarks.

Allusion has already been made to the doubtful position of *Elder Graves* upon the great and exciting question of slavery, in a former chapter of this work. The *secret* of his "armed neutrality" upon this great issue, and in this stirring period of the world, is two-fold: first, as a Northern man by birth and education, he is *anti-slavery* at heart, or, to use the language of a distinguished politician, he is "*pro-North and anti-South;*" and next, his slanderous book, now going through a second or third edition, was written and published with a view to make money; and to adapt it to the tastes of his sectarian friends on both sides of Mason and Dixon's line, he has passed the subject by with silent contempt, although he has ridiculed the separation of the Methodist Church, *South*, from the Methodist Church, *North*, which separation was caused alone by the *slavery agitation of Northern Freesoil Methodists* in the General Conference of 1844, in New York, which everybody outside of a madhouse or leading-strings is presumed to know. The *Southern* portion of the Methodist Church had no other alternative left them but to separate from their Freesoil brethren of the North;

and, as a Southern man, I endorse their act of separation most heartily. They sought to *ostracize* one of the Southern bishops, an able and experienced officer of the Church, eminent for public services and extensive usefulness, because, in a second marriage, he had selected a lady who owned *a few slaves!* The marriage was admitted to be a prudent one: the lady, now in her grave, was every way fitted for the wife of a bishop; but then a former marriage had left her in possession of a half-dozen slaves. Here was the *occasion* which abolitionism sought, at the North, to direct its shafts against the fortress of slavery; and they sought to carry it by their strong and powerful cannonading. The imprudence of the anti-slavery party in that General Conference did more to rouse the South to resistance, than all the belligerent attitudes assumed by the hotheaded politicians of the country—sending a thrill through the Southern States, and awakening sentiments of heroism and moral daring alike creditable to the Church and honorable to the country.

This is no time for frank and patriotic men to remain neutral upon a subject alike affecting the interests of the Church and the country. I *volunteer* to show my hand upon this great question, not caring one *dime* whether it array the entire North against me or not. And the people of the South should require this *adopted citizen*, Elder Graves, to state, in unmistakable terms, whether or not he now entertains the same feelings and views, touching the great slavery question, that he did while a citizen of the "Western Reserve," in Ohio, where abolitionism is a *trade* with nine-tenths of the inhabitants. Let Mr. Graves be interrogated, and forced to define his position at once, or leave the South in hot haste! Let him be driven at once out of the stagnant pool of abolitionism, that his whispers and insinuations may no longer send forth *malaria* and death among the institutions of the South! Political disquiet and commotion are daily giving birth and sustenance to new and loftier schemes of agitation and disunion among the vile abolitionists; to bold and hazardous enterprises in the States and Territories, and even in *Congress;* to insurrection and revolution throughout the entire country! Among political men, without distinction of party, the common virtues of honesty and truth have become superannuated and obsolete! The slavery agitation, that had been buried by the Compromise Acts of 1850, is anew lifting its head, and, under the piratical flag of "Black Republicanism," asserting the rights of "human liberty:" her infernal altars smoke with fresh incense, and, enlisted in her defence, are scores of designing men in the South—some filling pulpits, some occupying high positions in colleges and academies, and who, though among us, are "not of us," our Southern friends may rest assured!

I am not, and never have been, *interested* in the slave-traffic, or immersed in the cares, advantages, or disadvantages of the institution of slavery, and therefore I claim to be a *disinterested* looker-on. A native of Virginia, I have lived half a century in the South, and seen the workings of the institution of slavery, in its best and worst forms, and in all the Southern States. I have gone among the free negroes at the North, and, in every instance, I have found them more miserable and destitute, as a whole, than the slave population of the South. In our Southern States, where negroes have been set at liberty, in nine cases out of ten, their conditions have been made worse; while the most wretched, lazy, and dishonest class of persons to be found in the Southern States, are *free persons of color.* I therefore go against the emancipation of slaves altogether, unless they can be sent to Liberia at once. I take my stand with the friends of the institution of slavery in the South, and, in defence of the rights of the South, connected with this question, I will go as far as the next man—even dying in the last ditch!

It is a well-known *historical fact*, that slaveholders were admitted into the APOSTOLIC CHURCHES; nor would this assumed position of the advocates of slavery be at all denied by any intelligent and well-read men at the North, but for the fact that they think such an admission would decide the question against abolitionists. I have given much attention to this subject within ten years past, and I feel no sort of delicacy in expressing my views and convictions, as revolting as they may be to Northern men and Freesoilers, even among us. I believe that the primitive Christians held slaves in bondage, and that the apostles favored slavery, by admitting slaveholders into the Church, and by promoting them to official stations in the Church. And why do I believe all this? Because I am sustained in these positions by uninterrupted historical testimony! I have seen similar views, only not quite so strong, urged by gentlemen who even go against slavery, as it exists in the South—among whom I name the REV. DR. DURBIN, a gentleman of great learning, extensive research, and of undoubted piety. He boldly affirms that slaveholders were admitted into the apostolic Churches, in an elaborate paper which appeared in the NEW YORK CHRISTIAN ADVOCATE AND JOURNAL, in December, 1855. I took the same ground in a newspaper controversy with an Ohio abolitionist, even three years ago! The coincidence establishes only these facts: first, that candid men of reading must make the same *historical discoveries;* and next, if we all go to historic premises, the conclusions are easy and clear.

Well, for the information of *Elder Graves*, and other anti-slavery men dispersed throughout the South, I assume that the fact of the apostles admitting into Church fellowship slaveholders, and promoting them to positions of honor and trust, shows that the simple relation of master and slave was no bar to Church membership. Masters and slaves, in the days of the apostles, were admitted into the Church as breth ren; they partook in common of the benefits of the Church; they held to the same religious principles; they squared their lives by the same rule of conduct; acknowledged the same obligations one to another; and worshipped at the same altar. This was true of the first and succeeding centuries, when the relations of master and slave, and the practice of the Church in reference thereto, were very much like they are in the Southern States of our Union at present. But to the proof that slaveholders were admitted into the apostolic Churches.

1. Historians all agree that slavery existed, and was general throughout the Roman empire, at the time the apostolic Churches were instituted. I have at my command the authorities to prove this, but to quote from them would swell this chapter beyond what I have intended. I will cite the authorities only; and anti-slavery men who deny my position can examine my authorities. See Gibbon's "Decline and Fall of the Roman Empire," vol. i. See "Inquiry into Roman Slavery, by Wm. Blair," Edinburgh edition of 1833. See vol. iv. of "Lardner's Works," page 213. See vol. i. of "Dr. Robertson's Works," London edition. Other authorities might be given, but these are sufficient, as they show that slavery was a civil institution of the State; that the Roman laws regarded slaves as *property*, at the disposal of their masters; that these slaves, whether white or colored, had no civil existence or rights, and contended for none; and that there were *three slaves to one citizen*—showing something of a similarity between the Roman empire and our Southern States! Gibbon says that slavery existed in "every province and every family," and that they were bought and sold according to their capacities for usefulness, and the demand for laborers—selling at hundreds of dollars, and from that down to the price of a beast of burden! Now, it is notorious that the gospel made considerable progress among the citizens of the Roman empire; and, as nearly every family owned

slaves, it is certain that slaveholders were converted and admitted into the Church. It will not do to say that the poor, including the slaves, were alone converted to God, because the apostles make frequent allusions to the receiving into the Church of intelligent, learned, and opulent persons. The learned DR. MOSHEIM, in his Church History, vol. i., relating to the *first three centuries*, settles this question most effectually. He says:

> The apostles, in their writings, prescribe rules for the conduct of the rich as well as the poor, for *masters* as well as *servants*—a convincing proof that among the members of the Church planted by them were to be found persons of opulence, and masters of families. St. Paul and St. Peter admonished Christian women not to study the adorning of themselves with pearls, with gold and silver, or costly array. 1 Tim. ii. 9: 1 Peter iii. 3. It is, therefore, plain that there must have been women possessed of wealth adequate to the purchase of bodily ornaments of great price. From 1 Tim. vi. 20, and Col. ii. 8, it is manifest that among the first converts to Christianity there were men of learning and philosophers; for, if the wise and the learned had unanimously rejected the Christian religion, what occasion could there have been for this caution? 1 Cor. i. 26, unquestionably carries with it the plainest intimation that persons of rank or power were not wholly wanting in that assembly. Indeed, lists of the names of various illustrious persons who embraced Christianity, in its weak and infantile state, are given by Blondel, p. 235 de Episcopis et Presbyteris; also by Wetstein, in his Preface to Origen's Dia. Con. Mar., p. 13.

2. I come next to show, from scriptural evidence, that slavery existed in the earliest days of the Christian Church, and that both *masters* and *slaves* were members of the Church. I assert, without the fear of contradiction, that the apostles did not denounce slavery as an evil, after the fashion of New England preachers; nor did the apostles require that persons held in bondage should be emancipated, after the manner of *Theodore Parker*, and others of Elder Graves's New England brethren! Slavery was an institution of the State, in the Roman empire, as it is in certain States in this Union, and the apostles did not feel at liberty to denounce it, if indeed they

felt the least opposition to it, which I deny. Hear the apostles on this subject:

> Let every man abide in the same calling wherein he was called. Art thou called being *a servant?* Care not for it; but if thou mayest be made free, use it rather. For he that is called in the Lord, being *a servant*, is the Lord's freeman; likewise also he that is called, being free, is Christ's servant.—1 Cor. vii. 20–22.
>
> *Servants*, be obedient to them that are your *masters according to the flesh*, with fear and trembling, in singleness of your heart, as unto Christ. Not with eye-service, as men-pleasers; but as the servants of Christ, doing the will of God from the heart. With good-will doing service, as to the Lord, and not to men: knowing that whatsoever good thing any man doeth, the same shall he receive of the Lord, whether he be bond or free. And, *ye masters*, do the same things unto them, forbearing threatening: knowing that your Master also is in heaven: neither is there respect of persons with him.—Eph. vi. 5–9.
>
> *Servants*, obey in all things your *masters according to the flesh;* not with eye-service, as men-pleasers; but in singleness of heart, fearing God. And whatsoever ye do, do it heartily, as to the Lord, and not unto men: knowing that of the Lord ye shall receive the reward of the inheritance; for ye serve the Lord Christ.—Col. iii. 22–25.
>
> *Masters*, give unto *your servants* that which is just and equal: knowing that ye also have a Master in heaven.—Col. iv. 1.
>
> Let as many *servants as are under the yoke* count their *own masters* worthy of all honor, that the name of God and his doctrine be not blasphemed. And they that have *believing masters*, let them not despise them, because they are brethren; but rather do them service, because they are faithful and beloved, partakers of the benefit. These things teach and exhort.—1 Tim. vi. 1, 2.
>
> Exhort *servants* to be obedient unto their *own masters*, and to please them well in all things, not answering again; not purloining, but showing all good fidelity; that they may adorn the doctrine of God our Saviour in all things.—Titus ii. 9, 10.
>
> *Servants*, be subject to *your masters* with all fear; not only to the good and gentle, but also to the froward. For this is thankworthy, if a man for conscience toward God endure grief, suffering wrongfully. —1 Peter ii. 18, 19.

I have but a single word of comment to offer upon these passages of Scripture. The original words used by the Greek writers, both sacred and profane, to express *slave;* the most *abject condition of slavery;* to express the *absolute owner of a slave*, and the *absolute control of a slave*, are the *strongest* that the language affords, and are used in the passages here quoted. If the apostles understood the common use of words, and desired to convey these ideas, and to recognize the relations of *master* and *servant*, they would, naturally enough, employ the very words used. To say that they did not know the primary meaning and *usus loquendi* of the original words, is paying them a compliment I wish not to participate in! And to show that I am not singular in my views of the meaning expressed in the passages quoted, showing that they express in the one case *slaves*, and in the other *masters* or *owners*, actually holding them as *property*, under the sanction of the laws of the State, I quote from the following authorities:

That great commentator, DR. ADAM CLARKE, on 1 Cor. vii. 21, says:

> Art thou converted to Christ while thou art a slave—the property of another person, and bought with his money? *Care not for it.*

The learned Dr. Neander, in his work entitled "Planting and Training of the Church," in referring to *Onesimus*, mentioned in the epistle to Philemon, says of him:

> It does not appear to be surprising that a *runaway slave* should betake himself at once to Rome.

To the foregoing might be added other authorities of equal weight and importance, but I will not burden this chapter with extended quotations. Nor will I weary the patience of the reader with passages from profane history, in the centuries immediately following the apostolic, as I could do if I deemed it at all necessary. And, from the foregoing facts and authorities, I will make such brief observations as, to my mind, seem warranted, and then conclude this chapter.

First.—There is not a single passage in the New Testament, nor a single act in the records of the Church, during her early history, for even centuries, containing any direct, professed, or intended denunciation of slavery. But the apostles found the institution existing, under the authority and sanction of law; and, in their labors among the people, *masters* and *slaves* bowed at the same altar, communed at the same table, and were taken into the Church together; while they exhorted the one to treat the other as became the gospel, and the other to obedience and honesty, that their religious professions might not be evil spoken of!

Secondly.—The early Church not only admitted the existence of slavery, but in various ways, by her teachings and discipline, expressed her *approbation* of it, enforcing the observance of certain *Fugitive Slave Laws* which had been enacted by the State. And, in the various acts of the Church, from the times of the apostles downward through several centuries, she enacted laws and adopted regulations touching the duties of masters and slaves, *as such.* This, in my humble judgment, amounts to a justification and defence of the institution of slavery.

Thirdly.—My investigations of this subject have led me regularly, gradually, certainly, to the conclusion that God intended the relation of master and slave to exist. Hence, when God opened the way for the organization of the Church, the apostles and first teachers of Christianity found slavery *incorporated with every department of society;* and, in the adoption of rules for the government of the members of the Church, they provided for the rights of owners, and the wants of slaves.

Fourthly.—Slavery, in the age of the apostles, had so penetrated society, and was so intimately interwoven with it, that a religion preaching freedom to the slave would have arrayed against it the civil authorities, armed against itself the whole power of the State, and destroyed the usefulness of its preachers. St. Paul knew this, and did not assail the institution of slavery, but labored to get both masters and slaves to heaven, as all ministers should do in our day.

Fifthly. — Slavery having existed ever since the first organization of the Church, the Scriptures clearly teach that it will exist even to the end of time. Rev. vi. 12–17 points to "The Day of Judgment," "The Last Day," "The Great Day," and the condition of the human race at that time, as well as the *classes of persons* to be judged, rewarded, and punished! A portion of this text reads, "And the kings of the earth, and the great men, and the rich men, and the chief captains, and the mighty men, and every BONDMAN, and every FREEMAN," etc., will be there; evidently implying that slavery will exist, and that the relations of master and slave will be recognized to the end of time!

In conclusion, the Methodist Church, South, occupies true scriptural ground upon the subject of slavery, and is now exercising proper Christian authority over her slaveholding members, enforcing the duties which grow out of the relation of a *Christian master* to his *dependent slave,* whether the latter be religious or irreligious, and out of the relations of both to the Church.

TO THE METHODISTS.

OUR heading indicates that this is a kind of address to the members of the Methodist Connection. I do not claim to have a peculiar license to deal out general and extraordinary epistles to the Church throughout the South. It is a liberty which ought to be taken by but few men, and they should be men whose age, experience, and long periods of effective service, give them claims to be heard. If, however, any remarkable events have rendered it necessary that a distinct and an immediate appeal should be made, I will be tolerated in this, as I will be in the preparation of this work, notwithstanding more suitable persons could have been found to execute the task in any one of the Conferences belonging to the Southern division of the Church.

A century and a quarter have now passed away since the establishment of Wesleyan Methodism, and the experience of that extended period has shown that the fabric is not composed of those unsubstantial materials which its violent but mistaken enemies surmised. Assailants have arisen at different periods, in Europe and America; and in the earlier stages of its existence, on both continents, persecutions, "fierce as ten furies," were ever and anon let loose, followed up by the blows of men of tenfold more intellect and force of character than the miserable calumniator of the "Tennessee Baptist" can bring to bear in his feeble crusade. A half a century ago, in this country, often came "the world's dread laugh, which scarce the firm philosopher sustains:" to this, in most of the cities, towns, and refined circles, was added, *proud disdain.* But in the midst of this elemental strife, which has been a war both of *principle* and *practice*, the peculiar institutions of Methodism remained unshaken: the outworks have been pressed, but no breach was ever made. The more violent the assaults made, the stronger the defences raised up, while more advanced positions have been taken. The whole structure of Methodism, both in doctrines and discipline, indicates durability. Many who once opposed the system are now its open advocates and admirers. Others have moderated in their attacks; and those who are now openly in the field, as opposers, are men of rather small calibre, seeking to hide the defects in their own characters by a war upon a great system. The whole has resulted in this: it has demonstrated that while the members of the Methodist Church are faithful to themselves and to the professions they have assumed, no injury can be inflicted. The lucubrations of bad men like *Graves* may excite occasional notice, and their numerous unmitigated slanders may produce occasional apprehension; but, like ripples on the distant wave, they are formed but to disappear; and, as time has shown, they can have no effect on the course of the mighty stream to which they are indebted for momentary appearance!

It is no new discovery now that the founder of Methodism was a man endowed with the first order of intellect; but this one thing I can say, namely, that his ambition was not to astonish mankind by the display of talent, natural or acquired. He lived for others; and it is now history that he kindled a light, not to dazzle but to benefit his fellow-creatures. In disposition, John Wesley was kind, placable, and affectionate. He practiced a strict economy, not from any sordid motives, but for the purpose of administering extensively to the wants of the poor. His integrity was unimpeachable; and money would have been of no value in his estimation, but that it afforded him the means of increasing his utility. When a young man at Oxford, his income was thirty pounds per annum, and he gave two of that away. When his income was increased to sixty, two years after that, he still lived on twenty-eight, and gave away thirty-two. The next year he received one hundred and twenty; still he lived on as before, and gave away ninety-two. In the height of his power, the Commissioners of the Excise, supposing that he had silver-plate which, in order to avoid the duty, he had not returned, wrote to him on the subject. Mr. Wesley replied: "I have two silver spoons in London, and one in Bristol: this is all the plate that I have at present, and I shall not buy any more *while so many around me want bread!*" He even *studied* for the benefit of others. If his learning became prominent, its exhibition was incidental rather than designed. It came to his relief and aid only when called for; and among the many excellences for which his works are remarkable, the simplicity of his style, to the exclusion of verbiage and vain display, is by no means the least remarkable. To his mind, naturally powerful and comprehensive, was added a correctness of perception which, at the commencement of his public life, enabled him not only to prepare the most judicious rules for the government of his then infant societies, but to examine and compare their agreement with each other, their bearing upon the general system, and to choose the most proper agents in reducing the whole to practical purposes. The consequence is, as every intelligent Methodist knows, that where this system exists in healthful exercise, as it now does in our Southern States, each part is brought sufficiently forward, and no portion is overlooked: there is a place for every man, whether rich or poor, in high position or of low degree, and every man *ought to be in his place!*

Another main advantage included in the entire plan of Methodism, as organized by Wesley, is that it offers suitable employment to every member. Varied as is the capacity of the human mind in different persons, such are the general duties connected with works of mercy and benevolence, which have gradually arisen within the pale of Methodism, that no man need "stand all the day," or any part of the day, "*idle.*" As an initiatory step, and an exercise of humility, he might enter a Sabbath-school, and begin a course of good works, by teaching some poor child to read his vernacular tongue, as well as the first lessons of salvation. Engagements more extensive may follow, and will, as one progresses in works of goodness—more *honorable* they cannot be. The ignorant are not only to be instructed, but the sick are to be consoled, and the suffering are to be relieved. Contributions which we can all well spare, will go far to enlighten and convert our slave population, by sending among them reliable ministers, to labor exclusively for their benefit, as domestic missionaries; and as their benefactors, we cannot fail to feel ourselves amended. Religion without *practice,* like water without *motion,* is certain to stagnate. The founder of Methodism knew this fact, and acted upon this principle; and therefore it is that, next to an unblamable life, the best evidence that a man can give of the genuineness of his religion is to be found attempting to communicate it to others, and discharging those duties and obligations which true religion enjoins. The whole tendency of Methodism is to this kind of activity, and the natural tendency of Christianity in the heart is to the same activity. "*Up and be doing*" is the motto of Methodism, and it is the essence of Christianity. To an *inactive life* Methodism is constantly opposed; because, as in the grave there will be enough of leisure, *now* is the time, and "while it is called to-day," for improvement and usefulness.

This is, in part at least, what is meant by the apostle when he exhorts us to *work out our salvation with fear and trembling.* The work of salvation is no lazy man's business; but it is a work of great difficulty, which requires close application and constant labor. Are all the nobler faculties of the mind and the efforts of life devoted to the attainment of the goods and honors of this world? and shall we expect to obtain heaven by mere accident? Certainly not. He who made us without our aid, never intends to save us unless we first save ourselves from this untoward generation. He will not save us unless we ourselves fight the good fight of faith, unless we agonize to enter in at the strait gate. The most laborious servitude is rendered tolerable by an assurance that we shall receive its entire and ample product. In the work of salvation we secure our own peace and happiness, both in this life and in that which is to come; and unless we *work out our salvation,* in the sense in which both Paul and Wesley enforced the doctrine, we plunge our souls into guilt and fear in this life, and into eternal despair in the next. Solemn thought! Hence, says the apostle, "Work out your own salvation with fear and trembling."

Consider the difficulty of the work and the danger of miscarriage, according to our theory, and it is founded upon the word of God. No outward forms, such as *immersion,* can make us clean, or save us from apostasy. We have mountains of difficulty to pass over; we have many difficult duties to perform; we have many open enemies, as well as foes in ambush, to contend with—exposed as we are to the attacks of the Devil, our common enemy, and to a host of bad men, who, like this unregenerate preacher, *Elder Graves,* seek to aggravate, and drive us from the path of duty. These *pirates of hell,* who watch to make cruel depredation on all the ocean of life, are the more dangerous as they sail under the false flag of Christianity. At one point, they exhibit the presumptuous rock of the *apostolic succession*, to drive us from the channel of self-denial, faith, hope, and charity; at another, they invite us to the sand-banks of *immersion*, on which thousands have been eternally shipwrecked. To avoid all these dangers, we have only to consult the map of our voyage frequently, the word of God, obey the orders of our Captain, Jesus Christ, and follow the directions of our pilot, John Wesley, and pray much for the Holy Spirit—observing the progress we make, and keeping an exact journal of our voyage!

Finally, upon this point, let us be sure that our hearts are changed, and that the love of God dwells in us: let us continue to worship God in the spirit, rejoice in Christ Jesus, instead of our denominational peculiarities, and see that we have no confidence in *baptism*, save as an outward ordinance. Then, when clouds of opposition shall thicken around us, the storms of sectarian malice arise, and the furious waves of calumny dash against each other, our minds shall be calm, and our souls shall rest secure in the arms of Safety; and with our anchor of hope cast in the port of heaven, and we working our passage with all diligence, we cannot fail, according to the doctrines of Methodism, which are taken from the Bible, to land in that happy country where all is peace and joy for ever!

One thing is clear: While the Methodist Church preserves her primitive simplicity, prosperity will follow; and it is a remarkable fact, that although attempts have been made, the tendency of which is to undermine her security, they have uniformly failed, both in Europe and America. Another fact, not much less singular, is that, so far as the parties are known, almost every attempt of the kind may be traced to men of whose minds the canker of personal corruption, or of immoral practices, has eaten up the better part. In two instances in Tennessee, the one in East and the other in Middle Tennessee, condensed malice, which seemed to gather strength by confinement in corrupt bosoms, has suddenly exploded, and slanders of all dimensions have been let loose, as if the fatal box had just been opened. In this warfare, pious men of any denomination have never joined; and it is scarcely needful to add that they never will. A desultory warfare, to which the daring and vulgar assaults of Ross and GRAVES have led, has been carried on in Tennessee, Georgia, and North Carolina, but the little havoc they have made has been about what might be expected from men meddling with things beyond their reach. The few clerical bull-dogs in East Tennessee, who espouse the cause in which *Graves* has signally failed, are not likely to excite respectable opposition. These men have done their worst, and there has been no extraordinary shock in the kingdom either of nature or grace. The sun rises as usual. Men go forth to their ordinary occupations. Methodist chapels are still being built, sermons preached, circuits travelled, societies formed, classes met, children *sprinkled*, and souls saved! Even Ross and GRAVES may rest assured that theirs are not the *Atlantean* shoulders on which are reposed the interests of the religious world! These considerations are humbling; but as they are true, they must needs be *salutary*, to some extent, as they bear upon men who are in danger of thinking of themselves more highly than the occasion requires!

The observation is trite that "facts are stubborn things;" and apart from mere assertion and averment, the present pacific and united condition of the Methodist forces, in all the Southern States of this Union, is a fact palpable as the light of day, and encouraging as palpable. The discipline as well as the doctrine of Wesley will roll onward for many a year to come—yes, when the writer of this address, and the readers thereof, of the nineteenth century, lie silent in their graves. And still Methodism will be assailed, as long as bad men remain on earth, or the Devil finds his kingdom opposed by the spread of Methodist doctrines! From open violence the Methodists have nothing to fear. Truth, in one form or other, will force its way; nor can Methodism be frowned from the world. *Graves* is the last one of the "enemies of all righteousness" who has tried his hand, and he is by no means among the most successful. He professes to describe Methodism, but has not hit a single feature, nor succeeded in the outline. His is neither a cabinet painting nor a whole-length portrait. His "Iron Wheel" is a broad, palpable, and iniquitous caricature. The beauties of the original are vilely dropped; supposed deformities are embodied and distorted; new ones are invented and superadded. And the only method by which slanders of this character can be met is that every inquirer after truth resolve to see things as they really are, and to examine with his own eyes rather than depend on those of prejudiced men; not to take Methodism, or any thing connected with it, upon trust, nor pin his faith to a bad man's sleeve. Correct notions of Methodism can only be obtained by an examination of its standard writings and existing records.

There is no need of argument, I should say, to convince our members, and the intelligent friends of our cause, that it is important to our interests, and to the cause of Christian morality in our bounds, that there be a more extended circulation of our books and periodicals. MESSRS. STEVENSON & OWEN, our Book Agents at Nashville, two indefatigable and excellent men, are doing good work, aided, as they are, by DRS. SUMMERS, the efficient, able, and untiring General Editor, and HAMILTON, at the head of the Tract operations, who is also doing his work well, and giving satisfaction to our friends, who are looking on with interest at the progress of our new Publishing House, and the various branches of business connected therewith. DR. SEHON, a man of ability, and capable of much labor, gives all his time, and devotes all his energies, to the management of our missionary operations, and deserves the thanks of the Church for his self-sacrificing devotion to her interests. I have been frequently about the Publishing House during the past fall and winter, and I take a pleasure in testifying that the Agents are doing a good work, having a great variety of useful, interesting, and cheap books, handsomely printed. They are having the buildings, which are neat and substantial, made sufficiently spacious for enlarged operations, so as to meet the growing demand of our Church, South. Let our friends in the Southern division of our Church patronize our Agents in all their purchases of religious books, and thus sustain and build up a concern which is to be of vast service to the Church in all time to come. Our book depositories at Richmond, Charleston, and New Orleans, are only *branches* of the Book Concern at Nashville, keeping on hand full supplies of our books and publications, which are sold on the same terms as those at the Publishing House in Nashville. The Book Agents do not publish books at these depositories. I have been thus particular in stating the relation which these depositories bear to the Publishing House in Nashville, because some of our friends have erroneously supposed that they are *rival* establishments, and that their interests conflict. Not so: to patronize these, is to patronize the Book Concern at Nashville, they having been established to afford facilities to those Conferences bordering on the Atlantic and in the far-off West.

By all means, let our people, and the friends of our religious interests, patronize our periodicals. These are the Richmond, Charleston, St. Louis, Memphis, New Orleans, Texas, and Nashville *Christian Advocates*. In procuring subscribers for these excellent and most useful *weeklies*, our friends should not neglect the SOUTHERN METHODIST QUARTERLY REVIEW, edited by DR. DOGGETT, an able man; the HOME CIRCLE, edited by that excellent man and chaste writer, DR. HUSTON; and the SUNDAY-SCHOOL VISITOR, a publication which needs no eulogy from me.

Methodists throughout our bounds should subscribe for one or another of these Advocates, the great officials of the Church, as they are set for the defence of the doctrines and discipline of our Church, and all have at their heads men able to perform the task. Another reason why these papers should be sustained is that they devote their energies to the cause of holiness, and aid the ministry in the great work of "spreading holiness over these lands." Last, but not least, they will keep our families up with the general intelligence of the day; they will give them the latest foreign and domestic news; and they will furnish the last and most reliable market reports—in a word, any one of the "Advocate family" of papers will be found interesting and instructing to the general reader.

THE END.

www.ingramcontent.com/pod-product-compliance
Lightning Source LLC
LaVergne TN
LVHW020210110826
845151LV00003B/659

* 9 7 8 1 4 2 5 5 3 5 1 3 1 *